JOAN C. WRENN
27226 Dunbar Place, Hayward, CA 94544

D0057178

John

INTERPRETATION
A Bible Commentary for Teaching and Preaching

INTERPRETATION

A BIBLE COMMENTARY FOR TEACHING AND PREACHING

James Luther Mays, *Editor*
Patrick D. Miller, Jr., *Old Testament Editor*
Paul J. Achtemeier, *New Testament Editor*

GERARD S. SLOYAN

John

INTERPRETATION

A Bible Commentary
for Teaching and Preaching

John Knox Press
ATLANTA

Library of Congress Cataloging-in-Publication Data

Sloyan, Gerard Stephen.
  John.

  (Interpretation, a Bible commentary for teaching
and preaching)
  Bibliography: p.
  1. Bible. N.T. John—Commentaries. I. Title.
II. Series.
BS2615.3.S56   1988   226'.507   87-45549
ISBN 0-8042-3125-7

© copyright John Knox Press 1988
10 9 8 7 6
Printed in the United States of America
John Knox Press
Atlanta, Georgia 30365

SERIES PREFACE

This series of commentaries offers an interpretation of the books of the Bible. It is designed to meet the need of students, teachers, ministers, and priests for a contemporary expository commentary. These volumes will not replace the historical critical commentary or homiletical aids to preaching. The purpose of this series is rather to provide a third kind of resource, a commentary which presents the integrated result of historical and theological work with the biblical text.

An interpretation in the full sense of the term involves a text, an interpreter, and someone for whom the interpretation is made. Here, the text is what stands written in the Bible in its full identity as literature from the time of "the prophets and apostles," the literature which is read to inform, inspire, and guide the life of faith. The interpreters are scholars who seek to create an interpretation which is both faithful to the text and useful to the church. The series is written for those who teach, preach, and study the Bible in the community of faith.

The comment generally takes the form of expository essays. It is planned and written in the light of the needs and questions which arise in the use of the Bible as Holy Scripture. The insights and results of contemporary scholarly research are used for the sake of the exposition. The commentators write as exegetes and theologians. The task which they undertake is both to deal with what the texts say and to discern their meaning for faith and life. The exposition is the unified work of one interpreter.

The text on which the comment is based is the Revised Standard Version of the Bible. The general availability of this translation makes the printing of a translation unnecessary and saves the space for comment. The text is divided into sections appropriate to the particular book; comment deals with passages as a whole, rather than proceeding word by word, or verse by verse.

Writers have planned their volumes in light of the requirements set by the exposition of the book assigned to them. Biblical books differ in character, content, and arrangement. They also differ in the way they have been and are used in the liturgy, thought, and devotion of the church. The distinctiveness and use of particular books have been taken into account in decisions about the approach, emphasis, and use of space in the commentaries. The goal has been to allow writers to develop the format which provides for the best presentation of their interpretation.

The result, writers and editors hope, is a commentary which both explains and applies, an interpretation which deals with both the meaning and the significance of biblical texts. Each commentary reflects, of course, the writer's own approach and perception of the church and world. It could and should not be otherwise. Every interpretation of any kind is individual in that sense; it is one reading of the text. But all who work at the interpretation of Scripture in the church need the help and stimulation of a colleague's reading and understanding of the text. If these volumes serve and encourage interpretation in that way, their preparation and publication will realize their purpose.

The Editors

PREFACE

The commentary on the Fourth Gospel that follows in these pages lays no claim to novelty or exhaustive treatment. It is not exegetical except in a general expository sense. That is to say, it does not presume (or attempt to supply) the knowledge of Hellenistic or "common" *(koine)* Greek vocabulary and syntax required to follow a philological or grammatical argument—although at times one or another such argument may be alluded to. Some users of this book may know the Greek text of John well; others may once have been familiar with it as a student's exercise. Sufficient numbers, however, will be unfamiliar with the original language in its nuances or indeed at all that the insertion of words and phrases in Greek may be an intrusion or frustration.

Neither will this commentary contain textual study of the sort in which the case is made for the author's preferred reading. Here, again, a layperson's knowledge of the problems of text transmission will suffice. The settlements opted for in the twenty-sixth, most recent edition of the Nestle-Aland *Novum Testamentum Graece* (1979) are considered satisfactory. Any departure from those readings will be noted when it seems important to do so.

The commentary's chief attempt will be to provide or to invite certain religious insights into matters with which preachers and teachers have long been familiar. These will depend chiefly on the rich scholarship of the Gospel of John which has become available since the nineteen twenties. To it will be added certain of the writer's own insights. The body of available Johannine scholarship is daunting in its very bulk. Conflicting positions are taken by those expert in text, word-meaning and grammar, in the life world and thought world of Hellenist Judaism, in the attempted reconstruction of the history of early Christianity. The last is especially the case as this history reveals a development into Gnosticism on the one hand and the more catholic interpretations found in First John, Ignatius, and Irenaeus on the other.

No attempt will be made at a consensus position from among the modern giants like Bultmann and Barrett, Braun and Dodd, Brown and Schnackenburg, and Lindars and Morris. This commentary will not be a homogenized interpretation in which sharp differences among those authors are eliminated and major agreements are featured. One must turn to them, author by author, to see how they interpret various passages in John, especially the stoppers *(cruces interpretum)*. The task essayed here will be simpler than any such survey of what is called "the literature." It will be to hew to a single line on the meaning of the whole Gospel and various aspects of it which seem defensible to the writer.

Overall, this book will consider major themes or facets of the Gospel in preference to chapters or verses (which are respectively thirteenth and sixteenth-century divisions in any case). John is made up of vignettes, discourses, and narrative pericopes which are both shorter and longer than the traditional chapter divisions. Any analyses of the Gospel which were to assume the absolute rightness of these divisions would betray it. At the same time, chapter and verse divisions are those most familiar to any who know John well. Second in order, surely, comes the paragraphing courageously attempted by modern teams (like the editor-translators of RSV, NAB or NIV). A more recent element still in sense-division is the attempt of the framers of the four lectionaries currently in use—the Catholic, Episcopal, Lutheran and Common (produced by the Consultation on Common Texts)—to determine where portions of John chosen for public proclamation should begin and end. The four sets of choices in the three-year cycle will be indicated, normally at the beginning of a passage's treatment for commentary. In that scheme, readings from John are inserted into year-long continuous readings from Matthew, Mark, and Luke. Lectionary practices of this sort are the oldest way in which the Scriptures were shared with believers at the weekly assembly. The invention of printing, coupled with the theological principle that the Holy Spirit's prompting of the preacher should determine the portions to be read and preached on, did much to bring the practice into disuse. But some Christians never abandoned it and many churches in our day are returning to it. Attention is paid to the practice in the following pages not to promote it but as a convenience to readers. It should be interesting to all to see which portions of John are proposed for public worship services and how editors subsequent to those who produced the Roman Lectionary (1969) think the Johannine sense is better preserved both by non-omission and by starting and stopping the reading at places other than the ones first proposed.

For those who preach from one of the church lectionaries currently in use, the intermittent use of pericopes from John may create a problem. As selections from this Gospel are interspersed within the three "synoptic years," they seem to be used to complement the other Gospels rather than to have an independent existence. This means that developing a sustained Johannine outlook in the pulpit will not be an easy matter.

Any single development by John is an integral part of his project. This can mean that congregations who hear good preaching will have John's few major motifs made clear to them whatever the pericope in hand. Some people are by temperament already on the Fourth Gospel's wavelength. Others will never be. By the homilist's careful exposition, all hearers should be free to decide.

The chapter divisions in the commentary are in some cases dictated by the inner logic of the Gospel; in others they are the simple matter of conforming to the choices made when thirteenth-century Archbishop Stephen Langton of Canterbury divided it into chapters. Thus, the subject matter of John 18—19 makes those chapters a natural grouping. The case is similar with 13—17 and 20—21 (although the argument for treating the latter two separately could be termed as strong or stronger). John 1:1-18 and 19-51 deal with quite distinct matters, yet they will be commented on together. The same is true of 4:1-42 and 43-54.

One familiar division which this commentary will not employ, except to note its popularity, is that between a "Book of Signs" (1:19—12:50) and a "Book of Glory" (13—20), with chapter 21 as an appendix. The reason is that all such editorial helps for writer and reader—except for the last-named, which is a clear fact of the Gospel's composition—give the impression that the author had this distinction in mind. That would be hard to establish. Jesus' "raising up" in both crucifixion and glorification is the greatest of the signs in the Gospel, although not so designated by that word, yet it does not appear in a hypothetical "Book of Signs." Likewise, Jesus' glory with the Father is revealed, not merely anticipated, by his words and works in the first twelve chapters. The clear distinction between the two "books" proves inadequate although undoubtedly a convenient device.

ix

To be specific about the chapter divisions in the commentary to follow, obviously the new disciples of Jesus can be dealt with in their first encounter with him separately from "the first of his signs" in Cana of Galilee (chaps. 1—2). The accounts of Jesus and Nicodemus, Jesus and the nameless Samaritan woman, and Jesus and the equally nameless man born blind are the logical subjects of separate treatment. So are his discourses to the assembly in the Capernaum synagogue, to the hostile crowds in Jerusalem, and to his friends at the supper near the end. But once it has been discovered how internally cohesive the Gospel is, how continuous everything is with everything else despite certain convolutions (much like a Moebius strip without beginning or end), it becomes impossible to deal with it in neatly demarcated units. The plan to do so is attractive for reasons of order, like any categorization scheme. But the Johannine technique of cries and whispers, hints and guesses, and the "gift half understood" means that a thoroughly ordered presentation is simply not indicated.

One way around this is to provide numbered verse citations to apprise the reader of echoes within echoes as the kaleidoscope turns (to change the figure) and new configurations appear. The commentator, however, begins to wish after a while that there were a large projection screen instead of a solid text, or wide page margins as in the Talmud. On it would be flashed or inscribed cross-references and similar passages from John in full. Often these would prove to be repetitions or near-repetitions delicately altered. Crowding in upon each other, they would establish visually the allusive technique of which John is the master. Chapter and verse numbers beat a certain numbing tattoo on the eye. The reader tends to react by saying: "I am sure it is just as the writer maintains. Why bother to look it up?" But whether they are laboriously checked out or disregarded, the response in neither case is quite as it would be if the same phrases were to crowd in on the eye repeatedly. Only then would it come home to the reader what the Gospel's basic technique of composition is.

The literary style of this author is, in a word, concentric. More accurately, it is an upward spiral. A linear series of comments on the author's performance can easily give the wrong idea. In this Gospel everything constantly comes up for review until the last page. The commentary will be like that, a look at a spiral which has as its axis knowledge of who the Son of God is, a knowledge which should mean belief in him. The various narratives, speeches, and reflections of the Evangelist illumine and elaborate upon this central theme. Since each part of the Gospel is integrally related to every other, the best way to use this commentary would seem to be via the text-index at the back. This will lead to discovering texts of reader interest wherever they occur rather than simply having the reader scan the successive pages or Table of Contents to find the treatments of familiar places. To be sure, the bread of life discourse and the raising of Lazarus (for example) will be dealt with in the expected sequence in the Gospel. But references to verses in these two chapters of John are likely to be found in the commentary both before and after the formal treatment of these passages in chapters 6 and 11. Within the commentary on the chapters of John that are largely devoted to Jesus' discourses, the movement may be to and fro in the dialectical manner of the Gospel. It is hoped that this is not a sign of the book's disorder but a faithful reflection of the Gospel according to John.

The commentary assumes from the beginning, as a matter sufficiently established by modern study, that the Gospel reflects the faith and life of the Johannine circle as much as, if not more than, it reports on Jesus in his lifetime. No effort will be made to reconstruct the original author's or the final redactor's life circumstances, as if they were available by dint of the relatively brief Gospel text. It will be taken for granted, however, that the incidents selected for treatment by the Evangelist and the development given them was meant to speak directly to first-century believers who were already in his tradition. Their horizon or field of comprehension was primary for the author. The events of Jesus' life were made to serve *it* and not vice versa. Whenever it is thought that the horizon of contemporary Christians can be fused with that of the intended first recipients of the Gospel, it will be done. Fusing the horizon of our contemporaries with that of Jesus and his contemporaries is the far greater temptation. It must be remembered, however, that that of the Johannine circle *always* intervenes.

Whenever the present Gospel text seems to have taken its rise from a historical reminiscence from Jesus' career, that fact will be noted. But this commentary will not be an attempted reconstruction of the history either of Jesus' day or of John's day. It will be an attempt to proclaim in our day the Jesus Christ proclaimed by John. The commentary will try to be at all points an "Interpretation," as it tries to convey the significance of the person and teaching of Jesus to modern preachers and teachers. The task is not easy, for what we have before us is the significance of the words and deeds of Jesus for the Johannine church, not those words and deeds themselves. We need to derive from the Gospel a significance for us through the prism of the significance for them, our first-century co-religionists. The obstacles would be insurmountable if the figure of Jesus as an object of faith did not loom behind this Gospel.

A legitimate question as the following pages unfold is why certain passages are given an extensive modern application and others a modest one or none at all. The answer is that any writer, like John, has to decide on his or her intended audience beforehand. The present writer knows the language and cultural setting he shares with his audience. Likewise he knows some of the great questions which people, and in particular Christians of the West in the present age, have put to the Fourth Gospel. This writer further has in common with many readers the preaching and teaching offices in the church. Neither he nor they view the inspired Scriptures as primarily the subject of historical, geographical, archaeological, or theological inquiry. The Scriptures are open to all four types but were produced in the first instance as a proclamation of a word of God to the church. This word in John will be dealt with before all else as a proclamation to believers of our time and place. That is a risky business, of course, but the church in calling an ancient literature its own has always lived by this risk.

The best way to see that the task is done intelligently is first to try to learn what the ancient author meant to say to his contemporaries. From this flows the need to avoid any modern interpretation of his word that goes counter to this intention. Important modern questions which derive directly from the concerns of John are, What does a right faith in Jesus Christ for today consist of? What is right faith in the Spirit-Counselor? And how has God sent both to do the one redemptive and sanctifying work, not a different work from the work of creation? The inquiring mind needs a Johannine answer to all these questions. Again, what are the means God has chosen in our day to witness to the divine "glory," the reality of godhead? If, as Jesus says in John, the works of God which he did in his brief lifetime would be far outrun by "greater works than these" done through his "friends," what works are they and do they continue up to the present? These are some of the questions one can legitimately put to the Fourth Gospel once there has been a serious attempt to learn the Evangelist's message to his contemporaries.

Today's believers experience great problems with authenticity and integrity, with cleaving fast to the truth, to the evidence of the senses, and to the force of argument when it leads to unappealing consequences. Money and power and influence corrupt in special ways, because losing them or never gaining them is a prospect repulsive to the modern spirit. The Gospel of John speaks directly to these questions, hence so will the commentary.

There are special problems involved in the church's holding firmly to the conviction that it has received a unique revelation in Jesus Christ while knowing that those who cannot reckon it a revealed message are not thereby excluded from God's love. The church has not always succeeded in maintaining both truths simultaneously. Some believers in Christ who could not be less interested in the corporate life of the church have succeeded even less well. The commentary will try to acknowledge what is exclusionary in the Johannine spirit and how this must (and may), must not (and may not) be understood by a worldwide church which John could hardly have envisioned. For this Gospel has thrived over the centuries by the love it preaches, which *in*cludes, and languished by the love it preaches, which *ex*cludes.

The special hazards of being a preacher or teacher in the church as John touches on them are faced squarely in these pages. If the message of this Gospel is to be shared by human expositors, it needs to come through a prism of pure light. The tasks which are globally called "ministry" must be carried out by women and men whose motives are pure, who have experienced the pain of fidelity to God's call like the Johannine Jesus, who care much for the "truth" of the Spirit-Counselor and little for the "glory" which humans seek from each other. Numerous opportunities are taken to speak of the ways in which this Gospel speaks directly to inheritors of the apostolic task, both corporately and individually.

A final matter of concern will be the correct terminology for those most opposed to Jesus in the Gospel, which means primarily to the Johannine community in its day. John calls them "Jews." The problem is, no one knows which Jews. Because confusion in the popular Christian mind has always attended this question and because Jewish people corporately have often been identified with the "some Jews" of John, long dead, this commentary proposes leaving the Greek term *hoi Ioudaioi* untranslated—even when preaching to modern congregations! This suggestion is reasonable only for the preacher who is consistently with a congregation in and out of season. The usage will heighten awareness that the term is a calculated piece of obloquy, not a description of an entire people, and that it is directed against persons nowadays unknown. That they were Jews of a certain power class is clear, though exactly which class and where—Judea? a diaspora location?—is not clear. The one dichotomy which the present writer does not allow, for lack of evidence, is the one commonly assumed between the first-century Jewish people generally and a largely gentile John community generally. In this widely-held hypothesis, the latter have been clearly separated from the former by the time the Gospel is written. If such were surely the case, there would be no mystery surrounding the term. "The Jews" would be its correct translation in all the vernacular languages. Since matters are by no means so clear, and since the insertion of any interpretative assistance ("certain Jews," "the leaders of the Jews") is not warranted by the text, it seems best to leave the uncertainty in place as to who is meant. The Greek term does this. The problem should not be insurmountable for preachers whose life work is exposition and for people who use foreign words and phrases like *vice versa* and *Kindergarten* constantly.

If the solution seems to be based on modern concern for anti-Judaism—there being no matching concern for the Roman soldiery or the temple priesthood whose less attractive members are let stand for the whole—that must be granted. Modern preachers and teachers need to be on guard against making an easy target of *any* people or class by careless rhetoric. This they do by using the translation, "the Jews," unexamined. The woeful failure of Christian preachers over twenty centuries to make careful distinctions whenever they speak of the Jews in a first-century context has made this a question apart.

A number of grateful acknowledgments should conclude these prefatory remarks. Topping the list are Carolyn Nicosia, now of Wabag, Enga Providence, Papua, New Guinea, and Linda Hardy of the secretarial staff of the Department of Religion at Temple University. My handwriting is quite legible but the green screen is relentless. Without these patient practitioners of the "processing" of words—repulsive phrase—nothing!

Present at the creation were Edgar and Rose Marie Corkrey, who give the word "neighbor" fresh meaning, my ever-supportive sisters Jean (Sister Mary Stephanie) and Virginia, and Janet R. Haney. *His omnibus, gratias ago.*

Gerard S. Sloyan

CONTENTS

INDEX TO SCRIPTURE
REFERENCES TO JOHN

This Index shows all references in this volume to the Gospel of John. The lefthand column lists the divisions of Scripture used in the outline of the commentary. The *boldface* page numbers immediately following each listing are the primary reference, showing the part of the commentary which deals specifically with that portion of Scripture. The list of page numbers following the boldface entry shows all other references in the volume to that portion of Scripture, or parts of it.

INTERPRETATION

Abbreviations used in citations

JB   Jerusalem Bible
LXX   The Septuagint
NAB   New American Bible (1970 translation)
NIV   New International Version
Q   *Quelle* (source)
RSV   Revised Standard Version
TEV   Today's English Version of the Holy Bible

Introduction

The Gospel according to John has been written about voluminously but is preached on and taught selectively. Christians generally, and those entrusted with the ministry of the word in particular, are wary in its presence. It promises so much, yet raises the question whether the promise is that of Jesus or the Evangelist. It is a church document—canonical, inspired, itself the inspiration of all the christological councils—yet it is rumored to have a sectarian tone. It was late in gaining acceptance into the canon because of its gnostic associations. Older generations had no hesitation in proclaiming publicly: "Jesus assures us, 'I am the way, the truth and the life,'" but the present generation wonders whether to trumpet that as an authentic Jesus saying. If it is not, how much background material must be presented to make it ultimately his saying? And will not whatever is put forward lessen the impact of this trust-inspiring word as a word of Jesus?

The Fourth Gospel continues to baffle, to enrich, to infuriate, and to console as it has done for centuries. It is worthless as history, say some. It is more dependable as a source on Palestinian life than the Synoptics, say others. It had to have been written after the last of the Synoptics, the majority holds. It could have been composed as early as A.D. 50, a small minority maintains. Its author was a Platonist who was committed to the gospel tradition, said one group of scholars earlier in this century. It was written by a diaspora Jew whose milieu was the Hellenist Judaism characteristic of the Stephen party, it is more modernly said.

John was the document of a local church that had broken finally with the synagogue, we are assured. Alternatively, it comes from a Jewish believer in Jesus, one of a circle of the like-minded whose high Christology repelled equally other Jews who believed in Jesus and Jews of the synagogue.

Who wrote this Gospel and why? What are we to make of it, we who have the preacher's or teacher's office as our trust?

1

How can we regain the confidence we may once have had in this classic expression of the Christian message so that we will wish to preach it in and out of season—either its text directly or by way of citation and allusion?

Each of the Four Gospels represents the attempt of a particular community, working through a scribe or group of scribes, to set down dependable traditions about Jesus. These traditions, each writer claims, have been lived out faithfully by disciples down to his own day.

Each of the Four Gospels is likewise a piece of written rhetoric which has as its purpose to *proclaim* and to *persuade:* who Jesus is and why he should be believed in as one through whom God has accomplished uniquely great things.

All four evangelists draw on numerous sources that are no longer available to us. Presumably these include oral narratives of specific deeds and sayings of Jesus, some of the latter in quite developed form before they were put into written form. The proliferation of such written fragments, later used as source material by the evangelists, could render questionable all but a few theories of literary dependence among the four canonical Gospels. This or that evangelist, in other words, could have made use of sayings or parable collections or miracle *catenae* ("chains") which we no longer possess. Indeed, more than one evangelist may have employed—and edited—the same sources. Still, the non-extant character of such hypothetical sources renders theories based on their existence questionable. That is why the "two-source theory" has the attraction that it does. Canonical Mark and the extensive verbal similarities between some fifty-three *logia* or sayings of Jesus in Matthew and Luke (designated Q) *do* exist. Matthew and Luke can be shown to have drawn in all likelihood from Mark. Matthew and Luke also give evidence of having drawn not on each other but on the sayings collection just mentioned. There are serious difficulties with the hypothesis that these two documents, Mark and Q, preceded and contributed to the composition of the Gospels of Matthew and Luke, but other theories of Synoptic composition seem to be fraught with even greater difficulties.

The literary relation of the canonical text of John to Mark or Luke, the two candidates for any demonstrable relationship, is uncertain at best. The prevailing view is that the author of John in its penultimate form did not make use of any of the Synoptics but had wide access to the materials they employed, those in Luke as much as Mark. Where there are close verbal similarities and sequences of material (as between extensive passages of John and Mark) or content (material found in John and Luke only), the drawing of both upon a common source could probably account for these similarities. John's fidelity to Mark's order is a problem except for those few who accept an *Ur*-Mark, a first edition of that Gospel. The final editing of John by another hand than that of "the evangelist" with canonical Mark handy is a possibility. What must be acknowledged in any case is the genius of the final editor of John in producing the kind of Gospel intended. It is a twofold genius if a distinction is to be made, as indeed seems necessary, between the penultimate and the final forms.

Differences of opinion on Johannine origins and the manner of the Gospel's composition are so many and so great that they are not likely to be resolved in yet another commentary. Yet the progress of critical study by persons of profound religious faith has been such that we can open the inquiry with more certitudes than doubts. To begin with, the Fourth Gospel seems to have been edited thoroughly by the hand that appended the last chapter, twenty-one. The immediately previous version can be reconstructed with some confidence by distinguishing between what bears the mark of an editor's hand and what does not. As to what preceded the work of the "evangelist" (as contrasted with the "final redactor"), speculations proliferate. There is nothing like unanimity on the written sources employed by the first author, nor whether he was himself the editor of a second edition which preceded the further edited version we now have.

There *was* a Christian genius of the Hellenist-Jewish tradition who used the Septuagint Bible but was not unfamiliar with the Masoretic text of the Hebrew Bible or the targums on it, who decided to emulate the literary form-tradition "gospel" which was already in place. He had his reasons for adopting a sayings tradition (which he rephrased freely), plus a signs tradition, plus a final-days tradition, plus a risen-life tradition— casting them all in a familiar narrative form. He must have been convinced that extant exemplars of the Gospel *genre* known to him were inadequate to his purpose.

Studies have established the high percentage of synoptic-like materials which appear in John. He proposes teachings of Jesus, incidents in his life, parabolic materials, theological re-

3

flections, and a trial-passion account which much resembles Matthew, Mark, and Luke, but never in the same form (cf., e.g., John 1:41–42 with Matt. 16:16–17; Mark 6:34–44 with John 6:5–13; John 20:22–23 with Matt. 16:19*b*), or almost never in the same form. When he comes close to them in wording (as in the account of the multiplication of the loaves, 6:5–13) or in order of events (as in the walking on water immediately after it, vv. 16–21), the mystery is heightened. Did he know any Synoptic Gospel at first hand? An occasional scholar of quality like C.K. Barrett thinks he had the Marcan Gospel. Did he have only discrete reminiscences from the tradition which the Synoptics had? Most students think so. Did he have access to traditional materials worked up in a form that another or other evangelists had? Support for his possession of certain Lukan-developed narratives is quite strong, especially in the passion narratives. As to his previous heritage of Gospel traditions, however, and the form in which they existed, little can be claimed overall with certainty. John sets himself to do something quite like the Synoptics about Jesus, but in an all but unique fashion. This Evangelist's watchword is: "I did it my way."

More stress will be placed in these pages on the undeniable fact that the last editor of John recognized, retained, and intensified the homogeneity of purpose and literary style in the work that lay before him than on any theories of mutual dependence among the Gospels. The case has been made for the lack of understanding or the downright disagreement of the final redactor with the work he had in hand, which he corrected in another spirit. The present writer is not convinced by these revisionist theories. He inclines to the view that the editing was largely sympathetic and done from a standpoint similar to that of the author. The person from whom we have the final text probably recognized the inconsistencies which create *perplexities* in the reader's mind (the technical term is "aporias"). These inconsistencies, it can be assumed, were retained out of reverence for the tradition, its various sources providing data which at times did not accord well with one another.

Uppermost was the intention to memorialize, in apparent biographical form, Jesus, the founder of the tradition, and to legitimate the founder's positions by showing how they were being lived out by disciples in the writer(s)' day. Suffice it to say that the Evangelist or first author, both knowing the literary form "gospel" and meaning to compose one, probably edited

4

his own work in stages. The final editor gave us the highly skilled literary product we have in hand. It is upon this, and no hypothetical previous form of the Gospel, we mean to comment. The sole exception to this will be the transposition of what are now two chapters of the Gospel (chaps. 5 and 6).

The traditional witnesses Simon Peter and Andrew, Philip and Thomas appear in John's Gospel, but surprisingly, the sons of Zebedee, James and John, do not. Rivaling Peter in stature as a legitimating witness to all that took place is the anonymous "disciple whom Jesus loved." No little part of the mystery surrounding this figure is his belated first appearance at 13:23, followed by fairly frequent mention thereafter (19:26, 35?; 20:2–10; 21:7, 20, 24; cf. 11:36? 18:35? 19:35?), although some see him as the one who is Andrew's companion in 1:35–50. He seems to be this community's great one among the apostolic company. He is such, however, in a delicate balance with the acknowledged leader in the other New Testament books: Peter.

The evangelist John, however much he may differ from the other three in incidents chosen for development and literary style, resembles them in his desire to teach his contemporaries the authentic tradition about Jesus. He is above all concerned with the way the tradition is being lived in his community, which he views as the one authentic witness to it. "That the founder [Jesus] really did and said these things can be known with certainty because a line of tradition guarantees it," Charles H. Talbert writes of another Gospel (*Reading Luke.* p. 3). John's Gospel is a record of that tradition, hence Jesus' words and deeds, at least in substance—for they are much expanded in John—are rendered secure.

The Evangelist's technique is to employ large, thematic units that individual occurrences in Jesus' life serve to illustrate. Thus, there is the master idea that Jesus is the true teacher sent by God from heaven ("above"), his proper home (3:31–34), to a human world "below" (8:23), thence to go back to reclaim the glory which he had with God from the beginning (17:5). He has come to the world as its light to keep anyone who believes in him from remaining in the dark (12:46). He is a revealer of the reality of God who has no previous rival in his intimacy with godhead (5:19c–20a; 6:46): not Abraham, not Moses, not any of the prophets. John's favored term to describe God is "the Father," just as he inclines toward "the Son" for Jesus. Everything that Jesus says or does discloses who he is. His speech and action

5

in so doing likewise disclose no less than the mystery of deity.

Jesus is fully and indisputably human for John. He is also "the Son" in the meaning of God's Son, a person in a closer relation to "the Father" than anyone has ever been to God (5:17). After his death Jesus will be glorified by going back to where he was before. Meanwhile, he dwells in God's presence (10:30; 14:20; 17:21) and converses with God (chap. 17), even while discoursing with disciples and the crowds over the reality of obedience to the Father.

Jesus in John comes from Nazareth in Galilee and is Joseph's son (1:45; cf. 7:52). He and his mother are invited guests at a wedding in Cana, a nearby village (2:1–2). The Evangelist seems to know the tradition that Jesus made Capernaum his Galilean headquarters (2:12; cf. 4:44–46; 6:59). Yet there is a sense in which Jesus' proper homeland *(patris)* is Judea (see 4:44). It can be argued from the way John uses the proverb about no prophet's being esteemed in "his own country" that Judea is meant. Jesus must leave there for Galilee because of his non-acceptance. Perhaps, however, all Israel is his *patris.*

The people of Galilee are never described as inimical to Jesus in this Gospel. The hostile reception he receives in the synagogue at Capernaum seems to be an exception (6:30–31, 41–42, 60, 66), but it will be shown below that the resistance of *hoi Ioudaioi* (vv. 41, 52) may not originally have been described as taking place there. The Judean crowds are almost consistently opposed to Jesus (e.g., in chaps. 5—10), although at times he will have his partisans in the south (cf. 9:16; 10:21; 11:45).

Jesus is a sign of division throughout this Gospel. Faced with him, people either come to believe in him and thereby walk in the light or choose the darkness of non-belief (8:12) and can expect judgment, that is, condemnation (3:19).

There is thus a constant struggle over religious truth going on in the Fourth Gospel between Jesus and his protagonists and those who actively resist them. Its colors are primary; there are no pastels or shadings. The author is totally self-confident. Where he and his community stand, there is Jesus and vice versa.

The modern preacher of the Fourth Gospel has a powerful weapon in hand but needs to avoid self-righteousness. The weapon has to be turned most often upon preacher and congregation, not upon long-dead antagonists of Jesus. There will, of course, be times when contemporary worshipers must be called

6

on to stand with Jesus and against his opponents of the present age. John's Gospel is a sharp weapon that can be grasped by handle or blade to the grasper's advantage or destruction. Every paragraph is an invitation to do the one or the other.

"He and his community" is said consciously, for, like all the Gospels, this one came out of a particular milieu to which it was in turn primarily directed. The final hand that wrought it belonged to one who hoped that its invitation to a profound belief in Jesus as the unique revealer of God and its sharp polemic against all who thought otherwise would be effective. That required an intimate knowledge of his audience and their ways of thinking, possibly molded by the author himself.

There is enough of a grasp of the Palestinian scene reflected in this Gospel to inspire confidence in hearers who know the "land of Israel" well. At the same time the Gospel seems to be the document of a community of dissident diaspora Jews, whose Bible is the Septuagint, whose grasp of basic Hebrew words is tenuous, and who are at home in the sonorous prose of a post-biblical hymnody that can be set in poetry-like strophes.

The one who speaks for them, John, is not in the first instance interested in telling the story of Jesus' public career. He wishes to proclaim Jesus' identity to contemporaries so that their belief in him will be correct. There is consequently the appearance of historical narrative, but behind it lies the reality of messages directed to contemporaries, friends, and foes alike. It is to engage *them* in the story that everything is told. John like any good storyteller—and he is one—uses his characters and events, Jesus along with the rest, to say what he wants to say about the significance of his believing community by telling of the significance of Jesus. It is this Jesus who is the center of the community's faith.

John does not produce a work of fiction. His narrative is historically based. But its primary goal is persuasion, not a chronicle of events. In the interest of persuading the hearer, he will use every technique known to the narrator's art—some of them very effectively. That is why it is a mistake to approach the Fourth Gospel by putting to it a set of historical questions: Did Jesus make his utterances at the different feasts as recorded? Was his life threatened by hostile crowds bent on stoning him? Could Pilate have conducted himself in a legal proceeding in the way described? The questions are not so much unimportant as irrelevant. History is modern biblical

7

scholarship's primary category, largely for apologetic reasons originating early in the last century. But history is not the right measuring-rod to apply to works of religious literature. Literary canons are. This does not mean that historical and geographical questions are not to be put to the Fourth Gospel, only that they are not primary. The way the author goes about telling his story is primary.

Raymond E. Brown's *The Community of the Beloved Disciple* provides a helpful attempted reconstruction of the milieu out of which the Gospel and the later Johannine letters came. Oscar Cullmann's *The Johannine Circle*, while proposing numerous keen insights, is not quite so successful. Prior to both (1968), there appeared J. Louis Martyn's *History and Theology in the Fourth Gospel*, which assisted many who had not previously thought of this Gospel as operating on two levels to recognize the one of the author's present and the other of Jesus' past.

A real breakthrough in John studies has come with R. Alan Culpepper's *Anatomy of the Fourth Gospel*. This dissects the Gospel in the manner common to literary critics of the narrative genre. The book is somewhat daunting to the exegete and the preacher alike in its application of an art largely unfamiliar to both to a piece of writing which they know well under another aspect. Amos Wilder (1971) was a pioneer in identifying to students of the New Testament the language of the Gospel as early Christian rhetoric. Studies by Petersen, largely on Mark (1978), Nuttall, on Luke (1978), and Rhoads and Michie (1982) and Robbins (1984), on Mark, have brought the literary achievement of the evangelists to reader attention in important ways. This must not be thought of as a new "angle" in Gospel study, which by definition is constantly bent on novelty. It is a serious analysis of the founding documents of Christianity on their own terms rather than those of the source and form and redaction criticism that has been imposed on them. For while sleuthing into the component parts of the Gospels and how the various phrases and pericopes came to appear in each of the four in the form they, do is not valueless, it is not what the evangelists thought they were doing. They were composing narratives which were literary creations in the strict sense. Exploring how they went about the task of authorship should give keen insights into the construction of the homily and the teaching lesson, each of them distinct art forms.

When we speak of John—the author who gave us the Gos-

8

pel we have in hand—we refer to someone continually choosing what he means to tell us and how. We may try to infer from his narrative why he makes the choices he does. While John as a living human being eludes us, his character as a literary artist is fully available. The authoritative source or sources he employed have a certain interest for us, but what he did with them has a far greater one. He speaks to us as an unobtrusive narrator, not making himself a character in the story he tells. "In John, the narrator is the one who speaks in the prologue, tells the story, introduces the dialogue, provides explanations, translates terms, and tells us what various characters knew or did not know. In short, the narrator tells us what to think" (Culpepper, p. 17). We find ourselves accepting him as a reliable guide to the meaning of Jesus' life and death, not just because the church has declared his Gospel canonical and inspired but because as a narrator he inspires this confidence.

John as narrator makes explanatory comments throughout his Gospel (although not between 13:31 and 17:26). These interjected "footnotes" have been listed as being as few as sixty and as many as a hundred and twenty, depending on what counts as an informational aside to the reader. They are an essential part of the text. At the same time, their distribution is not related to the structure of the Gospel. The Johannine narrator speaks from a vantage point of omniscience. He shares his knowledge with the reader or hearer, including the identity of the central figure (1:1–18), from the very start. This makes the reader better informed than any character in the story. The teller knows what is going on in Jesus' thought (e.g., 5:6, 6:6, 64; 13:1; 16:19) and the secret reflections and actions of other characters (e.g., 4:27; 12:6; 13:28, 29; 21:4), although the plunge into their thoughts is never deep. John usually speaks in the third person but occasionally he becomes "we" (1:14, 16; 21:24). It is possible to assess the extent of his knowledge only from what he tells the reader. John is likewise omnipresent. "To the narrator . . . everywhere is 'there' and nowhere is 'here' " (Culpepper, p. 27).

As to time rather than place, John speaks retrospectively as in 7:39: ". . . for as yet the Spirit had not been given, because Jesus was not yet glorified." This means that the perspective of the Johannine community is presented as absolutely necessary if one is to understand Jesus adequately. Indeed, the whole Gospel is contributed to by memory, the interpretation of

9

Scripture, traditions based on the early church's post-Easter experience, awareness of possessing the Spirit, a reading of the glory of the risen Christ back into the days of his ministry, and "an acute sensitivity to the history and struggles of the Johannine community" (Culpepper, p. 30).

Does this mean that we have no assurance in this Gospel that the events and words conveyed to us really happened as described? They happened, to be sure, *but as described,* namely in John's narrative world. That is the truth of this Gospel, as of the other three. It gives us the significance or meaning of Jesus Christ as one author and his community perceived it. The Fourth Gospel gives us no raw data in the historical order on Jesus of Nazareth. All the data are processed. Given our modern historical mindset, we may think we are the poorer for that. John was convinced that we are the richer for the way he told the story, namely, that his community's defeats and victories were totally co-incidental with those of Jesus. Such has always been the view of the church, which canonized this narrative in its present form.

This book will attempt to be faithful to John's Gospel by commenting on it for preachers and teachers in the spirit in which he wrote it. It was for him a proclamation in story form, not a work of history, and in that form they must tell it again and again.

PART ONE

The Baptist and the Disciples Witness to Jesus

JOHN 1—4

John 1
A Word in Flesh Who Is Light and Life

The Fourth Gospel begins with the story of "a man whose name was John" (v. 6) who is not identified by parentage or place of origin, only by the fact that he was "sent from God." Later in the story it will come to light that he is baptizing in water (v. 26) beyond the Jordan (v. 28) in what he himself describes as "the wilderness" (v. 23), the desert. The place of John's activity is named: Bethany (v. 28). It is not the Judean village just east of Jerusalem on the way to Jericho but a town of the same name in Perea. Perea is the province east of the river which lies opposite the southerly part of Samaria and northern Judea. Later still, the baptizing activity of this John will be situated in Aenon near Salim, "because there was much water there" (3:23). The added detail would be needless for a readership familiar with a Semitic language since Aenon is recognizable as a transliteration of "springs." Whatever this writer's intended audience, since he is composing a Gospel in Greek, he feels required throughout to give the meaning of Semitic terms (cf. 1:38, 41; 4:25; 11:16). When he returns briefly to John's career (3:22) he will add that John "had not yet been put in prison" (3:24), as if the fact of his imprisonment were well known to the readership. At 4:1, but for two brief references back to the mysterious John as a witness to Jesus (5:33–36; 10:40–42), all mention of him ends.

11

That, indeed, is what the baptizing prophet chiefly is in this Gospel—not a preacher of repentance moving vast crowds to change their ways but a witness to Jesus, one who gives testimony to him (1:7–8, 15, 19–20, 29–34). If Jesus or the community of believers who came after him are conceived by the author as somehow on trial in this narrative, clearly John is being summoned as a leading witness on Jesus' and the community's behalf. One can know by heeding the testimony of this desert-dweller that Jesus is the Light (v. 8). More than that, he is the authentic or true Light (v. 9). He is the Lamb of God who takes away the sin of the world (v. 29). Jesus is the Son of God (v. 34) who baptizes with Holy Spirit (v. 33). John will prove to be the first in a series of witnesses in this Gospel giving testimony to Jesus. As the story develops, this is so much the case that some see in John's Gospel a protracted judicial process (the Hebrew term is *ribh*), in which favorable witnesses like John and later a series of things and persons like Jesus' "works" (5:36), the Father (5:37), and the Scriptures (5:39) are pitted against accusatory witnesses. The latter will say that Jesus breaks the sabbath and makes himself equal to God (5:18), that he has a demon (7:20; 8:48) or is a Samaritan (8:48) A few students of this Gospel go so far as to say that Jesus' appearance before Jewish priestly authority (18:13–24) is muted in the way it is because a judgment of condemnation to death has already been passed (see the repeated vocabulary about "killing" Jesus: 5:18; 7:19–20; "stoning" him 8:59; 10:31; "arresting" him 7:30). All of this his opponents were unable to achieve, the Gospel explains, "because his hour had not yet come" (7:30). It is unquestionable that, at the very least, the Evangelist will bring his narrative to a climax in Jesus' hour of testing after many witnesses have been summoned. Before Pilate, Jesus will give what the Evangelist thinks is the final, irrefutable testimony on his own behalf.

John 1:1–18

Portions of 1:1–18 occur only on Christmas (Catholic and Common) and the first (Episcopal) and second (Catholic and Common) Sundays after Christmas. The infrequent use should not prevent two important things from happening: preaching solidly on Johannine Christology (which is at the same time its soteriology) in the season when the incarnation is especially being observed and treating the Jesus of John solidly in the spirit of the prologue whenever the polemical exchanges of this Gospel are featured, since those earliest verses are the key to all.

The opening eighteen verses of this Gospel are often set apart in writings about it as "the prologue" as if they were totally different in kind from all that is to follow. Since they are nothing of the sort, we have tried to situate them in the total fabric of the Gospel. An alternation between a description of the ordinary or everyday and the transcendent that gives it meaning is a standard feature of this Gospel. This is first found in 1:1–18, which oscillates between the origins of Jesus in the deepest recesses of godhead and the events in the life of an apocalyptic prophet, John. Usually in this Gospel an incident will be described first as it occurs in a certain time and place. It is then followed by a religious reflection of the author which illumines it.

Here at the start the order is reversed. The setting in the innermost reaches of deity comes first. The activity of John the prophet is placed in relation to it. A man in time witnesses to a heavenly "Word" and "Light" who likewise has become a man in time. The usual order in John first sets down a miraculous deed of Jesus or a conversation he engages in, often expository but sometimes polemical in nature. The Gospel then goes soaring into the farthest expanses of deity, situating Jesus somewhere there because it is his proper sphere. The reversal of the technique that will later prove usual in this Gospel, as found in its opening narrative, should not put us off. The story features an ascetic figure in the desert who wishes to downplay his own importance and testify to what is true about "the Son of God" (v. 34). In actual history, the memory of the prophet John was probably still strong in Palestine (and farther east) at the time the Gospel was written. Many must have had the problem of setting him and Jesus in relation in this new age of prophets. Like the other evangelists, John lets history serve his purpose by placing the son of Zechariah in a subordinate position to Jesus. His technique is to make the Baptist a witness to him, that and nothing more. John's testimony, basically, is that Jesus is the sacrificial Lamb of God who will take away (or bear upon himself) the world's burden of sin (1:29, 36). The Evangelist is sure of this and has no problem in making John say it.

We would make a bad mistake if we found in the prologue—and it is such both because it comes first and because it sets the tone for the whole—a poem about life in the heavens, not life on the earth. It is primarily a tale about John the prophet and Jesus; better, Jesus as illumined by the reflected glory of

13

John. But it comes at the beginning and is intended by all means as an account of Jesus' beginnings. These are his absolute beginnings. The Bible's opening in Genesis is a series of narratives about the earth's origins and human origins from the creative hand of God. The beginnings of "the Word," hence of Jesus who is that Word, are in God. Genesis in Greek translation begins with the phrase, *"En arche,"* "In the beginning." The Fourth Evangelist chooses it for his opening phrase for evident reasons.

In an important sense the opening of the Gospel is as much about the origins of the believers to whom it is addressed as it is about the origins of Jesus. He came forth from God as Word or Life or Light (vv. 1–5), says the omniscient narrator, before he became flesh to dwell among *us* (v. 14). The Word's coming as Jesus is important in our regard; it is not an isolated marvel touching the man Jesus only. The purpose was to come to his own home place and his own people (v. 11)—those prepared for such an event by centuries of God's loving self-disclosure, *that they might receive him, believe in him, and thereby be empowered to become offspring of God* (v. 12). No less is envisioned than the new divine begetting of all who have already known God as Israel's LORD. This is to be a sonship and daughterhood of God other than that achieved by the creation of humanity. It will even go beyond the covenantal bond that is sealed by Moses' law (v. 17). This Gospel assumes at all points the truth of the Israelite revelation. It is a piece of writing that makes no sense apart from the chosenness of Israel, the people of God's election through Abraham.

Something has already gone wrong with the plan: "His own . . . received him not" (v. 11). The author is convinced that a people prepared has not fulfilled its calling. Nothing, however, can put him off from telling what he has to tell. It may be the story of a plan that has in good part gone awry, but the plan has at least come to fruition among those the author knows best. The Evangelist *has* to tell of a Word that was with God in the beginning and has become a human being in the midst of other humans. He has to record the birth of many from God which will result from this unique divine birthing. All who have received and will receive the Word that became flesh were born not in the ordinary ways—the mixing of bloods, passionate desire, the ordinary will to conceive—but "of God" (vv. 12–13). This is to be a story certainly not of John, not of "Jesus Christ" only (v. 17), but of a new race of humanity. Just as Genesis starts

14

out, "In the beginning" (1:1) to tell the origins of the cosmos and the human race, this Gospel of John will be a story about fresh beginnings, a new human race.

The idea has been widely entertained for three-quarters of a century now that the nameless Evangelist possessed a poetic rendition about a Light or Word that was the life of humanity— an account of human redemption—which had no special Christian or even Jewish reference. Into this cosmic poem the author inserted the details of a Jesus-John juxtaposition. There was, in this theory, already the myth of a redeemer whose origins were in the heavens and who came to earth to give those who would become his devotees the fullness of knowledge and wisdom. This was to be of a liberating kind, setting its possessors free from all earthly limitation. It would empower them to come back with the liberator to the heavens from which he had originated. Unfortunately for the theory, no exemplar of this pre-Christian myth has been found. A later gnostic baptismal sect called the Mandeans *did* have such a tale, but we first learn of them in the seventh century. We are right to presume that their myth was influenced by John, not vice versa. A host of Christian gnostic systems arose much earlier than the Mandeans. They had in common a profound appreciation of the divine Word which came from heaven and returned there as the exalted Christ. The earth-bound human character of John and Jesus in the Gospel prologue had no appeal for them. Most of this we know from the writings of church fathers like Irenaeus, who quoted these sectarians extensively.

There came to light in Egypt (beginning in 1945) a library of Christian writings cognate with one aspect of John's Gospel that conceived of the redeeming Christ as largely (in some of the writings, totally) unbound by human limitation. Close parallels to the Johannine prologue and the soliloquies of Jesus in John were almost entirely lacking until these finds. Extant were the Christian or Christian-edited "Odes of Solomon" and the pre-Christian poems in which the goddess Isis was the speaker, making the claim in a sonorous chant: *"I am* this" or *"I am* that." The Coptic monastic library of Nag Hammadi in upper Egypt, however, which is the one referred to above, revealed the Fourth Evangelist to be the unwitting poet-founder of a school that contrived great beauties of christological expression at the cost of losing its moorings on the earth. The "Word that became flesh" as Jesus, John makes clear, was a person who at

15

times, despite gifts such as knowing the Father intimately and knowing people's thoughts, was thirsty and hungry and at other times was emotionally and physically exhausted. He went to a shameful death. Not so the central figure of some of these Christian gnostic tractates. Thus, "The Testimony of Truth," 30–31 can say:

> But the Son of Man [came] forth from Imperishability, [being] alien to defilement. He came [to the] world by the Jordan river, and immediately the Jordan [turned] back. And John bore witness to the [descent] of Jesus. For he is the one who saw the [power] which came down upon the Jordan river; for he knew that the dominion of carnal procreation had come to an end. The Jordan river is the power of the body, that is, the senses of pleasures. The water of the Jordan is the desire for sexual intercourse. John is the archon of the womb.
>
> (*The Nag Hammadi Library*, p. 407).

The "Gospel of Truth" makes of the poetic seed sown by the Fourth Gospel the following:

> The gospel of truth is a joy for those who have received from the Father of truth the gift of knowing him, through the power of the Word that came forth from the pleroma [fullness]—the one who is in the thought and the mind of the Father, that is, the one who is addressed as the Savior, (that) being the name of the work he is to perform for the redemption of those who were ignorant of the Father, while the name [of] the gospel is the proclamation of hope, being discovery for those who search for him. . . . This is the perfection of the thought of the Father, and these are the words of his meditation. Each one of his words is the work of his one will in the revelation of his Word. While they were still in the depth of his thought, the Word which was first to come forth revealed them along with a mind that speaks the one Word in silent grace. It (masc.) was called thought since they were in it (fem.) before being revealed. It came about, then, that it was first to come forth at the time that was pleasing to the will of him who willed. And that will is what the Father rests in and is pleased with . . . . Now the end is receiving knowledge about the one who is hidden, and this is the Father, from whom the beginning came forth, to whom all will return who have come forth from him. And they have appeared for the glory and the joy of his name.
>
> (*The Nag Hammadi Library*, pp. 37–38, 46).

16   Those abstract and convoluted reflections are the work of a second-class mind. The evangelist John, who had a first-class mind, set the story of John's testimony to Jesus against the background of biblical and post-biblical Wisdom speculation in

which God achieves all that God plans through a companion of old: the divine Wisdom. This Wisdom in the Bible is both God and other than God, a partner in colloquy for the great Alone who has neither consort nor like but only the richness of the fullness of majesty:

> Before the mountains had been shaped,
>   before the hills, I was brought forth; . . .
> When [the Lord] established the heavens, I was there, . . .
>   when he marked out the foundations of the earth,
>   then I was beside him, like a master workman;
> and I was daily his delight,
>   rejoicing before him always,. . . .
>   (Proverbs 8:25, 27, 29–30).

> For wisdom . . . is a breath of the power of God,
>   a pure emanation of the glory of the Almighty;
>   therefore nothing defiled gains entrance into her.
> For she is a reflecting of eternal light,
>   a spotless mirror of the working of God,
>   and an image of his goodness.
>   (Wisdom of Solomon 7:24–26).

If the Wisdom of God could so speak, was not this Wisdom clearly the Word who was with God in the beginning (1:1, 2) through whom all things were made (v. 3)? Had John and the community of faith that gave rise to him not known Jesus the Christ, the Wisdom of God in mortal flesh, the Evangelist would scarcely have made the claim. Only the experience of him brought on the affirmation, not speculation on Word and Wisdom after the manner of a geometric theorem. The Johannine community had known a person in the flesh—not immediately but by a chain of tradition—of whom it could say in faith, "without him was not anything made that was made" (v. 3). It could also say of him, "what God was, the Word was" (1:1c, NEB)—a better translation, given the Greek word order, than the familiar but confusing "and the Word was God," which betrays John's clear attempt to keep God and Word distinct. This Word who was in the beginning with God was the source of all light and life for humanity (v. 4). But life and light in the sense intended are attributes of deity itself. The Light that would shine in darkness in the person of Jesus is the Light to which the baptizing prophet John came to bear witness (vv. 7–8).

Experience precedes faith in this as in every case. The Evangelist proclaims what he has known. His proclamation con-

17

cerns the great reality of his life. Modern preachers of the biblical word likewise proclaim faith in Christ as Word of God become human. Have they known him? They knew him once, as idealistic but often untested youth. Much experience of life has intervened: disappointment, a few evangelical successes, and the always perilous venture of knowing the divine Word enfleshed in the believing community. That assembly is always made up of saints and sinners and the lukewarm in-between. Experience of it is not always edifying. The Christian preacher's life is a constant mixture of experiencing a "world that knew him not" (v. 10), by painful paradox, often within the church, and others "who received him, who believed in his name" (v. 12), the ones who make the venture of faith credible to a person whose task it is to express it publicly. To look for a Word become flesh in Jesus only can be thwarting. He is nowhere available on those terms. In the glory of heaven, yes; on the pages of Scripture, perhaps, by a massive exercise of imagination; but in life-fact only in the believing community, which by definition is a mixed population. Yet, without knowing the enfleshed Word in those who have "become children of God" (v. 12), the preacher of Johannine incarnation has nothing to proclaim.

To preach John's kind of faith it is as necessary to believe in a solid, sooty, sinful creation as it is to believe in a God who utters a creative Word. Flight to gnostic categories is much more attractive. It is no wonder that many pulpit practitioners take such flight. The author of "The Gospel of Truth" is a man for all seasons. John—the real John, not his gnostic interpreters through rhetorical abstraction—is a man of few seasons. But the few seasons speak. They speak to real people who are trying to live the gospel, not to the large donors whose names are found on the brass plaques of a world-denying, gnostic Christianity. It is the faithful poor, those who have suffered grievous loss and who yet believe, those who have been sorely tried and who cling to faith, those who are patient endurers of life's injustices that are those in whom the Word becomes flesh along with Jesus the Son. To have been intimately in their midst is to be able to preach the truth of an incarnate Word.

The true Light was in the world—an enlightening Light for whoever would let it be such (v. 9). John came to give testimony to the Light "that all might believe through him" (v. 7). Some would not in Jesus' day, in John's day, or now admit this Light (vv. 10–11). A tragic question that needs facing constantly is,

Are the self-professed children of the Light in fact children of darkness, not consciously evil but in their self-absorption closed to the light of God's truth? How do preachers ask that question of themselves? Of the people who support them by their contributions? How do they pose it publicly to a world that gives every evidence of being a darkened world unfriendly to the divine Light?

Directly, is the answer. Point blank. If they ask it regularly of themselves, they may be able to put it to congregations and to the world at large. No one can ever be sure of one's fitness to throw this challenge. The only way to find out is to try—and to ask oneself (in the next pulpit assignment?) whether one would have the courage to do it again. The Light that is Christ means something only when the attempt is made to dispel the prevailing darkness.

"And the Word became flesh and dwelt among us" (v. 14*a*). The verb chosen means "pitched his tent." It is redolent of God's desert-dwelling with Israel (cf. Num. 35:34; Josh. 22:19, combined with descriptions of the cloud of glory that covered the tent of meeting, e.g., Exod. 40:34). The "full[ness] of grace and truth" was evident in the human face of Jesus, this ardent Jew whose glorification empowered believers to see in him the enfleshed Word of God. "We have beheld his glory, glory as of the only Son from the Father" (v. 14*b;* but cf. 7:39). We have beheld it in those whom the Father has begotten through their belief in the glorified Son or we have not seen this glory at all. It is through a chain of tradition—believers begetting believers—that any can presume to say over the ages that they have beheld the glory "as of the only Son from the Father."

John testified to Jesus—on what ground we do not know (v. 15). Simply upon seeing him, as the Evangelist tells it. It would have to be the work of God. He looked and he saw someone who though he came after him ranked before him. And he gave testimony. Whoever sees the Word enfleshed in an individual, a congregation, even in a segment of a larger communion, has to give testimony to that Word by the power of God. It is a law of the Spirit.

The Gospel to follow will be a book of testimonies, for the witness of the Evangelist is immediately appended to that of the prophet John. John the evangelist will proclaim too who Jesus is, namely someone from whom people have received a genuine, not a spurious, "fullness" described as "grace upon

19

grace" (v. 16). Believers in Jesus are those who have been made full with the gift of deity itself. It has been delivered to them in the person of the enfleshed Word. There is probably a quiet polemic here against claims for a *pleroma* ("fullness") of godhead on other terms. "Grace upon grace" seems to be an answer to the claim (we can only know this because of the arguments reported later in the Gospel) that the divine gift follows upon each successive fulfillment of a commandment. The law given through Moses is a great gift (v. 17a), as the Fourth Evangelist acknowledges. He will never deny this, no matter how bitter the debates may be between Jesus' followers and the protagonists of Moses and the law (5:45–47; 6:32; 7:22–24; 9:28–29; 12:34; 19:7). But the author will declare at every point in his Gospel that God has done something new in making himself known through "the only God [the easier, hence less likely to be authentic reading, says 'the only Son'], who is in the bosom of the Father . . ." (1:18). This Gospel declares a new epiphany of the God whom no one has ever seen. Jesus Christ has revealed him. That is the whole meaning of the document before us. It records a struggle between those who acknowledge Jesus as the revealer of God and those who will not. The struggle will go on until the end of time: in every Christian assembly, in every pulpit occupied by proclaimers of this gospel, at times in open engagement between professed believers in Jesus and deniers of him in deed.

Excursus on the Opening Hymn's Pervasiveness Throughout the Gospel

It is essential to grasp at the start the insight that the entire Gospel will be a disclosure of God by the one in the bosom of the Father who could say, ". . . I know him" (8:55), and, "I speak of what I have seen with my Father . . ." (8:38). The conviction that Jesus is the Word of God become human is never returned to in so many words, but it underlies all that will later be said. What Moses cannot do through the promulgation of law-observance can be done through Jesus Christ in grace and truth (v. 17). For while the lawgiver came down from the mountain having heard but not seen God (v. 18a; cf. 6:46), Jesus "who is from God . . . has seen the Father" (6:46). He is "from above" (8:23) and declares to the world what he has heard from the one who has sent him (8:26b; cf. 16:28).

The Fourth Evangelist nowhere attempts to *prove* the

20

marvelous allegation that underlies his Gospel, namely that Jesus is sent from the God with whom he has always enjoyed unspeakable intimacy (12:44; 13:20). This is already the faith of the Johannine community. John merely enunciates it. He is in a condition of seeing and knowing through witnesses who give their testimony, and have done so going back to Jesus' day. The chain of testimony is what matters; it is unbroken. Consequently the burden of the first twelve chapters will be the many persons and events that testify to who Jesus is. The best witness, however, is Jesus' own person, the words that he speaks (4:41–42; 5:47). Jesus gives the supreme testimony on his own behalf. The Evangelist can do no better than relay it.

The chief mistake one could make about the Jesus of John's Gospel is to conclude that the Christology of epiphany denies or diminishes Jesus' humanity. It does not. Numerous heresies, gnostic and other (notably the second-century Docetists or "seemists"), have supposed that the Fourth Gospel gives them warrant to place the redemptive deed of God firmly in mid-air: more elegantly, in the heavens from which Jesus came. The manifestation of the Word as Jesus in John is as indisputably an occurrence of the land of Israel—the lakeshore of Galilee and the hill of Golgotha—as it is in the other Gospels. The Jewish Jesus is as much a reality of this Gospel as of the Synoptics. Here, as in other Gospel places and Acts, he is made to distance himself from certain elements in the Jewish community by speaking of "your" or "their law" (8:17; 10:34; 15:25). He argues with his law-observant opponents passionately. He takes the pains to avoid a premature, violent death because his mortality awaits demonstration only when it is "his hour" (13:1; 19:27), an hour that previously "has not yet come" (2:4; 7:30; 8:20). Jesus is not a mere marionette in this Gospel, but he does do things only on his Father's schedule. He is, one must say, supremely in charge of his destiny (see 10:18). Witness the preternatural dismay that overcomes the soldiers at the sight of him in the garden (18:6) and the lordliness with which he conducts the exchange with Pilate (vv. 33–38). In that chapter it is Pilate and not he who is on trial. He fulfills the Father's plan, but he does it in sovereign freedom.

The Evangelist has taken the traditions he has received and read them, so to say, from God's side. Call it if you will the theologizing of a human drama. This Gospel tells how a man speaks and acts who is literally inebriated with the divine. The

21

two, human and divine, are distinct realities in John. Jesus is not God and God is not Jesus. Word of God he surely is, but this causes him to engage in no recorded internal conversations with God or to experience any confusion over what is man and what is God in him. Jesus is an integrated human being throughout. He has a lively consciousness of God as uniquely Father to him. He is by that fact "the Son." Later reflections in the church on the mystery of this intimacy, going back to Jesus' origins in God as Word, would yield the statement in faith that he "is very God of very God." Yet nowhere does John state this in its Niceno-Constantinopolitan clarity. The creedal affirmation is the deeply reflected-upon faith of the church.

Is the theological construct of a Word become human real, or does it exist only in the Evangelist's mind? The glorification of Jesus, a matter long believed in at the time of the writing, has made the unique sonship of Jesus eminently real to the Johannine community. This final flowering in the Jesus Christ of glory had its roots in the divine being, John is convinced, or it could never have been manifested in him as it was. "Glory," a divine reality, does not, cannot overtake a mere human being in its fullness. It must have been Jesus' condition from the beginning or it could not have been given him at the end. On such a premise the writing proceeds.

John 1:19–51

John 1:19–28 (and vv. 6–8) is the choice of all the lectionaries on the Third Sunday of Advent in Year B (2). This provides an excellent opportunity to stress the difference the Johannine perspective makes. John's treatment of John the Baptist and his role is quite unlike that of the Synoptics despite his use of common motifs. He makes John a witness, the first to bear testimony to Jesus the Light, and not the baptizer of Jesus. John affirms who Jesus is by denying who he is not. The proximity of Mark's development of the Baptist's place in the story of salvation on the previous Advent Sunday is an advantage. The way Johannine thought functions should be made clear at every opportunity. It is a distinct treasure of the church, not something to be incorporated carelessly with the various (likewise mutually distinct) Synoptic theologies.

John's testimony to Jesus in the Fourth Gospel occurs on the Second Sunday of the Year (or after Epiphany) in Years A (vv. 29–34) and B (vv. 35–42) in the Catholic and Common lectionaries, while the Lutheran and Episcopal use verses 29–41 for Year A, verses 43–51 for Year B.

22

The first eighteen verses of chapter 1 largely take care of the testimony rendered by the Baptist (who is never so designated in John) to the one who "was before me" even though he "comes after me" (v. 15). It continues briefly, however, by way of a grilling of this witness. In verse 19 priests and Levites are sent as emissaries of Jerusalem's "Jews"/"Judeans" *(Ioudaioi)*, here the power class that serves John in the way the "scribes and Pharisees" do the Synoptics. But the Evangelist also knows of John the Baptist's "testimony" (v. 19). The desert-dweller denies being "the Christ"—John uses the Greek term here— and then, on direct challenge, Elijah or "the [end-time?] prophet" (vv. 21–22). The prophet like Moses whom God will raise up (Deut. 18:15) is widely understood to be spoken of here. John is a "voice" crying out prophetically with Isaiah for a straight way for the Lord (v. 23). The Isaian passage is made by the Evangelist to begin: "Make straight the way . . .," more or less as in the Synoptics. Both are unlike the Hebrew which reads: "A voice cries: 'In the wilderness prepare the way. . . .' " (v. 23)

John possesses the testimony-tradition common in Christian circles, but his abbreviated version of what follows is his own. Like the other evangelists he uses the Scriptures not slavishly but magisterially—that is, to say what they mean in Christ. The Baptist's right to function as a baptizer has been challenged in the familiar threefold way (vv. 19–22, 25). He denies that he is the Christ or Elijah or the prophet, then points to an unknown of the future to whom he stands in the relation of a subordinate, even a servant (vv. 26–27).

"Among you stands one . . . the thong of whose sandal I am not worthy to untie" (v. 27). An Indian Christian of the writer's acquaintance raised in Kuwait, although his roots are in Kerala, is having trouble coming to terms with the new church he has encountered in the cultural West, specifically at a university program in computer studies in Arizona. Picking a volume of Christian "spirituality" off a shelf randomly—a work of the thirties by a French Dominican friar once read widely in Europe and elsewhere—he says: "I was raised on this." He only half expects the person near him to believe it. "This was the faith of my youth. I was taught to think everyone superior to myself, to prefer everyone's will to my own." Old, worn-out Flemish Christianity redolent of Bishop Jansenius of Ypres or the pietiest strain in Protestantism? Or the sentiment of the Baptist who saw God in Jesus but not in his own ascetic self? "I baptize with water; but among you stands one whom you do not know, even he who comes after me, the thong of whose sandal I am not worthy to untie" (v. 27). ". . . You are slaves of the Lord Christ"

(Col. 3:24*b*). ". . . In humility count others better than your-selves" (Phil. 2:3).

The Evangelist knows the veneration in which John is held as late as his own lifetime. He knows the lure of the ascetic and the capacity of a Jesus who converses publicly with women (4:27) to put off the pious. He must make the case for Jesus and against the Baptist. "You sent to John, and he has borne witness to the truth. . . . He was a burning and shining lamp, and you were willing to rejoice a while in his light. But the testimony which I have is greater than that of John; for the works which the Father has granted me to accomplish, these very works which I am doing bear me witness that the Father has sent me" (5:33, 35–36).

The Baptist's testimony to Jesus is delivered piecemeal as the Evangelist describes a series of days in which John gives his witness on the first (vv. 19–28), second (vv. 29–34) and third (vv. 35–36). It peaks in verse 34: ". . . I have seen and have borne witness that this is the Son of God." On day two John knows Jesus as the redeeming "Lamb of God" without having hereto-fore seen him. The God who sent him to baptize with water identifies to him, as the one who baptizes with the Holy Spirit (v. 33), the person on whom the Spirit descends as a dove. The testimony concerning the Lamb is repeated to two of John's disciples "the next day" (day three). With the transfer of these disciples to the new teacher Jesus thus achieved, John the Bap-tist slips away.

Is the Evangelist trying to construct a symbolic week? He has started his account with the phrase, "In the beginning." The Genesis narrative which opens in this way shortly begins to describe a symbolic week. The Gospel can be discovered to be doing the same, however, only by a manipulation of its data. The attempt is interesting, if not convincing, and is as follows: Day four would begin after sundown ("the tenth hour," i.e., 4 P.M. "that day," v. 39). The events surrounding Andrew's seek-ing out Peter and bringing him to Jesus would then absorb a fifth day (vv. 40–42); the "next day" on which Jesus decides to go to Galilee and finds Philip (and in turn, Nathanael) would be the sixth day; and the seventh or final day would be the mysteri-ously designated "third day" of the marriage feast (2:1). Aside from the impossibility of the literal northward journey on foot in one day, there is the more basic problem that John seems to have abandoned any symbolism—if he ever intended it—by

24

mid-week. His, "On the third day" (2:1) may be the fulfillment of a biblical third day (cf. Hosea 6:2) of the prophecy of 1:51 about angels ascending and descending on the Son of Man. It may be the more prosaic day of celebration after three hard days of travel. Or again, it may be the way the Cana story began in John's source, transmitted untouched.

None of these considerations of schedule is important compared to what is going on in the second part of the chapter. Jesus' acquiring two new disciples from John (v. 37) and others in turn (vv. 41, 43, 45) is the matter of paramount concern. In a pattern different from his calling them to follow him in the Synoptics, they discover *him.* Each immediately gives witness to Jesus by ascribing a title to him. Jesus' asking, "What do you seek?" (v. 38), is a surprisingly brief first utterance in light of all the lengthy discourses he will later speak in this Gospel.

Is it of any significance that Andrew's companion is unnamed (vv. 35, 37, 40)? There are those who suppose that the disciple whom Jesus loved is already being introduced here, even as some think that "the other disciple who was known to the high priest" (18:16) is the same figure. Much more significant than that speculation would seem to be the dispatch with which the Gospel deals with the various titles Jesus is known by. It is as if John wishes to tell the readers that he knows well that some are hailing Jesus as the Messiah (v. 41), the one spoken of in the law and the prophets (v. 45). The entire sequence exists for the sake of these and other titles of Jesus and his bestowing the title of Rock (Cephas) on Simon (v. 42).

One almost concludes that John wishes to assemble the expressions of faith in Jesus that he knows are abroad: true but insufficient. Yet when the climax comes at the end it surprises us: Jesus is, on his own testimony, "the Son of man" (v. 51). That this is not the Son of man of the Synoptics must be noted. That figure is always a simple human being or a present sufferer or a future reigning apocalyptic figure. John's Son of Man is a person on whom angels ascend and descend from the open heavens. He is God's man, even as the Jacob of the ladder was the man who became "Israel" and gave that name to his people. There is already a sense of mystery about Jesus' calling to which every phrase in the first chapter contributes. He is more than and greater than all the claims that are being made in his favor. Jesus is interchangeable with the whole Jewish people and they with him. He is the contact point on earth with the myriads of

25

heavenly messengers. This man who is "Son of man" must be heeded in his least utterance.

Already in the first chapter of this "spiritual Gospel," as Clement of Alexandria was to call it, there is impenetrable mystery. One perceives human contacts of a most dramatic kind, but the terms are not the ordinary human ones. A man is sent from God with the sole purpose of testifying to another who will be the very Light of God. Those are the normal terms of a prophet, so there is no surprise in the John portrait—only in the immense claim made in behalf of the one who is to come after him. The *Shekinah* (Mishnah *San.* 6:5; *Aboth* 3:2), a post-biblical term for the divine light or presence, is a symbol of deity itself, yet it is a human being who is the object of the prophet John's testimony. The outcome of the prophesied one's appearance is told at the start. He endured rejection by the very "world" that was made through him (1:10). His own did not receive him, yet those who did receive him became off-spring of the divine. To have known this man is to have beheld his glory, the glory of the "only God." The forerunner of the one announced confesses that he does not know him, yet he is sure that a sign from God will disclose him. And so it happens. The confirming sign is the Spirit descending in the form of a dove.

Jesus is recognized as a teacher by two disciples of John before he has spoken a word, then shortly as Messiah and the long-awaited one to whom all Scripture has pointed. The pace of the narrative is not real. Little is explained. When Jesus first speaks he gives Simon the name "Cephas" ("Rock") without explanation or background (v. 42). He exercises a preternatural recognition regarding Nathanael—"Before Philip called you, when you were under the fig tree, I saw you" (v. 48*b*)—and views himself in terms of a well-known tale of the patriarch Jacob. What is going on here? How can this unabashed theology "from above" prove acceptable to a modern age which says it can only make sense of a theology "from below"?

Johannine Christology and the Road to Nicaea

The Fourth Evangelist in taking his narrative stance at the vantage point of godhead runs a risk that he thinks the entire biblical history of the people of Israel justifies. This people, secure in its faith as the chosen of the God it called YHWH (*Adonai* or "LORD" being substituted in speech to avoid pronouncing the Name), assembled its writings after returning from exile and composed new ones in a spirit of perfect confidence. The action of this people's God was assumed to account for its slightest adventure. The LORD accomplished what was done in Israel's midst because it was the divine will to do so. Messengers were sent to express God's bidding, prophets were illumined to speak, warriors were to do battle and win. When things went against this people, a series of increasingly sophisticated explanations was brought to bear. Nowhere, however, was there either apologia or excuse for the activity of God. It was simply the given which underlay all. The faith of Israel in its God was sufficient justification for the assumption.

Whatever John may have known of previous approaches to setting down the traditions about Jesus, the Gospel he composed was the option he took. He set himself to write a book fully in the biblical spirit in which God's action in Jesus accounted for all that took place. How was that action so surely known? It had to be what was experienced in the community. Those who knew the ones who knew others who knew Jesus Christ glorified had always had this faith in him as indwelt by God. It was now being challenged; John knew that. It was being challenged unwarrantedly, he was convinced, even by those who professed themselves to be believers in Jesus Christ. This could not be let alone to continue. Some vigorous protagonists of Moses were setting themselves in opposition to the protagonists of Jesus, even to the point of violent challenge. Resistance seems to have been a matter of daily experience in the lives of John and his community.

Something far more subtle than a struggle between law-observant Jews and the followers of Jesus of Nazareth seems to have been going on. It appears that Johannine claims in favor of Jesus were being questioned by some who said they believed in him but could not relinquish Moses' role in their lives as the conveyer of ultimate divine authority. We cannot tell whether they thought Jesus was a second revealer of God after Moses. We only know that his intimate position as the Word ever with God was more than their Israelite monotheism could endure. It is not easy to know with whom the Johannine church is locked in mortal combat, nor over precisely what issues. The answer is that they fought with some who are Jews—but nearly all in this Gospel may ethnically be Jews—and they fought over the identity of Jesus in a context of the ancient Mosaic deliverance of commandments.

This is a terribly contentious Gospel. Its polemical character is as strong as its mystical strain. Our modern tragedy is that we know fragments of what the struggle was about but not the whole story. This Gospel reports on thought worlds in collision. Exactly what positions were held by the Evangelist's opponents, however, or what he thought they were and how legitimately they held them from their own standpoint, we cannot be sure.

All this makes the modern preacher's approach to the Fourth Gospel precarious. The document expresses an important aspect of the church's apostolic faith. More than that, it is the christological faith that came to prevail in the councils and creeds. The modern church of East and West is irrevocably Johannine. For that reason, to preach John's Gospel is necessarily to take a stand on the faith of the subsequent centuries. Christian believers hear it with their minds made up as to its meaning. Their whole formation as Christians has ensured this. A prime difficulty is that one needs to have a genuine Johannine faith to preach in this Gospel's spirit. That means there must be the unshakable conviction that God is at work in the community, in Jesus Christ through the Word and the Spirit Paraclete (cf. 14:16–17, 26; 15:26; 16:13–14). Without such a conviction, one had better fall silent.

It is easier to proclaim doctrinal positions with a confidence bordering on certainty than to profess the faith the Fourth Gospel demands. Mouthing its sonorous statements can be repulsive if Johannine faith is absent. Preachers are constantly being challenged by this evangelist as to whether they have the faith to proceed with the relating of a simple occurrence in Jesus' career from the standpoint of God. For that is what John does constantly. The problem of John in the church, paradoxically, is that so many have exposed this Gospel so readily! Instead of silence after proclaiming it publicly, they went on with a cascade of words about "glory" and "testimony" and "this world" and "condemnation."

They have done worse. Many have extracted from John a Christology that is formally heretical. Not taking the pains to struggle through the fourth and fifth-century debates, they have gone down the gnostic path of seeing a divine Logos briefly held captive in a body of flesh. "This man is God" they have thundered from the pulpit, setting aside all Johannine, not

28

to say Nicene and Cappadocian, subtleties. The Evangelist never makes that statement, even as the christological councils do not, but always something more nuanced. "This Word of God came to be the man Jesus," is closer to the mark. But, immediately, more has been said that is incomprehensible than comprehensible.

A temptation even greater than the theological is provided by this graphic author. It is especially serious in an age when people who have attended seminaries are increasingly less attracted to theological matters. John tells engaging stories with such swift strokes that the modern homilist is inclined to take the disciples' discovery of Jesus or the Cana wedding or his exchanges with the Samaritan woman and construct from them pulpit parables of psychological response. In a way, that is fair enough since the Evangelist was the first to play the game. But to rest on a human plateau of encounter with the human Jesus is surely to betray the Johannine intent. He is always operating symbolically and on the plane of deity as well. This does not mean that his symbolism must be ours in every case. Often we cannot be sure what his symbolism is or, discovering it, make it useful for contemporaries. That can settle the matter from the start. But the human in Jesus is always a parable of the divine; it is not a veil but a disclosure. Not to let the symbolism soar to the point where it discloses the divine glory in Jesus is to betray the Evangelist's purpose.

An attractive route is the allegorical. You cannot choke it off. The Evangelist often gives evidence that he himself has an allegorical intent. His work is perverted only when a metaphysical principle is attributed to him other than the one on which he is operating. He does not have a matter-spirit opposition. Only a faulty hermeneutic can discover that in him. John's "genuine" (or "authentic" or "real") is, in fact, the divine. This is set against the inauthentically human, which is a bad copy of the "Light" or "Word," the "Vine" or whatever it may be that is not demonstrably of God. John the Evangelist is not the enemy of the temporal or the material or the human. He is the friend of all that comes from God and, by way of belief in the Son, goes back to God. He interprets all human reality by asking, implicitly, the simplest question: How can it come to share in the divine glory proper to Jesus Christ for which it is intended?

29

John 2—4
A Wedding, a Night Visitor, a Conversation at Midday

Chapters 2–4 are important to what will follow in this Gospel, especially the first half, because they set the tone for a certain kind of testimony to Jesus. The first chapter was concerned with the witness to Jesus provided by John the Baptist and by Jesus' earliest disciples. This only Son, in turn, testifies to the Father. He who has been in the Father's bosom makes God known. The pattern of testimony to Jesus so that he will be trusted as an authentic revealer of God continues here. It takes the form of "signs," identified as Jesus' "first" (2:11) and "second" (4:54). In between these two miraculous deeds there are provided other signs of a new order of the ages, the upraised temple of Jesus' body (2:18, 21), birth "from above" in water and Spirit (3:3, 5), and a time of future worship in spirit and truth that will not be bound to a sacred site (4:21–24). In the midst of all this, the testimony of John the Baptist begun in chapter 1 is completed (3:22–30; cf. 5:36).

John's narrative style in the first half of his Gospel (chaps. 1–12) is largely the same throughout. He will tell a story of the most deceptively simple kind. It may be a miracle story either of healing or control over nature, but that does not tell against its simplicity. Incorporated into the story will be a conversation between Jesus and another person, which shortly proves to be the reason why the tale is told. There may be a healing in circumstances which embroil Jesus in a debate with unfriendly onlookers. Sometimes the follow-up to the wonder he performs is developed very little, as in the case of the Cana miracle with which chapter 2 opens. There, Jesus' deed comes to the steward's notice but to no one else's except his disciples', in whom it causes belief in him (v. 11b). Whole companies of people come to have faith in the "signs which he did" (v. 23), as in Jerusalem during his first recorded Passover when he cleansed the temple and his disciples believed "the scripture and the word which

Jesus had spoken" (v. 22*b*), or Sychar of Samaria where many believed in him (4:39, 42). The signs seem to trigger belief if not to act as its cause.

One marvel of healing—in this case of an official's son—is told just as it might have been in a Synoptic Gospel, with the brief concluding statement that the official at Capernaum "believed and all his household" (4:53). Such lack of development, however, is rare. Most of Jesus' "signs" are worked in John to give the Evangelist an opportunity to comment at length on their significance. They all illumine the same point, namely who Jesus is in relation to God ("the Father"). Once this has been established, John has little more to say; but his Jesus may say quite a lot to establish it. A discourse of Jesus will be followed, in certain cases, by a reflection of the Evangelist. The two are barely distinguishable. Together they give meaning to the observation that the Jesus of John is "the first Christian believer."

Are all of Jesus' miraculous deeds "signs" for John, and are signs by definition miraculous? Neither can be established with certainty. Two of Jesus' miracles are described as signs (2:11; 4:54), yet others have intervened and will follow which are unspecified as to number or numbering (2:23; 3:2; 6:2). When the term is used generically, it describes events which are both public and marvelous. A "sign" and a "work" appear to be interchangeable (6:30). The greatest work of God, however, is belief in the Son (6:29) which, however marvelous, is not public, or is such only by dint of verbal proclamation. Must not Jesus' final lifting from earth, then, the crucifixion part of that twofold "raising up" which gives eternal life if it is viewed in faith (3:14), be a sign? And what of Jesus' driving the money changers from the temple? Does John mean to include this as one of the signs Jesus performed which made many believe in him (2:23)?

Those who make a list of the signs in John 1—12 usually give seven, culminating in the raising of Lazarus, which points to the greatest of all: Jesus' death and resurrection. To make a list of seven, they must include only miraculous signs. John is not of much help here. Those who say he had a "signs source" available to him are able to tell its probable content only by defining beforehand what the term "sign" meant to John. Whatever the signs that Jesus performed were for John, they were numerous in his public life (20:30). The ones that were written about were set down to encourage or confirm belief in

31

him (20:31). Numerous though they were, they did not compel belief (11:47). Indeed, faith seems to be required in John to make a miracle a sign.

John's career as forerunner was marked by no signs whatever but by something much greater: Whatever he said about Jesus was true (10:41). Testimony, therefore, precedes signs in importance, although the signs occur to give testimony. It seems to be John's considered view of the works which Jesus did that they are subordinate to belief in his words—words not spoken on his own authority (14:10b). Jesus solicits from Philip belief that he is in the Father and the Father is in him (14:10a)—on the authority of Jesus' words alone (14:10b). Only if Philip cannot believe in Jesus' person may he fall back on the works the Father does, the God who dwells in Jesus, as leading to faith (v. 11).

Not a moment's doubt surfaces in the Fourth Gospel that being sent by God as Jesus was does not include his authority over nature. He is nature's master, to the end that people may marvel (5:20) and, marveling, believe. There is the tragic possibility of profiting from the marvelous—namely, being fed, a type of personal advantage—without seeing it as a sign (6:26). John reports on the signs that Jesus does in a context of belief in him. He has no other interest in them.

> John shows that . . . for the people to see through the miracle to the sign (i.e., to Jesus' identity) some preliminary faith is sometimes present (2:11; 4:46–54; 20:30–31; 21:6–7), but at other times is not present (2:23; 3:2 . . . 11:45): when faith is already there the miracles deepen it (2:11; 4:46–54; 20:30–31); when miracles evoke faith or openness to faith, a further development is necessary if Jesus is to be understood properly (e.g., chap. 3; chap. 9) (Charles H. Talbert, p. 60).

John 2:1–12

The Cana story occurs on the second Sunday after Epiphany (second in the year) in Year C in all the lectionaries, halting at verse 11 in all but the Catholic, which includes verse 12.

In an abrupt opening, John situates the mother of Jesus at the Cana wedding, then makes Jesus and his disciples appendages to her presence. The choice of "the first of his signs" (2:11) is governed by a reminiscence of his family piety, his filial devotion. Mary is never named in John. She is always "the mother of Jesus" (v. 1; cf. v.12; 6:42; 19:25–27) or "Woman" in the

32

vocative case (v.4; 19:26). The Evangelist uses her here as a paradoxical symbol of both intercessory power with her Son and the impropriety of anyone's having a claim on him except the Father. She will first be told, in a stroke of psychological distancing, that it is not his "hour" (v.4). Only *God's* demands on Jesus, in other words, are to be heeded. Then the deed requested is done. Later she will be made a symbol of concern for the needs of believers in her son, typified by the disciple whom Jesus loved. The disciple will be described as taking her to himself "from that hour" (19:27). The disposition of events is always in divine hands, not human, Jesus seems to say in verse 4.

Every character in this Gospel has to bear more than an ordinary human burden. All are there to carry forward the design of the Father to beget "children of God" (1:12) in the Son. At the cross the disciple whom Jesus loved seems to stand for all believers in a relation to "the woman" and she to them: the church as a family of believers. This apparent Eve symbolism of John made Saint Justin Martyr in the mid-second century, and after him Irenaeus and Tertullian, create a "new Eve" of Mary—the companion of Paul's second Adam, Christ, in the work of redemption, just as the woman was the companion of the man in the fall. Some think the symbolism is not there to be seen, that John tells the story of the initial refusal of the request only to show that ties of blood could not prevail in the new community. The writers of the early centuries, in the typology they adopted, read the story otherwise.

Cana is a village of no special consequence. It does not appear in the Hebrew Scriptures, even as most of the tiny settlements in Galilee do not. Yet its situation in the north, Jesus' homeland, is important to John's carefully crafted narrative. Galilee is the place where he is almost universally received, Judea the place where he is widely rejected. An important exception to the latter is the poor reception given to his discourse in the Capernaum synagogue about being the bread of life. There, uncharacteristically, the Jews (*hoi Ioudaioi;* the question throughout this Gospel is, *which* Jews?) who murmur and dispute him are to be found (6:41, 52). We shall see later what these normal denizens of Judea—inclining some to translate *hoi Ioudaioi* "the Judean opposition"—are doing there, that is, resisting Jesus' teaching about himself in Galilee.

The wedding tale is told almost laconically. "When the wine failed" (v. 3) is a genitive absolute, having in this context of celebration some of the characteristics of the sun's rising or the tide's going out. Jesus' mother alerts him to the problem of the exhausted supply. There are no details provided, no moralizings proposed. The party has come to a dessicate halt: bone dry. The maidens cannot rejoice in the dance nor the young men and the old be merry (Jer. 31:13a), for there is no new wine on which the virgins may flourish (Zech. 9:17). Jesus' response to the observation of his mother is hardly gallant. It is hardly acceptable Greek. It is, however, recognizable Septuagint Greek as we shall see shortly. This puts us on notice that something different is going on than a family vignette about concern for a host's embarrassment.

We have been given a clue, by the designation of Eve at her creation as "the woman" (Gen. 3:23), that the mother of Jesus is being placed in an archetypal role. But first the Evangelist must distance the woman of his story from the man by putting on his lips the familiar biblical challenge, "What do we have in common?" or "What do you have against me?" (v. 4; cf. Judg. 11:12; II Sam. 16:10; I Kings 17:18). The basic problem is then disclosed: The hour of his full manifestation has not yet come. John will spend much time in his narrative on the disclosure of Jesus' glory in its proper time. The Son can do nothing but what the Father would have him do. The final epiphany is reserved for his being lifted up from the earth. All depends on the careful outworking of the divine design.

Clearly the scruple of Jesus is required only to send the narrative forward. The mother's word to the servants follows quickly. She is as peremptory with them as he will be in his disposition of her from the cross. Her word is not a pragmatic suggestion at a village wedding. As John frames it, it is a watchword for the Christian ages: "Do whatever he tells you" (v. 5). Like the Pharaoh's command to the Egyptians, "Go to Joseph; what he says to you, do" (Gen. 41:55; the LXX wording is the same as John's except for the tense of the verb for "says"), it is an instruction to seek life at its source. Jesus is the possessor of life and the dispenser of life (3:36a; 5:24). The woman's word of command to the servants foreshadows the instruction of her Son regarding prayer: "Ask whatever you will, and it shall be done for you" (15:7b). Though there he counsels petition to God, here she is proposing recourse to him. John has the mother know the power of the Son. Doing whatever Jesus commands is for John the essence of discipleship (cf. 15:14, 16).

34

Stone jars (v. 6) would have required less purification than jars of baked clay. Their non-porosity made a great difference to the laws of purity. Is their being six a detail of significance? It is attractive to say that the fact that they are short of the sacred number seven is important to John. We cannot know. We need to be on the alert, however, for symbolism everywhere. The amount of water in the restocked jars—some one hundred and fifty gallons—would have provided a great amount of "good wine" (v. 10) for a party already in mid-course. This does not seem to be the Evangelist's point. He is more concerned with the implications of the purification requirement for the dusty hands and feet of travelers who are ritual observants: namely, that the water of one epoch—that of the narrative—must be replaced by the wine of another, the age inaugurated by Jesus' words and deeds. In this account the symbolism is everything.

The instructions of Jesus to the servants about filling the jars with water to the rim, then making a draught for the steward's examination, make a great deal of sense as story. As a description of their conduct, they create a problem of sequence. What did the servants know, and when (v. 9)? The origins of the water? the wine? John's interest is centered on "where [the water now become wine] came from" (v. 9) in a "whence" *(pothen)* that is central to his tale. This is a verbal clue to his readers. It prepares them for the mystery of the origins of the "living water" Jesus will promise the Samaritan woman (4:11), and indeed for all later mention of the origins of Jesus himself (7:27; 8:14; 19:9). John's great question is, "Whence" is he? In this Gospel Jesus does not "come from" Nazareth in Galilee or any other physical location (despite 1:45). He comes from above, from God, as does the gift of water he gives, "welling up to eternal life" (4:14). The servants know, at the level of fact, that the water which became wine had its immediate origins in Jesus; yet John does not equate that knowledge with faith in Jesus. As so often in the chapters to come, John is operating on two levels—both of time and meaning. He sets up his *double entendre* (the phrase has been debased) and, like a good raconteur, looks on with suppressed expectancy to see if the reader follows him. He is not a heavy-handed narrator who says: "Where it came from! Do you get it? From Jesus who gave the order or from on high, which is where Jesus originates?" That is not John's style. He prefers to plant clues around

35

the landscape and wait to see who can interpret his entirely serious theological charade.

The order of life is reversed by Jesus, this master of the revels who gives new life to the nuptial celebration. He does not provide vintage wine at the start when palates are sharp but when the party is in full swing. What kind of Jewish Dionysos is this (the pagan god had his shrine not far off in pagan Beit Shan, the Greek Scythopolis)? The Jesus of John has saved the good wine until the "now" of a first disclosure of his glory (v. 10). It was a manifestation, an epiphany, and it was meant to be that—observed later in the church as the Epiphany on the feast of Dionysos, January 6 in our calendar, when it was reputed in the Greek world that the god turned water into wine.

Water is the great elixir of the Bible. One must have lived in a dry country for even a little while to know the force of the symbolism of thirst and its slaking, rivers and streams, dry river beds, and exhausted wells. No one speaks ill of water in the Middle East. Similarly, no one should suppose that wine flowed freely and was drunk everywhere in lands of the Bible. It was a cash crop for vintners, like olive oil. Many a peasant was busy in its production. But the poor drank little wine and ate less meat. Cheese and bread and olive oil were their fare, with water for their daily thirst. At a wedding or other family celebration, it was different. There, a couple's parents would have scrimped and saved long to do it right. Family and friends passed harsh judgments on those who could not carry a wedding off in style. Sheep and calves and every delicacy would have been served in profusion and the wine would have flowed freely. There can have been no misprizing of water in the situation described in the Johannine tale, only a praise of wine as uniquely befitting the occasion.

In the late pre-Maccabean book of First Enoch, the vines planted "in those days"—the last age—will produce wine for plenitude (10:19). Philo the Jew of Alexandria, who outlived Jesus, has a treatise *On Dreams* in which he speaks of the divine *logos* (ordering of creation) in terms of rich, red wine. The same is true in some rabbinic writings descriptive of the messianic days, which set the wine of the future against the present age of water. Surely the glory of the age to come is being heralded by the Evangelist, who knows of a stream that runs red in the presence of one greater than Moses (cf. Exod. 7:17).

We must not forget that the author has let his reader in on

36

his faith conviction about Jesus from the start. Knowing his view of the power of God residing in Jesus, we are prepared for a series of disclosures of God at work in him. After the Baptist's testimony and the early faith of his disciples ("Thus did he reveal his glory, and his disciples believed in him," 2:11*b*, NAB), nothing should surprise us. Yet the muted quality of the first story takes us off guard. How would a crowd of merry-makers react to such a marvel? John solves the problem of keeping it from becoming public knowledge. The event is a reality for Jesus' mother and his new disciples only. The response of the latter is a confirmation of their incipient faith (v. 11). The drama then moves back to the privacy of a stay at Capernaum "for a few days" (v. 12). How can the busy commerce of this lakeside town contain the secret, especially as the fishermen resume ties with old friends in the company of this new one? That is the genius of this Gospel. It goes back and forth from one world to another, one eon to the next with silent ease. A small company's life is totally transformed, yet existence goes on as before. The orchestrator of this symphony will alternate fast movements with slow, the joyous with the somber, simple airs with symphonies of crashing majesty.

John knows from the experience of years now that to believe in Jesus as the Christ is to live a life within a life. Nothing is changed but everything is changed. What had been water is wine. Word has become flesh. An hour that has not yet come is here. This is existence at the edge of the ages, a point at which the old eon and the new dance a figured minuet. What will be *is.* What seems to be *is no more.* In this Word and Light of God who is a man, all is new. How else can the transformation be conveyed except in quiet parables of cosmic change?

The Cana miracle was read aloud annually in older lectionaries, surely too often, given the riches of all Four Gospels, a wealth which the practice impeded. But once in three years seems by any standard too infrequent. Homilists should not hesitate to introduce this most attractive of narratives into their preaching on other occasions. There it reposes in John for use whenever this seems fitting. When it is referred to, the temptation of the Catholic preacher may be to overstress Mary's intercession with her Son; of the Protestant, her initial rebuke by her Son. Both will be wrong, of course, for the story is at root about neither. It tells about the disclosure in ordinary family festive circumstances of the hidden glory of Jesus the Son. Cana's

37

meaning is not the expression of divine power in a miracle. Neither is it the relief of human discomfiture. Its meaning is that the hidden life of the children of God will inexorably be revealed. Moral lessons about excessive drinking are out of place in conjunction with this tale: elsewhere, perhaps, but not here. So are tidy moralities about family life. Not even marriage is in question except incidentally. This quiet tale is about a shift in eons, nothing less. It says nothing about the replacement of Judaism with its worshipful, extra-biblical ritual of purification—an important part of what would later be "oral Torah." It tells something profound about a fulfillment in history by the power of God through an uttered Word; of a promise made to the patriarchs, peaking in Moses the lawgiver and culminating in Jesus Christ. It is a story of the life of God with a beloved people continued.

It is well worth the preacher's while to meet the challenge of this wedding-feast pericope. It is easy to speak about a worn-out Jewish past and a vibrant Christian present, neither of which ever existed on quite the homilist's terms; but this is to be resisted. Dealing in caricatures is much easier than coping with religious realities. It is never more useful.

As with all Gospel truth, we are confronted at Cana by an interpretation of the hoped-for final age. John situates the age in his own time. This fact makes it both easier and harder for us to take in the reality, so foreign to our thinking, of first-century Judaism's "end-time." We modern Christians tend to relegate the last age as an event of the future to some never-never land or to the hour of our death. The cartoons of sign-carrying fuzzy-wuzzies announcing "The End" are our means of coping with a myth in which we only half believe. Even the Christians who say they take biblical apocalyptic literally have to put some modern construct in its place. Placing the last age in the middle of our lives, as John does, provides a certain immediate comfort; but it holds the possibility of long-term distress. Is the time of fulfillment really here? Has the life of the believer, on the believer's best day, filled any but the greatest "enthusiast" with the conviction that this age is a time of fiery red wine and not pallid water? Only preachers who by long meditation and prayer have experienced a new order of the ages can convince hearers that such an order has overtaken them. John's genius is that of the totally committed believer. Without belief in the hearer his prose is proper to the genial madman. Angels ascending and descending, the Messiah discovered, six jars of twenty-five gallons each of the finest vintage turned loose on an already incandescent peasantry. This is the poetry of absolute newness. Only those who live in newness know what to make of it.

In January the year is new. On the Jordan's bank of a baptismal font, life is new. The believer drinks from the cup of a renewed covenant (the *kaine diatheke* of Jesus' words at the supper table) and says: "It is the Lord." To believe is to know that the old order has passed away and the new has come. The Cana story invites congregations to consider seriously whether they think that the master of the feast who gives the brisk command, "Fill the jars with water. . . . Now draw some out . . . ," makes all things new. "Thus did he manifest his glory, and his disciples believed in him."

There must be newness of life in the many places where Christians assemble if this is not to be an idle winter's tale.

John 2:13–25

The church's ancient use of the Fourth Evangelist's temple-cleansing account continues into modern practice. It occurs but once in the three-year Sunday lectionary. That is on the third Sunday of Lent in Year B. The pericope is also traditionally to be found on Monday of the fourth week. The cleansing of the temple has long been taken as symbolic of the purification of candidates in preparation for their baptism on Easter eve. In union with the risen Christ they are to be members of his body, the believing people now become a new temple. The significance is therefore a baptismal and a pre-paschal one—which is the whole meaning of Lent. The liturgies in their selection and adaptation of Bible readings for the feasts and seasons have always taken the symbols they find there and moved them one step further.

John has situated Jesus until now only marginally in the religious life of his people. He has confronted him first with a desert solitary who is challenged by members of the temple priesthood (1:19) and the rigorously observant Pharisees (1:24). Family life is religious life for the Jew, so the wedding feast must be reckoned a religious event. Now, after a respite in what will become Jesus' adoptive home, Capernaum (v.12), there is a clash of Jesus with the commerce of religion in the temple area on a major feast. Today's newspapers have alerted us to enough bloody conflicts occurring on feast days on modern Israel's West Bank, in Saudi Arabia, and in the cities where Hindus and Muslims live that we should not be surprised by the relatively mild challenge that Jesus mounted. More surprising, perhaps, is its

39

containment. What survives vestigially as the report of a religious challenge may have had the aspects of a popular riot, *if* Jesus expressed the revulsion of many at what went on in the forecourt to the holy place. We do not have any strong evidence, however—only our imaginations—to bolster the view that the necessary trade in birds and beasts was thought to be an abuse or that this was Jesus' main concern with it. Once again, in this Gospel, the symbolism assigned to the historical event is more important than the event itself.

John places the occurrence early in Jesus' career for programmatic reasons. In the Synoptic tradition the cleansing occurs within the Passover during which he was arrested and condemned. Here in John it takes place during that spring festival, but in the first of the three Passovers which John records (v. 13; cf. 6:4; 11:55), not the last. The tendency of Christian tradition to assign Passover status to "a Judean feast" (5:1), although there is no reason to do so, has given us four Passovers in this Gospel, hence the familiar three-year public ministry. The historical grounds for such a three-year span are thoroughly shaky. We are sure only of John's desire to give Jesus' activities a liturgical framework. As part of this, John symbolizes him as Israel's paschal lamb, slaughtered on Preparation Day (cf. 1:29, 36; 13:1; 19:31–33).

The differences between John's account and those of the Synoptics are slight. He alone has Jesus make a whip of cords and drive the livestock and the money-changers out, spilling their coins (v. 15). Only John of the four quotes a verse of Scripture (v. 17; Ps. 69:9). The narrative is a diptych in two panels, 2:13–16 and 18–21, of which the second is a theological commentary on the first. Jesus' dismissal of the offenders is not the stitched-together Isaiah 56:7 and Jeremiah 7:11 of Mark 11:15–17 (which the Matt. 21:12–13/Luke 19:45–46 version largely resembles, "house of prayer *'for all the nations'* " having been removed). John has Jesus eject them with a paraphrased word from Zechariah 14:21 about traders in the LORD's *house"* (v.16). "My Father's" (v. 16) or "the LORD's *house"* (v. 17) is important to John because he means to use it interchangeably with the "this *temple"* logion (v. 20) of the Synoptic trial accounts: "Destroy this temple and in three days I will raise it up" (v. 19; cf. Mark 14:58: ". . . that is made with hands . . . not made with hands"; Matt. 26:61: "the temple of God").

40

Jesus is challenged in panel two on the meaning of his

action in panel one: "What sign have you to show us for doing this?" (v. 18). A proof of authority is here demanded, not a sign as a motive for belief. The answer Jesus gives is the sole Johannine prediction of the passion, and it is delivered thus early in the narrative. He acts authoritatively in his Father's house, the temple, because the basic dwelling place of the LORD, the God of Israel, is henceforward to be Jesus' body. This body is the "temple" of the Evangelist's concern (v. 21). The deed of Jesus indicates that the final days have arrived—in his person.

What is the Scripture that his disciples believed after he was raised from the dead (v. 22b)? Not Zechariah or the Psalm so much as all that was said on the sacred page concerning the house of the LORD. Every reference to the temple was fulfilled by "the word Jesus had spoken" (v.22b), a word as binding as Scripture itself.

Especially worthy of note is John's intimation in verse 22 that nothing concerning Jesus could be fully comprehended until he was raised from the dead. It is an important caution to us who preach or teach. We tend to pass judgment on the people of Gospel times—and even our own—for their lack of faith, when John makes confrontation with the risen Christ the reason why anyone *could* believe in him. Yet most who are not believers have never encountered the risen Lord. The paradox is that John has a stiffer standard for his contemporary antagonists—whom he regularly charges with failure to believe—than for disciples of Jesus like himself. And we follow him into the trap.

Jesus' sign of water become wine, John has written, helped to make believers of his disciples. Jesus' mother is not mentioned in this connection; she is made to speak with the conviction of a believer. His deed and word in the temple was another kind of witness to himself: possibly a sign, although not designated as such. What other "signs" did he do in Jerusalem at the Passover feast (v. 23)? We are not told. Whatever they were they made many "believe in his name"; but Jesus is wary—actually, John is wary—of this kind of human testimony (v. 24). Here we have the first indication in this Gospel that there is a witness to Jesus available which the Evangelist questions. Jesus knows the human heart (v. 25b) and does not commit himself to its fragile support (v. 25a). But is not belief in him the very search that John has Jesus intent upon? Evidently not *any* belief. Subsequent chapters will reveal a faith in Jesus that John

41

finds woefully lacking. Meanwhile, the division of the Jerusalem crowds over Jesus as a result of his signs continues to grow. There is faith, but not all of it is trustworthy because not all of it is authentic.

A Rebirth of Images

A catalogue in John of antitypes of newness up to this point would surely bring us to four: the Light corresponding to the witness to the Light; grace and truth through Jesus Christ corresponding to the law given through Moses; wine answering to water; and an upraised mortal body corresponding to an edifice of stone. In each case the first symbol is not abrogated by the second but given new meaning. A simple "replacement" theory, the curse of centuries of Christian preaching, is not in question here. John has no such theory. Yet he very clearly lives in a religious thought world where the book of biblical symbols is being read with fresh eyes. The later biblical writers did this with the work of earlier ones; authors later reckoned to be apocryphal (or in some cases deuterocanonical) did it with the subsequently declared canonical corpus. The covenanters of Qumran, the Tannaitic commentators who wrote the Mishnah, and all the other New Testament writers besides John similarly reworked the symbols contained in biblical passages (cf. Jacob Neusner, *Midrash in Context; Messiah in Context; Torah*). The evangelist John oversaw, in Austin Farrer's memorable phrase, a rebirth of images. To preach effectively on Johannine texts one must achieve a certain mastery of the author's symbol system. It is a self-contained universe that owes much to the Bible and a little to Synoptic Gospel material. A complicating factor is that John uses the words of other Gospel material but never the tune. His is a kaleidoscope which employs traditional data. The patterns which emerge from the turning cylinder are entirely his own.

John 3:1–12

The Episcopal and Common Lectionaries propose 3:1–17 for the second Sunday of Lent in Year A (1). All four lectionaries read 3:14–21 on the Fourth Sunday of Lent in Year B (2) and on Trinity Sunday in the same year the Lutheran and the Common have 3:1–17 while the Episcopal stops at verse 16.

The manifestation of the Son of man to those who will believe in him continues. Multiplying dependable witnesses is the Evangelist's chosen means. As he piles up testimony through signs and the words of Jesus himself, he knows that not all believe. Of those who do, some do not believe rightly. There is a brand of human testimony offered to Jesus that he has no need of (2:25). In the next story—the encounter of Jesus with a man of learning—well-intentioned adherence to ritual purity as the way to be a faithful Israelite is challenged. Nicodemus is called "a man of the Pharisees," "a ruler of the Jews" (v.1), and "a teacher of Israel" (v. 10).

The geographic pattern up to now has been Perean Bethany (immediately east of Judea), Galilee, then Judea again, through its capital Jerusalem. If a north-south alternation is being established, we should expect a vignette of Galilee next. The Nicodemus story is quite without locale, but at its conclusion Jesus and his disciples are reported going "into the land of Judea" (v.22). Nicodemus will be designated one of the Pharisees when he reappears in 7:50, but not in his final appearance as a burier of Jesus, along with Joseph of Arimathea (19:39). There the latter is said to be a secret disciple "out of fear" (19:38), as Nicodemus *may* be because of the detail in verse 2 that he came by night. Such has been the assumption of the ages, but it is nowhere stated in the Gospel. The influence of 19:39 has carried the day. One wonders immediately how much John wishes to say to his contemporaries about men of learning and influence who do not have the courage to profess their faith openly. Nicodemus will be portrayed as a "teacher of Israel" opaque about fundamentals, which may be his "night."

At this point, the Evangelist chooses to introduce into his narrative the distinction between flesh and spirit. He does not have Jesus work a sign for the benefit of Nicodemus (who makes the connection which good will ought to make between the signs Jesus has done and God's power in him, v. 2). John prefers to let the words of Jesus have their impact as testimony. The author portrays Nicodemus as resistant to this witness because of an incapacity for the obvious (v. 11). Here for the first time John employs the technique in which a conversation partner of Jesus' responds uncomprehendingly as a means of encouraging Jesus to further exposition. One wonders if the Evangelist may wish to characterize the learned generally as lacking in courage—doing their incipient faith in Christ to death by a thousand qualifications. Such pusillanimity has always resulted in *la trahison des clercs*—betrayal by the learned class—down to the ca-

43

pitulation of intellectuals (even theologians) to totalitarian ideologies. Its much commoner form, however, is a failure to face up to the demands of truth lest position or advantage be lost. Nicodemus is an important Gospel figure in the lives of preachers, teachers, and laity deep in the life of the churches. He is so familiar in his earnest spinelessness that he makes birth in the Spirit a very attractive option—for whoever will admit this beginning of new life on Jesus' terms.

The compromises of those for whom temple sacrifice means income have been dealt with in the cleansing narrative (cf. 2:16), although that concern does not seem uppermost for John. The men of holy commerce have their rationale. Jesus and his Johannine disciples question the use of the holiest site in the nation for this exchange. In its original historical setting this might have been a protest against temple sacrifice. The leaders of the teaching community, through their good-willed representative Nicodemus, may be fearful of losing respect, influence, tenure in office. Surely they are permitted a few scholarly scruples. What can birth "from above" be? (The "anew" of RSV seems a less apt rendering of the adverb *anothen*, 3:3, cognate with the "whence," *pothen*, of 2:9.) How is the blowing wind like birth in the Spirit (v.8)? And whatever does John mean by birth of water and the Spirit (v.5)? Who can be expected to comprehend a religious tradition of centuries like the Jewish in this unfamiliar vocabulary? Rather, in this familiar vocabulary put to unfamiliar use? A traditionalist like Nicodemus may acknowledge Jesus as a teacher come from God and, after his tragic death, consider that he deserves a decent burial. It was the strange, non-Jewish direction in which Jesus' followers went later that caused the mischief. Birth from above in the full maturity of life was not a recognizable Jewish category at the time John wrote. He wants to record the mystification with Jesus' teaching of those he calls Pharisees—and his own impatience with them.

Using the doubled "Amen" of John for the first time, Jesus takes the initiative by saying that birth from above is required to "see the kingdom of God" (v.3). "Kingdom" is unusual in John (elsewhere, in a dynamic sense, it is found only at 18:36). "Seeing" the rule or kingship is otherwise confined in the Gospels to Mark 9:1 and the parallel in Luke 9:27. Nicodemus takes the reference to birth literally, challenging Jesus' statement thereby. He is told in response how the figurative "birth from above" operates. Water and Spirit make it real. It is Spirit-begetting that is in question here, with water as its sign. The normal birth of infancy is not in question.

This has to be the ordinary vocabulary in John's community of new life in Jesus Christ. What we seem to have here is a snatch of religious debate. It undoubtedly comes from the Evangelist's time. The litigants are far apart. One party rejects the other's speech as literalist; the other responds by complaining of an unwarranted use of figure. There is no resolution. Communication breaks down when a simple example is rejected as making no sense (vv. 8–12). The two, in modern parlance, are "talking past each other." The teachers of Israel, it seems, are being charged with declaring the Spirit vocabulary of the Jesus people incomprehensible. The question is left hanging with the exasperated conclusion of Jesus' remarks at verse 12. (Something quite like this will happen at 5:47.) How can the heavenly—by definition all that touches on God's dealing with humanity through Jesus—be understood if the earthly—by definition all things besides—cannot be grasped?

John 3:13–21

There seems to be no way out of the stalemate. Flesh and Spirit as here represented by Nicodemus and Jesus simply do not comprehend each other. Yet all is not lost, for the stage is set for the development the Evangelist wishes to make. He does this in a kerygmatic exposition of his own (vv. 13–21), a proclamation of faith, which may very well have been led up to by verses 31–36 before the final editing. John has had Jesus say that the best thing he, Jesus, can do is to bear witness to what he has seen (v.11). This Gospel, we may assume, summarizes the Evangelist's preaching career. It has been a lifelong attempt to testify to a life lived, a glorified man "seen" (i.e., believed in). Nothing more can be done to convey the reality of Jesus, especially to a learned class which seems to have a talent for multiplying difficulties. Very well. In the absence of the heat of exchange, the effort will be made to state the case calmly.

The reflection attributed to Jesus in verses 13–21 seems to have originated as part of a kerygmatic discourse which the final redactor incorporated without troubling to smooth it out. In it the question of verse 12 about "earthly" and "heavenly" things is left hanging (like that of 5:47 which, again, is not

45

developed). This is strange, even though it is a rhetorical question. Verse 13 begins, moreover, with an "And" that most translations do not bother to render, a clue to its having been a continuation of something. Here the heavenly ascent of Jesus, which the writer knows of from the tradition, is tied to the descent of the Son of man from heaven (v. 13). Was that basically what 1:51 was about—the Jacob's ladder figure put to use in aid of the descending and ascending Son of man whom angels attend? Verse 13 is certainly related to 1:1–5 in its claim of a heavenly origin of Jesus ("who descended from heaven"). Verse 14 says, in a reversal of the old gravitational principle, whatever goes down must come up. The Son of man descends from heaven. He must be raised aloft if anyone is to believe in him. This is the Johannine double "upraising" in crucifixion and resurrection that will occur more than once (cf. 8:28; 12:32, 34). Moses' serpent of bronze, if looked upon with trust in God, preserved the Israelites from death (cf. Num. 21:9). The exalted Jesus, looked on believingly, gives the life of the final eon ("eternal life") to those who believe (v. 15; cf. Dan. 12:2). "Eternal life" occurs fifteen times in John, as does "life" used in the same sense without the adjective. God's love is such that this God wills life and not death for all who believe in the only Son. That indeed is why God gave him (v. 16), not for the world's condemnation but its salvation (v. 17). For many, the Gospel peaks here.

Clearly, life—in the sense of being saved from death in the new eon—is the great benefit which John knows lies in store for the believer. The antithesis between the true Light (vv.19–20)—the Word that becomes Jesus—and a world that did not receive it (1:9–11) is identical with the Light's clash with darkness (v. 5). This figure in which one who comes from God is described as Light and all that is opposed to God is described as its absence would be familiar to the post-biblical Jewish world. Living and perishing, being saved and being condemned are other expressions of the same clear opposition. It is blameworthy not to believe in the only Son of God, John is convinced, hence deserving of adverse and lasting judgment (v. 18).

Nicodemus is a bumbling figure, rather than a resistant one, whose case is not resolved. But apart from him there exist evil men who love darkness rather than the Light. They are fearful that if they come to the Light their deeds will be exposed (vv. 19–20). Does John know any such persons? He hints at it strongly, but it is hard to be sure of his meaning. He stays so close to the rhetoric of apocalyptic, and the Qumran writings in particular, which divide the world into a virtuous "we" and a wicked "they," that his actual judgments are not clear. John's is the rhetoric of exclusion into the night of darkness of whatever does not accord with his convictions. His commitment to God and Jesus Christ may not be questioned. His strictures on living persons who do not believe as he does have to be questioned. John is obviously writing polemically and directing his fire at those who culpably do not have faith—his faith which is the sole correct one—in Jesus. Who exactly they are we do not know.

Another important category surfaces: "doing what is true" (v. 21) as opposed to doing evil (v. 20). A performer of such deeds does not first do them and then come to the Light. Deeds "wrought in God" (v. 21) are by definition of the Light, not of darkness. They need to be seen clearly but they do not become "what is true" when they are made manifest, rather the reverse. "The truth" that is done, as the Greek has it (v. 21), is interchangeable with light and life. All three bespeak the reality of God which Jesus Christ shares with God and which the believer in some sense shares with Christ. But this development will surface slowly. For now, the basic vocabulary of the Gospel is being set.

John 3:22–30

Chapter 3 brings Jesus and his disciples to some unspecified place in Judea at verse 22. This is so even though the colloquy with Nicodemus may well have been in Jerusalem while Passover was on (cf. 2:23). John is meanwhile baptizing in Samaria just west of the Jordan and east of Mounts Gerizim and Ebal (cf. v.23). The pericope may not be historical but intended to settle finally the relative positions of Jesus and John the baptizer. The latter has been left abruptly at Perean Bethany in 1:36. He resumes the testimony to Jesus he has given earlier, but the Evangelist means to be the last arbiter. He, or more likely the editor who placed verses 31–36 after the Baptist's witness, settles the question from the by now familiar faith position on Jesus' heavenly origins. The stance attributed to the Baptist in verses 29–30 is consonant with the role he has been asked to play in 1:19–34. Only verse 27 is a clear piece of Johannine theology. The Baptist there identifies "heaven" as the necessary source of anyone's "receiving anything"—the heaven from which Jesus descended (v. 13).

What kind of Jew is the *"Ioudaios"* (v. 25) who could have engaged John's disciples in a dispute over purifying? Since the context of Jesus and his disciples is "the land of Judea" (v. 22) and since the presence of a Jew like John in Samaria is improbable unless there were Jewish settlements on the road to Beitshan, "Judean" might be the better translation. Here, as frequently in this Gospel, the term can be taken to describe the men of the south committed to emerging oral Torah. Perhaps John requires the Baptist's testimony to Jesus *in Samaria* before Jesus arrives there (chap. 4). The discussion "about purification" (v. 25)—was it over the Baptist's bath in water as it related to Jewish observance? to Jesus' baptizing?—leads to John's disciples' questioning their own position. Who is this Jesus who baptizes (v. 22) and attracts such a following (v. 26)? The Baptist's first response is quite general. He cannot give what he does not have; another can give "what is given him from heaven" (v. 27). The Baptist then reiterates his testimony that he is not the Christ (v. 28; cf. 1:20) and provides the memorable disclaimer unique to John's Gospel about not being the bridegroom, saying that he is a friend who is fated to decrease (vv.29–30). It is a watchword for the Christian ages. There has never been a follower of Jesus who has not at some time been tempted to displace him. The Baptist of the Fourth Gospel knows the folly of the move.

John 3:31–36

The translators (RSV) do well to insert quotation marks at the end of verse 30 to indicate the end of the Baptist's speech. As has been said, the remainder of the chapter is a Johannine meditation of the sort the final editor distributes throughout the Gospel. The light-darkness, truth-evil pairings of verses 13–21 yield to the spatial metaphor in verses 31–34*a* of "above" (heaven) and "being sent" (not "below" but "to earth"). The previous affirmations that Jesus Christ makes the Father known (1:18), in testimony based on what he has seen and known of heavenly things (vv. 11–12), are repeated. So is the most sweeping charge to date that *"no one* receives his [Jesus'] testimony" (v. 32; cf. v. 11*b;* 1:11). Yet anyone who does "seals" it as a fact (v. 33) that God is truthful. The same verb, *esphragisen* ("sets

48

his seal") will occur in 6:27, but there God has set his seal on the Son of man. In speaking the words of God, the one whom God has sent certifies that the Spirit is not doled out parsimoniously (v. 34). The Father's saving love for the world (vv. 16–17) is here rephrased so that it becomes a love for the Son. Yet the effect of the love is the same, namely, eternal life and not the wrath of God for all who believe in him (vv. 35–36).

Jesus, Healer of Wounds and Divisions

We shall not be encountering any new themes from this point on in the Gospel. The Johannine vocabulary is set. What we can expect is an ingenious reworking of the few motifs which the first three chapters contain. All primacy of action lies with God who is the first to live, to speak, to send. Jesus is to be heeded because of the true testimony provided him by the signs he works; by the Baptist; by the Father; but most of all because of the witness he provides to himself by his own words.

Jesus is submitted to a testing throughout this Gospel. Many cultures of the world including the Babylonian, the ancient Hebrew (Num. 5:11–31), and the Amerindian are familiar with the determination of the guilt or innocence of the accused by "ordeal." It may take the form of making a woman drink "bitter water," as in the biblical passage cited above, or drawing lots, or drinking a poisoned cup. Nothing so primitive appears in John. He creates a full-scale drama of legal process. It is not of the formal courtroom kind but of witnesses summoned for and against Jesus the accused, who is a surrogate for his faithful followers in the John community. Jesus is allowed to speak. He proves to be the most effective witness of all because of his credentials. These turn out to be his origins, his "pedigree."

The Evangelist, having stated his belief that the Jesus who came to birth is no ordinary man but one who has originated with God, has challenged himself to put on Jesus' lips words that bespeak the divine wisdom. Only a prayerful person who has meditated long and hard on the love of an outreaching God, an inspired person in the biblical sense, could have brought this off. John has lived his life in a circle that has long considered the utterances of Jesus in a certain way. The Johannine school, if the expression is not too strong, is skilled in this interpretative technique. That fact does not make the achievement any less. The Gospel's consistency, its soaring beauty, its rootedness to the earth in contrast to later gnosticisms, make it a memorable piece of faith literature.

The differences between the gnostic fancies that sprang from John and the Gospel itself may above all not be forgotten. Later Christian heresy would find a full-scale dualism in this writing: spirit set against matter, deity against humanity, heaven against earth. John does not have such a dualism. God is God for him, all that is true. Jesus is a Galilean Jew in whom the Truth (or Light or Word or Life) of God dwells. This Son of man is not an automaton, a machine entertaining a divine Ghost. He is someone who has always known the truth of God through intimate presence (how, the Evangelist does not presume to know). He speaks what he has known. The writer John does the same at one remove, having experienced the Son of man in the community of faith.

Like any author, John can influence our perception of the dramatic conflict he presents by the way he arranges his narrative. He has elicited reader sympathy for Jesus from the start, presenting him as someone sent by God who speaks only the truth that he knows. The Evangelist has portrayed a Baptist who, under the impulse of the Spirit, is subordinate to Jesus because he does not have the role or function that Jesus has. The men who are to be Jesus' followers are immediately attracted to him in a way bordering on religious faith. Jesus first performs a marvel, then lectures a man of learning on the power of the Spirit in human lives. If this were not enough, John engages in theological asides to the reader (couched in the third person), which attempt to make the writer's faith stance the reader's if it is not such already. From what we know of the techniques of rhetoric we can identify this Gospel's first three chapters as a strong appeal to the reader to identify not only with Jesus but with a specific view of him. Convictions opposed to those of the author are polemicized against. His own are presented in the most favorable light. Those who preach on John's Gospel are invited to do the same—always with the caveat that their faith must aspire to that of the author if they are to speak in authentic tones.

John 4:1–54

The story of the woman at the well (vv. 7–30) occurs only once in the lectionaries, on the Third Sunday of Lent in Year A. The Catholic and Episcopal lectionaries propose that it be read in full up to verse 39; the Common Lectionary proposes verses 5–26, with 27–42 as optional. The Lutheran proposal is that verses 5–26 be read on the previous Sunday. None of them, unfortunately, requires that verses 39–42, which give point to the story, be read. Yet, belief in Jesus by a religiously ostracized group is what the story is about. Hence all moralizing about the woman's irregular life or Jesus' relations with women, interesting as they are, are not especially useful as an exposition of the text. The story is about religious tensions and a church which, in its origins, sought to overcome them, even while the attempt itself caused new tensions. John 4 should be preached in the spirit in which it was written. If it is not, the Gospel is betrayed.

Verses 31–38 do not occur as a Sunday lectionary reading, possibly because of their complexity. That Jesus' food is to do the will of him who sent him (v.34) is the memorable expression of an important Johannine theme. The subsequent verses about sowers and reapers (35–38) create serious exegetical problems even though their general drift is evident: Subsequent laborers profit from the exertions of those who went before them. The sentiment is important in all church work whether of the laity or clergy, where the unconscious yearning for human glory interferes seriously with promotion of God's glory.

Verses 43–54 do not occur as a Sunday reading in any of the lectionaries, probably because its Synoptic character (a version of Mark 8:5–13; Luke 7:1–10?) is thought to render this needless. As the healing of the official's son appears in John, it is numbered as the "second sign" which Jesus did when he came from Judea to Galilee (v.54). The wide conjecture is that it was so designated in a source which the incorporator of the narrative into the Gospel left untouched. Like the other Cana story, it has hardly any characteristics of Johannine style; no explanatory words of a revelatory character are provided. The healing is achieved at a distance and as a result of the trust of the official in Jesus' word (v.50). Because of the sign of healing, "he and his whole household believed" (v. 53*b*).

The next chapter, four, is largely a single literary unit. Toward the end there is a bridge that takes Jesus from Samaria, where the action has been located, to Galilee, specifically Cana and Capernaum (vv. 43–46). The chapter closes with Jesus' first miracle of healing in this Gospel, his "second sign" (vv. 46–54), esp. v. 54). Like the first sign, it takes place in Cana, the two narratives bracketing chapters 2—4 as a literary unit. The pattern of geographic alternation we have observed, namely from Judea to Galilee (v. 3), continues as the narrative opens with a stop-off in Samaria. The reason given for Jesus' departure from the region is his success at baptizing in Judea and its adverse effect on the Pharisees (vv. 1,3). Why the Pharisees are opposed to Jesus and/or John is not spelled out. As in 1:24 they are presumed to be unfriendly, although the mention of them as the party of Nicodemus' allegiance (3:1) does nothing to advance this idea.

A corrective editorial hand seems to be at work in verse 2, indicating that the claim that Jesus baptized more persons than John (v. 1; cf. 3:22, 26) may not be a felicitous way of establishing

51

his superiority. The Synoptics' silence about Jesus' having done any baptizing inclines the reader to think that the more solid historical tradition is that he did not, hence that the correction is justified. We seem to have here a case of historical realism prevailing over Johannine symbolism, which made Jesus a baptizer so as not to be subordinate to John the Baptist in any way.

Everything about the telling of the tale of the Samaritan woman is by now familiar Johannine style. There is a simple exchange at the outset that, like that with John's disciples or Nicodemus, immediately has religious implications. The anonymous Samaritan does not speak like the learned Nicodemus. She is a woman of the people, fully aware of the terms of traditional rivalry between Samaritans and Jews. Jesus' simple request for a drink from a historic well at mid-day becomes a discussion of water in a double sense. Nicodemus had not let Jesus' references to birth or breath (wind, spirit) get very far. The Evangelist broke that conversation off with Jesus' frustration at the man's density. After a few verses of response attributed to Jesus, John turned to soliloquy. He lets the exchange at Jacob's well in Sychar proceed much further, possibly because of its favorable outcome. It is presented between two references to food in the "inclusion technique" of written rhetoric, the first being John's dismissal of the disciples to buy food to get them off the scene (v. 8), the second a statement by Jesus that his food is not the ordinary kind but "to do the will of him who sent me, and to accomplish his work" (v. 34). In between, the discussion is not of food but of drink.

As is usually the case with a Johannine vignette, this one is so attractively presented that it can be considered on a human level without higher reference. That would surely defeat the Evangelist's purpose. His colorful narrative is the vehicle of a more serious intent. Any dwelling by the preacher on the details of the story would merit from the Gospel writer the same censure for opaqueness that Jesus visits on Nicodemus. The one detail that is *not* expendable, however, is the locale of the patriarch's well in what, for the Jew, is enemy territory. Essential to the account is its setting in the midst of a people which, since destruction of its temple on Mount Gerizim by John Hyrcanus in 128 B.C. and the town of Shechem in 109, had been considered an alien folk (*goy;* cf. Sirach 50:26*b*) by the Jews, not even a nation or people *(am)*. The biblical account of the schism in II Kings 17 is heavily redacted and scarcely trustworthy historically. Critical examination of it, along with the pertinent data from Josephus' *Antiquities,* Books XI and XII, reveals that until the northerners—who were not carried off in exile (the people of Israel or Ephraim called Samarians)—permitted Alexander the Great to build them a temple on Gerizim there was little enmity. Earlier, the returning Judean exiles under Ezra could not stomach any shrine for the restored nation except the one they rebuilt in Jerusalem. The situation worsened steadily between 300 and 100, yielding "Samaritans" as a term distinct from "Samarians" in Hebrew and Greek (cf. the present writer's "The Samaritans in the New Testament," pp. 7–21).

The tension between the two closely related peoples, although at its New Testament peak demonstrably only a century and a half old, would have been thought to be age-old by Jewish Bible readers. The tension would at the same time have required an explanation to non-Jews—perhaps even to some diaspora Jews at the time John wrote. John supplies this in verse 9c, which is better translated "do not use vessels in common with" than "have no dealings with" Samaritans.

Important to John are "the gift of God," "who it is that is speaking" to the woman, and "living water" (v. 10). He is, above all, aware of the ancient antipathy, but only incidentally aware of the anomaly of Jesus' conversing with a woman publicly (v. 27b). Once again, however, John's main concern is the heavenly authority of Jesus the speaker and the gift of life he holds out. "Living water" at a literal level is a running spring or stream as contrasted with well water in John's by now familiar contrived ambiguity. The woman's puzzlement at Jesus' ability to make good his promise of supplying living water has to be spelled out (vv. 11–12). If she were to comprehend him at a hearing, it would be death to John's enterprise. Jesus' superiority to Jacob in all respects is the point at issue (v. 12). He promises a spring of water that wells up to eternal life (v. 14). She asks for it, but on terms that indicate she does not grasp his meaning.

One could almost play a guessing game with the Gospel by this time. In the game a biblical symbol like water from the well of Jacob is put forward. The participants are asked to imagine how the Evangelist will elaborate on it. Their responses, if not identical with John's, will be in the realm of a transcending symbol which fulfills the ancient type. This Gospel is sacramental, even incarnational, in its use of everyday realities to convey the divine or heavenly. The objects that make up daily life are

53

not despised and set aside. They are not merely used illustratively. They are part and parcel of the new existence that Jesus invites to. He approaches people not randomly or casually but as possible bearers of witness to him to whole populations. To believe in him is to begin to give testimony about a "life" completely new.

The female member of a people despised by Jews is provided with a disorderly life (vv. 16–18) to make her trebly a minority person: woman, Samaritan, polygamist. The contrast is with Jacob whose credentials are in impeccable order. The paradox is that the water even Jacob could not supply she shall have. One important fact is set aside, namely that in Moses' day Mount Gerizim was a mount of blessing and Ebal one of cursing (Deut. 11:29; 27:11–13). John confines himself to the Judean reality of his own day that Jerusalem had within its limits the right mountain for worship for Jews, Samaria the wrong one (vv. 20–22). Without some resolution of the enmity between these two peoples the story is purposeless. It ends with: "Many Samaritans from that city believed in him because of the woman's testimony" (v. 39). This summary means to account for the origins of a substantial Samaritan component within the Christian community which John knows. That clearly is the basic reason why the story is included.

This accounts for Jesus' insistence on Jerusalem's superiority to Samaria as the place for acceptable worship. Not only would the historical Jesus have thought so, but the inserted phrase "salvation is of the Jews" (v. 22) would provide the Johannine community with the cachet of religious respectability in Jewish circles which subsequent chapters indicate it did not have. It is questionable, of course, whether such an awareness by Jews would be of any use once it was known that Jesus' followers had embraced the Samaritan "enemy." But the Evangelist cannot be faulted for trying. The woman's identification of the one whom her people expected as "the Messiah" or "Christ" (vv. 25, 29) would be the author's accommodation of the Samaritan hope for a Restorer *(Ta'eb)*. "Savior of the world" (v. 42) is equally uncharacteristic of Samaritan vocabulary. It is part of John's "saving" language (3:17; 5:34 and elsewhere), with a global claim for Jesus' role included. The Samaritans did not share the Jewish view that a Davidic king would come to inaugurate the final age. He would be, rather, a Restorer of all observance in the mold of Moses. We have to rely on Samaritan

54

writings from the patristic and medieval periods to discover the end-time hopes of this people. Its faith in the exclusive witness of the Pentateuch—presumably the Samaritan-text version of it—was known in Jesus' day. There is little other contemporary evidence about their views except their conviction that Gerizim was God's holy mountain, not the Ophel-Zion of the much later conquest of Jerusalem's indigenous Jebusites. But the Jewish antipathy to Samaria was bitter, as the Mishnaic tradition already in the making attests. The Johannine community is aware of the contempt Jews have for a Jewish group that can accept Samaritans as members. The latter community's sign of outreach to Judaism—that is, the believers in Jesus among them—consists of showing that they have accepted a Jew as Messiah. The "many more" who believe in Jesus (v. 41) must have believed that, through him, the ancient Jewish-Samaritan hatred had been healed on Jewish and not Samaritan terms. This is of no little importance to an evangelist to whom a successful apologia to Jews in behalf of the alienated part of the old Northern Kingdom is mandatory.

The whole story is fraught with symbolism, so much so that we are right to doubt the literal truth of the woman's having had five husbands and not being married to her present partner (v.18). Aside from the inherent improbability of such a career, there is the fact that the Samaritans were stigmatized as "Cuthians" (*Berakoth* 7, 1, and so throughout the Mishnah), a tribe of the Assyrian Empire in II Kings 17:24, 30. These were one of five idolatrous peoples of the East identified in Second Kings by their gods and consorts (vv. 30–31). If the woman's five husbands were these peoples, the present liaison of the Samaritans at the stone surface of sacrifice on Gerizim would be the sixth: an idolatrous cult in Jewish eyes.

John makes Jesus' knowledge of "all that I ever did" (v. 29) the argument that convinces the Samaritan women that he is the Christ. The Evangelist has previously put on Jesus' lips the declaration which is the faith of the Johannine community: "I who speak to you am he [the Christ]" (v. 26; the Greek reads: "I am, the [one] speaking to you; cf. commentary on 8:38). Evidently John wishes to make this faith statement to his readers to confirm them in their faith; perhaps to motivate them to it if they have not held it. The identification of the Christ or Messiah was a matter of supreme interest to Jewish populations in John's century. The Gospel author is presumably having a

55

hard time proclaiming a crucified insurgent as Messiah, like any proclaimer of Jesus of the first apostolic generations. The case he makes with Jews is that God has endowed this Jesus with special powers to know what is going on in the human heart (vv. 16–19). That is how he is to be recognized and known as the Messiah. Nathanael became a believer because Jesus said: "I saw you under the fig tree" (1:50). Before that, Jesus simply looked upon him from a distance and was able to declare his guileless-ness (v. 47). The Jerusalem crowds, in their new condition of belief at his signs, are not immediately trusted by Jesus "because he knew all [people]" (2:24) [and] knew what was within the human [heart] (v.25).

In the present narrative this man who requires no human testimony and who entrusts himself to no one can inform a stranger about her entire career. Jesus is speaking to a Samaritan, symbolic of her people in the terms of the Johannine Gospel. Hence Jesus knows everything Samaria ever did from a Jewish viewpoint: false worship, consorting with Judah's enemies, whatever the Jews of Judah in the south ever thought the kingdom of Israel in the north was guilty of. Despite this complete knowledge of Jesus about them, the Samaritans are portrayed as a people accepted. Nothing is forgotten but all is forgiven. The Evangelist, speaking in Jesus' name, goes on record as totally aware of the alleged Samaritan sins of the past. There is no naïveté in him. There is, however, full acceptance despite full knowledge.

Equally important to the Samaritan-Jewish healing, so capable in itself of creating a new breach for the Johannine church, are this Gospel's radically altered terms of faith in the Messiah of the Jews. All the apostolic preachers had the problem of altering the symbol "Messiah" from that of the victorious warrior-king to a new understanding. This understanding had to include the triumph of God in the last age but had to be free of the trappings of earthly power. In the victory of Jesus over the grave, alone, lay the symbol of end-time conquest. As to the rest, he was a sufferer in the recent past whose disciples had to suffer in the present until their future victory. Each New Testament writer went about his task differently, holding fast in general to a modification of the symbol like that suggested above. John introduces the idea early that Jesus is the Messiah, putting it as a faith statement on Andrew's lips after the latter has spent only part of a day with him (1:41). A final editorial hand thinks that the Hebrew word transliterated as *"Messias"* needs to be translated *"Christos"* for readers who know only the Greek term. The Baptist testifies that he has been sent before "the Christ" (3:28). The Samaritan woman is made to puzzle over whether Jesus can be the Messiah (or Christ) (vv. 25, 29). All this use of the term early in the Gospel indicates that by the time the Gospel was written it was an appellative of Jesus (cf. 1:17), and that as applied to him its content had been substantially altered. Chapter 7 reproduces arguments, probably from the Evangelist's day, about whether someone whose identity is known can be the Christ (7:26–27, 31). But when the question arises in 8:22 and 11:27 it is evident that in John's time Jesus is firmly believed in under this title.

PREACHING ON THE BELIEF OF THE SAMARITANS THROUGH THE WOMAN'S TESTIMONY

There ought to be no pulpit embarrassment, no extended theorizing about the difference between the Johannine Jesus and the Synoptic Jesus. At times, to be sure, there should be some brief distinction made between the two approaches to proclaiming him. In the period which the church reckons its primordial age, Jesus was believed in as the Word of God through whom human words from God were heard. This apostolic conviction should be presented at full strength. It may not, however, be used as the Christian heresy of a later age: God in the body of the man Jesus or a Word replacing the human soul and spirit of Jesus. Apollinarian, Eutychean or Monothelite this Gospel is not; it is Johannine. Yet its appeal to subtle and pious minds of the past in ways the church came to brand heretical means that it will always have the power to do this. The perversion of Johannine thought crouches at the door of the preacher who puts this Gospel to use. The church is the arbiter of what is the use and abuse of Johannine thought. Conciliar christological teaching, it is true, suffered from ignorance of the Semitic thought world out of which this Gospel came. Still, church teaching on the Johannine Christ is a dependable guide to what the author did *not* mean. The history of the christological debates and the councils in which they peaked is a fruitful study for anyone who would proclaim the Fourth Gospel boldly. A book like *The Christological Controversy,* by Richard A. Norris Jr., can be helpful here.

The fourth chapter on the Samaritans does something that

57

no Gospel passage does, except perhaps the one on the man not of the disciples' company casting out demons in Jesus' name (Mark 9:38–40=Luke 9:49–50). It gives guidance about how to deal with wounds and divisions, especially those of long standing. Jesus is described elsewhere (Matt. 10:34–36=Luke 12:51–53) as having come to divide, not to make peace. In the Samaritan pericope, he is presented as a reconciler of ancient enemies. Jesus was a Galilean Jew, hence a man of the old Northern Kingdom. There is no evidence that Galilean Jews were better disposed to Samaritans than Judean Jews or vice versa. The Samaritan documents reflect no special piety toward Elijah or Elisha, the prophets of the north, nor do they claim a special affinity with the Northern Kingdom. Still, the fact is that John testifies to an early spread of the gospel to the "non-Jews" of Samaria (so proclaimed less than two centuries before), which he roots in a historical reminiscence from Jesus' life.

Synoptic tradition (Luke for his theological reasons proves to be largely an exception) attributes to Jesus brief sorties to gentile territory across the Sea of Tiberias *(Kinnereth)*, toward Tyre and Sidon and the "ten cities" area. From what we know of Jesus, the ancient schism with Samaria would have struck his Jewish heart as all wrong. There is a community remembrance of post-Pentecostal outreach to this despised people (4:39–42; Acts 8:1, 4–25). The present passage situates its origins in Jesus' having preached there.

There is no Christian body unfamiliar with ancient antipathies or old wounds. Black and white, Catholic and Protestant, Jewish and Christian are the most familiar. The resentment of the native-born for the immigrant population sundered this country anew after slavery had done it for the first time. Economic stratification may have been the actual reason, but in time all irrational positions are given a specious rationalization by recourse to religion. There can be religious divisions between very close cousins, as in the Samaritan-Jewish split. One thinks of churches broken off from other churches or synods of the same church; Germans and Scandinavians, Celts and Slavs within the same religious family. The antipathies run deeper as the years pass and the legends grow. Jesus in John's Gospel is on record unequivocally as against this prejudicial antagonism.

58

The whole story may be an attempt to legitimize a mission to Samaria in circles where it is disputed (cf. "Do not go into the cities of Samaria" Matt. 10:5), by putting prophecy of a future mission to Samaria on Jesus' lips in a conversation with a representative of that place. In such case, others than Jesus (viz., the Hellenist Jews of Acts 6—8) would have labored while "You [Peter and John, for the Jerusalem church, Acts 8:14] have entered into their labor" (v. 38*b*).

In another interpretation, the parabolic language about fields and reapers (vv. 35–38) represents a reconciling of two elements, the disciples of chapter 1 and the Samaritan converts of chapter 4. "One may posit that the second group in Johannine history consisted of Jews of peculiar anti-Temple views who converted Samaritans and picked up some elements of Samaritan thought, including a Christology that was not centered on a Davidic Messiah" (Raymond E. Brown, *Community of the Beloved Disciple*, p. 39). In either case, earlier and later claimants to the evangelizing role are being reconciled in this carefully crafted tale.

Preachers of healing must themselves be healers. It is a long and laborious task. People are prepared for embracing unity by apostles of unity in the spirit of Jesus. The story of the people of Sychar who came to faith in him, first because of the woman's testimony (v. 39) and then their experience of Jesus (v. 42), is a paradigm of all reconciliation. A report which one thinks one can trust has great value but there is nothing like first-hand experience. There has to be face-to-face contact with the Catholics or the Baptists or the Puerto Rican Pentecostals of whom one grew up hearing the worst. As the subjects of unconfirmed myths, these flourish as "others." As people with common human problems they lose their mythical status. Yet not all cultural differences evanesce upon contact. Often contact heightens them. There has to be understanding, and that takes a long time to achieve. Multiplied human contacts in and out of season can contribute much. Nothing, however, is so forceful as being faced constantly by the gospel imperative.

An important avenue to reconciliation is acknowledging the full religious and human capacities of the "other." Common work in common causes—the relief of the needy, the living of the gospel—is best of all. Yet the healing of old divisions needs to be kept to the fore constantly. It is part of the preacher's office. It is the main concern of John 4.

The first four chapters of John move along briskly in narrative style. There are numerous time clues provided (cf. 1:29, 35, 43; 2:1, 12, 13; 3:24; 4:40, 43). With the exception of the soliloquy to Nicodemus there has not been much discourse material attributed to Jesus. By contrast, subsequent sections begin to be introduced by the vague phrase "After these things" (cf. 5:1; 6:1; 7:1) and a reference to a religious feast, indicating that a selectivity among episodes has set in. Discourses of Jesus grow more frequent. Undeveloped signs like the miracles at Cana and Capernaum cease altogether. These factors in combination point to a natural break in the Gospel after chapter 4, although whether it originally resumed at the beginning of chapter 5 we defer to the next chapter.

PART TWO

After These Things

JOHN 5—7

The Probable Original Sequence of Chapters 5 and 6

The arguments are strong for the occurrence of chapter 6 after chapter 4 in a version of the Gospel previous to its final editing. Either way, problems remain. Those of logical sequence that are solved by the transposition of these chapters are balanced by the new ones it causes. Still, the bulk of argument favors Jesus' continuance in Galilee in an earlier narrative, as in 6:1, rather than his abrupt departure for Jerusalem in 5:1 and totally unexplained presence back in Galilee in 6:1. The remark in 7:1 about Jesus' not traveling in Judea for fear of being killed follows logically on 6:18 without the interference provided by a long chapter 6 spent in Galilee. Similarly, the "one work" of 7:21 is best explained by the more recent healing of the paralytic at the sheep pool in 5:2–15.

Without suggesting that Jesus' actual movements are involved—only the probable state of the Gospel before its final editing—we shall proceed to a consideration of the sixth chapter on the multiplication of the loaves and the fish and the discourse on the bread of life it led to. Chapters 5 and 6 are both self-contained units; thus, little compelling argument can be derived from their respective contents; neither one requires absolutely that it be preceded or followed by the other. In both, there is a new audience for Jesus' utterances, *"hoi Ioudaioi"* (5:10, 15, 18; 6:41, 52), whomever the author intended by it. If the word originally meant "Judeans," it occurs more fittingly in chapter 5 in Jerusalem than in chapter 6 where Galilee is the locale. But the term arises with equal abruptness for readers in

61

either case, since only 1:19 and 2:18 have prepared them for it as designating a group of Jews especially hostile to Jesus.

John 6
The Bread of Life

If the entire Fourth Gospel is devoted to disclosing who Jesus is so that people can believe in him, this long narrative does it by showing him to be nourishment for the soul better than the manna of Moses' day. The lawgiver by his petitions kept alive a people fated nonetheless to die. Jesus is the person who, "devoured" in faith, will keep a people alive forever.

Chapter 6, in the transposition theory, contains the culmination of Jesus' activity in Galilee. Reception of him has been generally favorable there. This ceases to be the case with the opposition to him represented by the (geographically displaced?) *"Ioudaioi."* He even experiences the loss of "many of his disciples" (v. 6⃝) as a result of his demand that his flesh be eaten and his blood be drunk since he is the bread that has come down from heaven (vv. 53–58).

The chapter is developed in orderly fashion. First there is the great "sign" (v. 14) of the feeding in verses 1–13, which peaks in Jesus' popular acceptance by the crowd. The storm on the lake follows (vv. 16–24), as in the Marcan sequence after the first multiplication narrative (cf. Mark 6:45–52). The latter was probably created by Mark and modeled on the fixed text underlying the multiplication story of 8:1–10 to prepare for it (see Robert M. Fowler, *Loaves and Fishes*). Jesus explains the significance of the sign in a discourse delivered the next day (vv. 26–59). This section ends with the brief editorial note that the revelatory remarks were spoken in the synagogue of Capernaum of Galilee (v. 59), as if the locale had somehow befit the hostile disputation that took place (cf. vv. 41, 52). Verses 60–66 are a theological observation cast as history. It is as if many disciples of Jesus known to the Evangelist have not continued in fidelity because of the stern faith demand made upon them concerning the person of Jesus and eating and drinking him in some fashion, which by that point in the narrative would seem to have been the community's practice.

62

The refusal to believe follows the Synoptic tradition of the sign of the loaves as a turning point (cf. Mark 8:11–13). The "disciples" in John 6 are not an especially intimate group, just ordinary followers. They are to be contrasted with "the twelve" (vv. 67, 70, the only usage of the term in John), whose fidelity to Jesus is given expression by the confession of Simon Peter. Verses 68–69 are this Gospel's equivalent of the Caesarea Philippi exchange (Mark 8:27–30=Matt. 16:13–20), although John has prepared for it by recording that Simon, who did not initiate the conversation, should be called "Cephas"—after a look from Jesus—"(which means Peter)" (1:42).

We have said that the concepts and vocabulary that will mark the whole Gospel are already fixed in the first four chapters. It is also true that chapter 6 is a perfect paradigm of the disputes over faith that will ensue in this Gospel: The litigants, the issues, the rhetoric of the disputes are all here *in nuce*. Faith in the person of Jesus is the great matter at issue. The question of his status as the perfect fulfillment of the type of Moses as prophet-king and wonderworker is the form the bitter controversy takes (cf. vv. 2, 15, 45). There emerges from this chapter a strong declaration of what Johannine faith in Jesus consists. Opposed to it is a mentality which cannot admit this faith because of its presuppositions. John is convinced that these must yield to the fact of *seeing* the Son (v. 40).

John 6:1–15

Jesus has been in Capernaum in 4:54, a town almost due north on the shores of "the sea of Galilee . . . of Tiberias" (v. 1), just west of the point where the Jordan river debouches into it. The "other side" is commonly taken to be the east bank: from the Jewish point of view gentile territory. Yet a northeastward crossing to Capernaum or a southwestward one to the Galilean town of Tiberias could qualify technically as "the other side," consuming almost as much time as a crossing from west to east or conversely. Great pains have been devoted to plotting Jesus' movements and those of his disciples and the people. The question is all but impossible to settle, since any point in any direction might have been the original "other side of the sea." "Tiberias," similarly, which appears as the second noun in the double genitive of verse 1 (and which RSV translates as an appositive—supplying the words, "which is the Sea of") may

mean the town on the west shore as well as the lake (the meaning it probably has in v. 23). Added to these uncertainties there
is the fact that the text we now have has probably received
editorial attention to remove ambiguities, an effort which has
only created new ones. The original author undoubtedly knew
the movements of Jesus he meant to describe. It is not necessary for the modern expositor or reader to understand these
movements, or to arrive at the redactor's understanding of the
text as he incorporated it, in order to grasp the religious and
theological meaning of the chapter.

"Multitude" (v. 2) is not a normal Johannine word. The
whole multiplication narrative betrays an awareness of traditions about a Galilean ministry like those of the Synoptics. The
ascent to an unspecified mountain may be intended to give the
miraculous feeding a Mosaic character. The reference to the
proximity of the Passover (v. 4) certainly has that intention.
Designation of it as "the Judean feast" (author's trans.) seems
gratuitous except for the author's conscious desire to establish
a contrast between Jewish observance and a new one centered
on Jesus. The exchange with Philip and Andrew, two who have
already emerged with roles in the John narrative (cf. 1:43–44),
is described as a test for Philip; but it is just as much a claim for
Jesus' superior knowledge and power of decision (cf. 1:48; 2:7,
25; 4:16–19). The similarities in this narrative to the first of
Mark's multiplication accounts (cf. Mark 6:30–44) are evident,
but the one in John is developed quite independently. Note,
however, the three verbs "take," "give thanks," and "distribute" which occur in some form in the Synoptic stories of the
miraculous feeding and in the words of Jesus at the last supper.
John's "distribute" departs from the Synoptics' "give," but he
has "give thanks" in common with Luke's supper narrative
(22:19a) and that of I Corinthians (11:24), as opposed to Mark's
and Matthew's "bless."

The tendency of the tradition behind the New Testament
to foresee the church's liturgical practice in the multiplication
of the loaves and the fish is as marked here in John as in the
other Gospels. An important difference is that in John's account
Jesus does not "break" the bread, a detail of Jewish meal behavior (cf. Luke 24:35; Acts 2:42) that came to describe the Eucharist in post-New Testament times ("the breaking of the bread,"
for example, Theodore of Mopsuestia, *Catechetical Homilies*
15.15–20). On the other hand, the action in John of "giving

64

thanks" (v. 11) is heightened by the later use of the verb in the narrative to describe what "the Lord" had done over the bread (v. 23); and, in fact, "thanksgiving" *(eucharistia)* won out in popular parlance over "praise" *(eulogia),* although there is no compelling New Testament reason why this should have been so.

The possibility is strong that the editor(s) of the present text "eucharistized" the passage by the addition of verse 23: "However, boats from Tiberias came near the place where they ate the bread after the Lord had given thanks." The use of the verb seems perfectly natural in this synoptic-like account of Jesus' action over the food. Unlike the Synoptics is Jesus' distributing the loaves and the fish himself to the seated five thousand; the other evangelists have him delegate this. This way of describing Jesus' behavior relates to the food (v. 27) or bread (v. 51c) that he, the Son of man, will distribute as God's greatest gift. Jesus is concerned that "nothing may be lost" (v. 12) of the gathered fragments. This is precious food, a kind that does not perish but endures to eternal life (cf. v. 27). The reader is well prepared by the end of the multiplication account for a significance of the event far beyond the merely miraculous.

John uses verse 14 as his theological comment on what has just happened. Jesus has performed a genuine "sign" and the "people" (not the "multitude" of v. 2) respond to it by acknowledging him as "the prophet" (cf. 1:21) who "comes into the world." The latter is an important Johannine phrase (cf. 1:19; 3:19; 9:39; 11:27; 12:46; 16:28; 18:37). This acknowledgment on their part of Jesus' status as that of one who comes to prophesy, that is, to teach in God's name, is for John the sole appropriate response to the sign. In the next verse, 15, the Evangelist is back in history or at least his version of it, which contrasts earthly power with the true mission Jesus has come to fulfill. John takes an enthusiastic mob filled with the spirit of zealotry (the A.D. first and early second century Jewish desire to throw off Roman rule forcibly) and puts it in contrast with someone whose power is from above. John will do the same in the trial before Pilate (cf. 18:33–37; 19:11–15). Kingship for the crowd is national liberation at the hands of a powerful messiah-figure. For John it is the solitary condition of Jesus, the ruler of the end-time (cf. 18:37), as he communes with God on the mountain to which he has withdrawn (v. 15).

Homilists and teachers who expound this pericope must be

on their guard against dealing with it as a marvel of power exercised by Jesus in a way divorced from the Evangelist's interpretation. This deed for him is an authentic sign, one that believers will know how to intepret but those looking to Jesus as a short-term solver of their problems will not. The miracle reveals Jesus as the latter-day prophet whom Moses promised in his own image (Deut. 18:15, 18). Believers in Jesus recognize him to be such. They see in him the giver of a holy, imperishable food, none of which is to be lost. This passage is eucharistic in the widest sense. It invites to thanksgiving for every gift of God. Chief among these is the prophet Jesus who has come into the world. It urges thanksgiving for the loaves, multiplied after recourse to an already hallowed liturgical formula (v. 11). They are symbolic of Jesus himself, the "food which endures to eternal life" (v. 27; cf. v. 12).

John 6:16–21

The pericope of Jesus' walking on the sea is not read on any Sunday, probably because the Matthean account which it resembles is chosen in its stead (Matt. 14:22–23) for the Nineteenth Sunday of the Year or Twelfth after Pentecost. The similarity of John to Mark 6:45–52, which is not read in the Marcan year, is greater than to Matthew.

The Fourth Evangelist sends Jesus' disciples back to Capernaum in a single boat from the mountain region where he had left Jesus. His "walking on the sea" (v. 19) is a starker telling of the marvel than the more nuanced Synoptics accounts. The disciples' fright upon seeing him betrays adaptation from a source, for nowhere else does John report this as their response in Jesus' presence. The setting is a Johannine "darkness" (v. 17), which Jesus overcomes. He similarly overcomes their fear of death from the strong wind buffeting the boat (vv. 18, 19). John opts to tell the traditional tale in terms of Jesus' sovereign power. He stills their fears as he stands alongside their boat on the turbulent sea. They "were glad to take him into the boat" but "immediately the boat was at the land" (v. 21). As in the healing at the exact hour Jesus spoke (4:53), everything gets a little more miraculous in John than in his sources. Here the prophet who prefers solitude with God to the power of kingship is the one who brings his troubled companions calmly to their goal. A symbolization of the Passover reading of the Israelites' safe progress though the Sea of Reeds may be intended by this placement of the storm on the lake. This is less likely, however, since the Gospel gives no indication in this place that such typology is at work.

John 6:22–24

With the telling of these two stories from the tradition, John has once again employed the technique we are becoming familiar with: a narrative which prepares the way for a revelatory discourse of Jesus, which in fact is a reflection of the Evangelist. The baptizing of John, the visit of Nicodemus, and the conversation with the woman at the well have all served this purpose. The wonder is that the marriage feast of Cana and the healing of the official's son at Capernaum have not. By the time of verse 21, we have been told of two signs performed respectively for the multitude and Jesus' disciples, on the basis of which he will discourse in order to solicit or strengthen faith. The immediate setting for the discourse, however, must first be established narratively. An editorial hand seems to be at work in verses 22–24, getting the "crowd" of verse 24 (RSV, "people") to Jesus' new location in Capernaum via an implausible convoy of boats. The crowd has seen that the disciples had set out in boats without him, as the previous passage had stated. We must conclude to editorial activity of some sort by a person or persons made nervous by inconsistencies and silences in the account.

John 6:25–59

Once arrived at Capernaum, the crowd expresses a natural curiosity about Jesus' movements in getting there before it (v. 25). They address him by a title previously accorded to both him (1:38, 49; 4:31) and John the Baptist (3:2, 26), namely, "Rabbi." Their innocuous inquiry about the time of his arrival leads to a dialogue in which Jesus' responses grow increasingly longer. ("When did you come here?" v. 25, is the same verb as "come to be" or "be begotten"; cf. the questions about the origin of the wine [3:9] and the living water [4:11] and birth "from above" [3:3, 7]. Hence, "When did you come to be here?" meaning "on earth," cannot be ruled out as a cryptic, second meaning; cf. 3:31; 6:42.) The passage may be thought of as going from verse 26 to verse 58. A challenge directed first to his wavering disci-

67

ples and then to the Twelve comes as an epilogue (vv. 60–66; 67–71). The discourse may also be viewed as one in two parts: verse 31 (where the quotation from Wis. of Sol. 16:20 [cf. Pss. 105:40; 78:23–25; Exod. 16:4, 13–15] is introduced) to verse 51*a;* then verses 51*c,* 53–58, the professedly "eucharistic" section. In either case, the technique employed is midrashic: a series of successive probes of the biblical verse cited above, "He gave them bread from heaven [to eat]." The purpose of the probes is to reveal Jesus as the object of faith, the "true bread from heaven" (v. 32).

The exchange begins with an accusation by Jesus that the crowd's prevailing interest is in full stomachs, not the power of heaven-originated signs (v. 26). He proposes giving them enduring food, not the kind they consumed the day before (v. 27). This elicits a question in the next verse about the "words of God" which Jesus reduces to one, namely belief, belief "in him whom he has sent" (v. 29). A circular questioning about a trustworthy sign or work follows in order to get the biblical quotation about bread from heaven out in the open for commentary. By it, the manna of the exodus is understood. The crowd challenges Jesus to provide a better sign than this. He responds by denying that Moses gave "you" (through their forebears) the bread of heaven. The "true bread" of God, "which comes down from heaven, and gives life to the world" (vv. 32–33), alone deserves the name. We have already encountered Jesus as the "true light" (1:9) and "true worshipers" as those who in the future will worship "in spirit and truth" (4:23). A proverbial saying is likewise "true" (v. 37), all in the same sense, namely that it bespeaks the truth of God.

Noun, adjective, and adverb in the "true/truth" family in John describe what is of God. The opposite is what must be identified with resistant humanity. Here the antithesis is between the manna of old, a symbol of the disciples of Moses in Jesus' (viz., John's) day, and the true bread from heaven which that bread was not. "My Father" gives the true bread (v. 32) and it in turn "gives life to the world" (v. 33). Thus goes the first midrashic comment on Wisdom of Solomon 16:20.

A demand of the crowd for this true bread (v. 34) leads to the next comment. John creates the confusion latent in their question in order to further the discussion. In having them ask for this bread "always," he hints at the wrong notion of a never-ending food supply. It is the same opaque request as that lodged by the woman at the well (see 4:15).

Before preachers exploring this text for purposes of pulpit preparation rush too far ahead, they should perhaps try to deal with it as if they did not know the outcome. They cannot suppress the knowledge that John is having Jesus speak cryptically of himself. Even if they were reading this Gospel attentively for the first time and had gotten only this far, they would have deduced that much. We suggest here only a reading that does not get *too* far ahead of itself. Jesus knows what the true bread from heaven is. It is neither the manna of old nor the miraculously multiplied food of the previous day. The crowd does not say, "What is it?" as they did to Moses (the pun on *"Man hu?"* and "manna" of Exod. 16:15) but, "We want it." Knowing what you want out of life is half the battle, if you want the right things.

Here the Evangelist proposes the wrong "bread from heaven" in order to identify sustenance for the final eon: nourishment that will give health, prolong life, promote a genuine existence in God. It is figurative language, all of it, for in fact a person is being spoken of. The modern Jew has *torah* to live by, the Muslim the revelation of God through the Prophet. Christians say they live by faith in God through Jesus Christ. The question they need to ask themselves after this first segment (vv. 32–34) is, Do they want this bread "always"? Faulty though their perception of their need may be, they must at least know they are in need and have an inkling of what their need is. Do they turn hungrily, even greedily, to the source that might fulfill their need? How fitting is the title of the old Sidney Howard play, "They Knew What They Wanted."

Clearly self-disclosure comes next, just as it did in the Jacob's well story, although here, "I am the bread of life" (v. 35a) comes in place of, "I am he, speaking to you" (4:26, author's trans.). We shall save for a later section discussion of the self-designation of Jesus "I am" *(ego eimi)* which occurs twenty-six times in the Gospel (see The Origin of "I Am"). The claim is the same in verse 35a and in 4:26: for those who come to him Jesus brings an end to all hunger and thirst. "Bread of life" is almost a Johannine *novum* but not quite. It does not have a biblical history and has very little Jewish history, but an apocryphal book of the first century B.C. or A.D. *Joseph and Aseneth,*

69

contains it. Needless to say, the idea of a person or a teaching under the figure of nourishment is found in some form in most of the world's religions. Here, an end to hunger and thirst is promised to those who believe in Jesus (v. 35).

The place where Jesus had previously said, "You have seen [me] and yet do not believe" (v. 36) cannot be traced. Such is frequently the case with assertions like this in John. The textual variant on this passage provides little help. A general disbelief must be meant.

"For I have come down from heaven" (v. 38) is a clear identification of his person with the bread of the text that is being commented on (v. 31 = Wis. of Sol. 16:20). Jesus has come to do the will of him who sent him. That will is to "lose nothing of all that he has given me, but raise it up at the last day" (v. 39). Thus, the resurrection of the elect at the end is named as the Son's life mission. This is to be achieved in the chosen by their seeing him and believing in him (v. 40). He will not rebuff any who come to him (v. 37). The theme of Jesus' accomplishing God's work has already surfaced (4:34). If Jesus is the food of believers, his food in turn is to do the Father's will (4:34). The eating and drinking language is fully revealed now as a figure to convey achieving God's sovereign will for Jesus and those whom God gives him on the last day.

It simply is not the case, as is sometimes said, that John has no future eschatology, only a present one. Solidly implanted in this discourse is the end-expectation of Jewish apocalyptic. Translated into modern categories, it says that there is an over-all divine plan for the vindication of the just and that Jesus is at the heart of it. The Father's giving the elect to the Son and their freely coming to him in faith are equally essential to the hoped-for consummation. There is no Jewish (or Christian) thought in which the divine will renders the human will inoperative. The elect must choose in response.

The exchange goes into a new phase in verse 41 with the wilderness-like murmuring of Jesus' opposition. His repeated claim to be the heavenly bread has the same net effect as the hunger of desert days (cf. Exod. 16:2, 7, 12; Num. 14:2), later of the sameness of the diet of manna (Num. 11:4–6). Then, the Israelites' murmuring was no less than a rebellion against the LORD (Exod. 16:8). The anger of the LORD blazed hotly, and Moses' displeasure was no less. John intends to convey the same in this place, identifying the words of Jesus as the reason for the angry resistance (vv. 41, 43, 61) and his no less angry response (v. 43).

Familiarity with Jesus' origins is thought to be sufficient justification to dismiss him from serious consideration (v. 42; cf. 1:45). John has already raised the question of Jesus' heavenly origins (1:1–18; 3:31) and will later make them the subject of overt dispute (7:27–28). For the moment, two previously mentioned themes are repeated and intensified: coming to the Father (cf. v. 37), which is a matter of the Father's drawing (v. 44) those who have already been taught of God (v. 45); second, the claim that the Son alone, who has revealed the Father (cf. 1:18), has seen the Father (v. 46).

The pericope seems to end at verse 48 with the solemn assertion, marked by a doubled, antecedent "Amen": "I am the bread of life." But the next two verses advance the idea almost imperceptibly that it is this bread which Jesus is: "And the bread which I shall give for the life of the world is my flesh" (v. 51c). Recent study has seen here the word of Jesus at the supper table in the Synoptics ("flesh" for "body"), an example of the rephrasing that is so often the case with a Johannine logion. Verses 32–35 have been replicated by 48–51, but with the introduction of the graphic concept "my flesh." This flesh is somehow to be offered vicariously so that in this giving the world may have life. The Word became flesh in order to give this flesh over to death—for the life of the world.

Verses 51c–58 are widely taken to be a theological expansion of the metaphorical language that has gone before. The language is sufficiently Johannine that the same author could have written it, perhaps at a later date. Yet the main idea is new. It is, in brief, sacramental in a eucharistic sense as the bread of life discourse up to verse 51a (or 51b; cf. 58c) is not. The earlier pericope had required only faith in the revealer sent by God. This new one interposes a material medium, some real and not merely metaphorical flesh and blood of Jesus to accomplish "living because of me" (v. 57) "for ever" (v. 58). Every conceivable interpretation has been put on the two distinct kinds of writing. Bultmann's exegesis (followed by that of Bornkamm and Koester, among others) is perhaps the best known. The Evangelist has reckoned exclusively with faith in Jesus, actively eschewing any professedly sacramental language. An editor has betrayed his intention by going in a sacramental direction. Again, futurist eschatology has crept in with this interpolation

71

(v. 54 later inserted at vv. 39, 40, 44), which the Evangelist would have had nothing to do with (Georg Richter, among others). Verses 30–31 of chapter 20 announce the whole purpose of the book to have been faith in Jesus elicited by signs. But this passage falls outside of that purpose, hence it cannot accord with the original intent.

An opposite view sees this passage as not providing a new interpretation but building on what has gone before, either in a way that the Evangelist planned from the start or a rethinking after a gnostic challenge. There are theories of the application in eucharistic circumstances of a symbolic christological metaphor, and of a final midrashic comment in verses 51c–58 on the "eating" verb in Wisdom of Solomon 16:20. Underlying these conflicting opinions seems to be a predisposition on the part of modern authors to a faith-alone or sacrament-alone outlook. Some applaud the move to the sacramental plateau, others deplore it—but both seem to do so more on the basis of a Catholic or Reformation heritage than of hard data provided by the Fourth Gospel. The clear fact seems to be that verses 53–58 are sacramental, whether or not they appeared in the original text. The problem of preachers, from the perspective of the Christian tradition in which they stand, is what they are to do about it.

In so disputed a matter, a verse-by-verse consideration should be helpful. We find first *"hoi Ioudaioi"* disputing among themselves (v. 52), in a further Septuagintal echo of Israelite conduct in the desert. Their challenge of Jesus' giving his flesh to eat is total (v. 53), in the sense that all that went before concerning him as living bread from heaven is branded incredible. The impossibility derives from the same apparent literal outlook as that of Nicodemus (3:4) and the Samaritan woman (4:11–12). This is a faith challenge, but it is couched as if the literal impossibility of eating Jesus' flesh is the matter in question. Following his usual technique, John does not have Jesus back down but has him wade in deeper: Not only must his flesh be eaten but his blood must be drunk if *"hoi Ioudaioi"* are to have a life within (v. 53).

Previously, belief in Jesus could achieve eternal life (vv. 40, 47). Now, there is a food and drink requirement. What has brought on the new affirmation? Probably resistance to Christian meal behavior anticipatory of the Lord's coming and, later,

72

commemorative of his death and resurrection. Jews not of the Jesus company may have been rejecting the symbolism attached by the John people to the Eucharist which was superior to that of the everyday or the Passover meal. A greater likelihood is that docetic spiritualism has raised its head within Christian ranks, of the kind identified by Ignatius of Antioch in his letters. Abstention from a symbolic meal in bread and wine would then be a logical corollary of scandal at a Jesus crucified in the flesh. Consuming the flesh and blood of the heavenly Son of man as the essential means of acquiring life is the sacramental sign of faith in a crucified Jesus, but some will not have it (v. 53). John's Jesus reaffirms the necessity, probably using the adjective "true" twice in the sense of "reliable" (rendered as the adverb "indeed" in RSV, v. 55). The one who has life from the Father, namely Jesus, conveys something of this life immanently to whoever consumes him (v. 57). It is a bread from heaven quite unlike that of desert days, in that the life it gives is "for ever" (v. 58).

PREACHING ON THE BREAD OF LIFE DISCOURSE

Whoever opts to preach on this chapter needs to stay close to the Johannine intent, which is to make Jesus as the food of the believer the deepest meaning of the multiplication story. Those who seek the life of the final age—which in New Testament apocalyptic begins with a being raised up in the flesh—must have the prerequisite "nourishment." This nourishment is strong and intimate faith in the person of Jesus. No ordinary evangelical exhortations to trust in Jesus can do full justice to John 6. This chapter is about believing without seeing (v. 36), about coming to God through Jesus and being assured that trust in him cannot be misplaced (v. 37), about the certainty of being raised up at the last day if one has believed in him (v. 40). "Belief" in the Johannine sense is impossible apart from a close, personal relationship with the Son of man who is in heaven. It is the "abiding" in another in an almost unheard of intimacy (v. 56), a living by the other's life (v. 57) for which the only fit parallel is the coinherence of Jesus with the Father in which he lives with the Father's life (v. 57). No Pauline language of faith is too strong to convey the reality of Johannine belief in the Son. If a homilist is convinced there is a sharp turn toward sacramentalism in verse 51c, faith is nonetheless the absolute condition

73

of the sacramental eating and drinking. The homilist who does not recognize that shift in the chapter is equally right to see faith as the meaning of eating and drinking in those verses.

Pulpit polemic on whether there is or is not a sacramental understanding here is out of place, if only because the fathers of the church were not fully agreed on the question. Neither were the fathers of the Council of Trent, for that matter. The Alexandrian spirit tended to see the whole chapter as a parable of faith in Christ, but various Latin and Greek Fathers were inclined to the eucharistic interpretation. This is a case where the highly influential Augustine (for the West) was found on all sides of the question: urging eating as belief; assuming a sacramental eating; seeing the food and drink as symbolic members of a church predestined to glory—among other interpretations. In the latter connection he wrote in a baptismal homily: "Take, then, and eat the body of Christ, for by the body of Christ you are already made members of Christ. Take also and drink the blood of Christ. Lest there be division among you, eat of what binds you together" (*Sermo Denis* 3.3). "There you are on the altar, there you are in the chalice. In this sacrament you are united with us—we are joined together, we drink together, because we share life together" (*Sermo Denis* 6.2). Writing in the traditional sacramental sense he says: "Until now, as you see, it is simply bread and wine. But once the consecration takes place, this bread will be the body of Christ and this wine will be the blood of Christ" (*Codex Guelferbytanus* 7.1).

Saint Ambrose wrote "This food which you receive, this bread which comes down from heaven, holds the substance of eternal life," (*On the Mysteries,* VIII, 47), which together with his citation of 6:53 (Vulg., 54) in *On the Sacraments* (VI, 1) makes it pretty clear where he stood. Saint Cyril of Jerusalem in the fourth of his *Mystagogical Catecheses* (at 4) had the same view. He quoted John 6:53 in a sacramental context, saying that Jesus' opponents misinterpreted his invitation to eat his flesh. Origen could say of the same verse, however, that it referred to the divine Logos who feeds believers with the word of God (*Commentary on John,* VI, 43).

Consequently, anyone who maintains publicly that any segment of this chapter bears but a single interpretation blunders through a misplaced certitude. Accusing another Christian body of twisting these texts, as polemical manuals from the fifteenth to the twentieth century tend to do, is indefensible both on patristic and modern exegetical grounds. The evangelist John is so consciously polyvalent in his symbolism that we impoverish him when we settle for one understanding of his words. He is likewise served badly when we weigh him down with modern Western debates on the word in preaching versus the word in sacrament.

Homilists are equally wrong to take after "the Jews" in their pulpit expositions of this sublime material. The Evangelist knew whom he meant to designate by this term and what he thought their unbelief consisted in and why he thought it blameworthy. We are not sure of any of these things. The danger of holding modern Jews at fault who know nothing of these first-century debates—through our careless use of John's term *hoi Ioudaioi* in translation, which will inevitably encompass *them*—is a danger that should be evident. Unfortunately it often is not. Referring throughout a homily to "the opponents of Jesus as John sees them" (never "the enemies of Jesus") should handle the delicate problem best. This is not, it should be noted here, a simple question of modern ecumenical conduct. It is the profound historical question of not knowing exactly who John's *Ioudaioi* are. That they are ethnic Jews is not in doubt. But the possibility of the term's at times indicating some Jewish believers in Jesus who are quite wrong in faith by a Johannine standard cannot be discounted totally.

John 6:60–71

This key New Testament chapter is, surprisingly, not read on any Sunday other than the five in mid-summer of the second or Marcan year (B), namely those that occur between July 24 and August 27 (the 17th–21st of the Year or 10th–14th after Pentecost). These verses (60–69) are read on the Twenty-First Sunday of the Year (or Fourteenth after Pentecost) in all the lectionaries. Summer preaching schedules are affected by clergy vacations and the appearances of guest preachers, not to speak of oppressive weather in some regions. These factors may result in diminished attention to a central Johannine treatment of right faith in the rabbi Jesus (v. 25). The adverse circumstances should not lessen the attempts of preachers to master the profundities of John 6. It is central to much that the church believes and does, not least in its varieties of eucharistic practice as they epitomize faith in Jesus' person. It should be wrestled with for the riches it contains and shared—whatever the weather is like at "home beach" or the resorts.

When we reach verses 60–69, the same cautions as above still hold. "The flesh is of no avail" (v. 63*b*) is a favorite text of anti-sacramentarians of the last four centuries. What did it mean to the Johannine author? It could equally be the state-

75

ment of the Evangelist, who puts a high value on "spirit" (cf. 3:4, 8*b;* 4:23–24), or an editor who is dismayed at the people in his community who are eating the eucharistic meal carnally, that is, not perceiving the faith in the person of Jesus required to understand the rite. The "many of his disciples" (v. 60) almost have to be those of John's acquaintance who are identifying Jesus' teaching as a hard saying. The comment should not be confined to the last thing said, namely, "This is the bread which came down from heaven, . . . the one who eats this bread will live forever" (v. 58, author's trans.), but applied to the entire discourse. Everything from Jesus' heavenly origins to his being food and drink to those who believe in him, from accepting his intimate relation to the Father to consuming his flesh and blood as genuine food and drink are the *skleros . . . ho logos* ("hard saying," v. 60) in John's sense, not any part of the utterance in isolation. He knows those who cannot hear his words in faith.

The whole Johannine version of the Gospel is in question here. The meaning of right faith is set in contrast to unbelief, namely accepting the ascent of the Son of man to "where he was before" (v. 62). He is that same Son who has first descended from the heavens as "true bread" (v. 32). The life-giving spirit that Jesus' spoken words constitute, if received in faith, make everything spirit not flesh, life not death (v. 63).

The Evangelist knows the historical tradition well and takes this opportunity to name the betrayer as one of those who in Jesus' day did not believe (vv. 64, 70–71); likewise, to record Simon Rock's faith (v. 68). The Father, mysteriously, has not given to Judas, or indeed to any of those who do not believe, the power to come to God (v. 65).

Judas is a "devil," that is, an adversary of God (v. 70). Jesus embodies the divine holiness (cf. 17:11). The Father is responsible for the faith of Simon and the others who remain faithful. The dilemma that accounts for their perseverance is as touching as any sentence in the Gospels. The alternatives to belief in Jesus as Lord and Holy One of God are simply worse: "To whom shall we go?" (v. 68). Believers are driven, so to say, into the arms of faith. Their acknowledgment of the truth of Jesus' words of eternal life is as much a matter of having no alternative as of positive reasons. This is the great minimum of Christian faith. In times of intense trial it can also be the maximum.

The taciturn expression of Petrine faith in John is as pregnant of good homiletic reflections as anything the Caesarea Philippi telling may offer.

John 5
The Testimony of the Father's Works

Chapter 5 does not contribute to any Sunday lectionary reading. That is not a reason to take it any less seriously in these pages. It is an important bridge between the ideas already put forward in chapter 6 and those which will follow in chapters 7—12. It must be studied with care as a means of following the flow and momentum of the whole Gospel, especially because of its strongly polemical tone.

If our hypothesis about the original precedence of chapter 6 to chapter 5 is correct, moving into the fifth chapter, which sends Jesus "up to Jerusalem . . . after these things," is the beginning of the remainder of the Gospel. He will be found in Galilee no more, only in the city where hostility to him is concentrated and he must die. The actual southern province Judea and its capital city do not seem to have special historical significance for John other than that it was the place where he was "lifted up from the earth." Symbolically, it stands for religious opposition to Jesus—which was probably the historical fact. It is where the power classes that contrived his death, a hostile temple priesthood and a hostile imperial functionary, were aligned against him. Each consulted its own ends in conspiring with the other to destroy him.

Civil power achieved his actual dissolution. Given the way Roman authority was exercised in the provinces, such had to be the case. John tells the story as if the sole effective agency were religious, just as all the evangelists do (cf. 19:16). In John's case the reasons seem clearer than in the Synoptics. He, more evidently than the others, is accounting for the opposition to faith in Jesus which his community experiences. He does nothing to set his beleaguered flock at odds with the Empire. John reports on hostility from a certain segment of ethnic Jews, probably protagonists of Mosaic observance, in such a way as to indicate that the situation between them and his group has thoroughly deteriorated.

John 5:1–18

The pattern of the chapter is one that is by now established. There is a synoptic-like healing narrative, identified—for the first time in John—as an offense against the sabbath (5:10, 16). Charged with doing a "work" on the day of rest, Jesus responds in unique Johannine fashion: "My Father is working still, and I am working" (v. 17). In response there is the anguished charge that by this utterance he was "making himself equal with God" (v. 18). A revelatory discourse not only begins at this point but goes to the end of the chapter (vv. 19–47).

Of all the places mentioned in the Fourth Gospel, Jacob's well in the Greek Orthodox church in Nablus—ancient Sychar but now within the city limits of Israeli Shechem—and the pool by the Sheep Gate off the Via Dolorosa, are those most likely to have been seen by Christians visiting Israel. "Bethzatha" (the textual reading favored by Nestle-Aland, the United Bible Societies, and RSV), is a memorable site for the Christian. The present writer favors the reading "Bethesda," under the influence of the description of the place in the A.D. mid-first century Copper Scroll as Beth Esdatayin, a Hebrew plural describing the pools (3Q 15:XI, 12–13). But this is a difference that should be aired only to indicate that the familiar reading from the Authorized Version of "Bethesda" is by no means groundless. For Josephus, followed by Eusebius, Bezetha was the Aramaic designation of the section of the city north of the temple area.

"Bethesda" both gave its name to a city in Maryland that lies northwest of the District of Columbia and—according to a brochure published by the National Institutes of Health—accounted for President Franklin D. Roosevelt's selection of the site. When his advisor Harry Hopkins reminded him of the then little town's name as they drove through it, Roosevelt said that this was his choice.

The Jerusalem Sheep Pool ("gate" is supplied to "pool" in English in 5:2, probably under the influence of some O. T. references) is surrounded by a memorable piece of stone work, a ruin, which can be visited on the property of the Missionaries of Africa (popularly the "White Fathers," from the habit they wear), who did the excavation. The medieval church of Saint Anne built by crusaders stands nearby. Herod the Great was

78

probably responsible for the porticoes which surrounded the two pools with another portico between. In the modern excavation the stonework lies very low. Even though the streets of Jerusalem in Jesus' day were several yards below the present level, the pool was probably below street level even then to catch the rain as a means of supplementing the underground sources. Any pulpit description of the excavation is helpful because so few New Testament sites are secure beyond a general location. This one is exact. For those who have not been there, Jack Finegan's *The Archaeology of the New Testament* has a good summary of the 1966 monograph of Joachim Jeremias about the site. That latter contains the information which Eusebius (ca. 325) and the anonymous Bordeaux pilgrim (ca. 333) both convey, namely that the pool's waters are periodically disturbed. Eusebius speaks of a purple-red color, which he ascribes to the blood of animals once sacrificed there.

John does not name the feast, hence any attribution is unwise even though there is some manuscript support for *skenopegia* ("Tabernacles")—perhaps contributed to by 7:2. John does not designate the man's illness either (v. 5). Does the detail of thirty-eight years signify anything to the symbol-prone author? Probably not, other than that it may have been a historical reminiscence. Yet Cyril of Alexandria might be right in assigning to the man's thirty-eight years of affliction the number of years Israel spent in the desert (Deut. 2:14). For Cyril this was a sign of Israel's achieving grace at the end. The "paralyzed" of verse 3 are the withered or dry *(xeron)* of limb. (Modern Xerox-users might be interested to know that the inventor of that dry process substituted a final "x" for the adjective's proper ending.) The scribal addition of verses 3*b*–4 (the "Other ancient authorities" of RSV's footnote being later manuscripts) about the angel's moving the waters should occur only in older pulpit Bibles, hence will not affect most preachers. The only problem is why the glossator thought it right that the person should be healed who reached the water "first." He was probably making specific the practical problem of precedence in verse 7.

Jesus asks the victim if it his will to be healed (v. 6*b*). When he is assured that it is, he heals by a word of command (v. 8). The exchange between the *"Ioudaioi,"* distraught at Jesus' sabbath cure, and the one healed follows, bearing a close resemblance to the story of the man blind from birth in chapter 9. In neither case does the beneficiary know the identity of the one

79

who cured him (cf. v. 13; 9:12). The similarity of these two poolside healing stories, the second one listed among Jesus' numerous signs (9:16), is a strong indication that they were found by the Evangelist in a source, probably in this sequence. Both, in any case, lead to christological expositions. The two men are "found" by Jesus (v. 14; 9:35), a soteriological phrase. This one is admonished to sin no more although there has been no indication of his special sinfulness. Jesus will later deny a tie between illness and moral fault (9:3). The "worse" thing that could befall him is divine punishment for wrongdoing greater than his physical disability—in other words, not coming to "life." This is the intended outcome of all the Johannine signs. Why the healed paralytic should have gone off unmotivated to identify Jesus to his opponents is not clear, except that John requires the confrontation for his theological purposes. He achieves this by having Jesus make the claim that just as the Father continues to work—presumably after the sabbath rest of Genesis 2:2 (as the source of all action)—so Jesus works on the sabbath as on any other day.

Examination of rabbinical sources discloses that human need takes precedence over any prohibition of activity on the sabbath. Since this is the principle Jesus follows in all four Gospels, we must conclude that his followers and those of the rabbis were in constant confrontation after his death over how the principle they held in common was to be applied. The Christians must have relaxed sabbath rest drastically in Palestine (or not concurred in the new rabbinic strictures on it). Perhaps this began with not holding gentile converts to its observance. We have in all the Gospels a record of remembered exacerbations on the point. John in particular has a charge against Jesus' followers that in their claims of Jesus' intimacy with the Father they have him "making himself equal with God" (v. 18). These struggles about setting sabbath observance aside and Jesus' exact status before God must have been a matter of decades-long dispute in the city from which John writes.

Threats of violence because of the nature of the christological claims could likewise have been a reality of long standing. The seeking "all the more to kill him" is first reported in verse 18 but will be encountered again in 8:59 and 10:31 (cf. 11:8). In all those instances it is by stoning. The same reason is given in 10:33 as here; "because you, being a man, make yourself God." That Jesus should have made any such claim in his lifetime is

80

quite unlikely, on the Synoptic evidence alone. It surfaces in John in these terms because of the peculiar nature of the Johannine Christology. Jesus' sonship of God, understood as a coming forth from God as Word in human flesh, is the test for right faith in Jesus, even if not couched subsequently in the words of the prologue. The violent shouting matches between the Johannine circle and whoever *"hoi Ioudaioi"* were must have ended more than once in a death threat which the latter thought fidelity to the torah required.

John 5:19–29

The first part of the discourse contains familiar material about the Son's seeing the Father's deeds and doing likewise. Greater than what the Father has done for the Son out of love is what he will yet do (v. 20; cf. 1:50*b*). God, the only lifegiver in Jewish thought, empowers the Son to give life to whom he will. At this point the discourse takes a sober turn. The Father has committed all judgment to the Son, made him the complete surrogate as it were. Judgment here is not the evenhanded divine declaration on the righteousness or unrighteousness of a life lived. It is condemnation, the opposite sentence to a decree of life. We are on familiar ground when we are told that hearing Jesus' word and believing the one who sent him brings eternal life. Here we are faced with the sharp opposite of life: condemnation, presumably eternal death (v. 24).

The pericope that follows, verses 25–30, repeats the idea of the Son's having life in himself because the Father does. It also contains the apocalyptic notion that the dead will come forth from their tombs on the last day, the good to life and the evil to judgment (v. 29). Not all Jewish apocalyptic was monochromatic, but this is one familiar pattern of it. John introduces a change by saying that the hour "now is" when the dead will hear the voice of the Son of God (v. 25). His "dead" are evidently not only those in the tombs but the present dead who are capable of present life. Up to this point the language has been that of the last day, which lies in the future. Now John seems to say that the object of apocalyptic hope can be present reality.

This anticipated existence of the final age can be very comforting for those who wish to be aligned with Jesus, the Father, and life. There is at the same time a problem which must be faced. How does the homilist handle the severity which accom-

81

panied the Fourth Gospel's hope, its rhetorically black and white character, its total lack of nuance? One way was discovered long ago, namely to preach it "straight" and delight in the condemnation *(krisis)* of the unbelievers as the Jesus of John seems to. If they do evil, that is close their ears to appeals for faith in the Son of man, so much the worse for them. They are the sightless of this Gospel, the unbelieving, the recipients of the judgment which the Father has given into the Son's hands.

A Reflection on Those Condemned in the Fourth Gospel

The first thing to do about the persons subject to condemnation in the Fourth Gospel is to identify them gingerly, if at all. They were very real in the Evangelist's mind but ever since then they have been an unknown class. They are certainly not the Jews of any age or place outside the time of John, possibly outside his thought. There may be people in every age known to God alone who refuse to believe in the Jesus Christ whom God has sent. They cannot be many, for experience teaches that large numbers of Christians (to whom alone the description would nowadays apply) do not care much about Jesus one way or the other—certainly not that much. Their sin may be indifference, but it is not rejection. The formal rejectors of Jesus on John's terms are probably few and known to God alone in any case.

An important consideration is that many churchgoers are people of delicate psyches. The well-adjusted and the bovine stay home in remarkable numbers. To share the categories of John's apocalyptic as if it were a product for immediate export can be devastating to some listeners. Jesus is apodictic in this Gospel, to be sure. He divides the world into the lovers of darkness and light, of truth and the lie. The Hellenized Jewish thought of this day was prepared for this. It lived by these categories. Are there any modern equivalents? The search for authenticity and its opposite, the refusal to search for it, come to mind. Bultmann certainly had "authentic" and "inauthentic" correct as useful translations of ancient into modern categories. There is self-deceit in every age and its opposite, the persistent refusal to deceive oneself. Religiosity (an *Ersatz* Christianity) versus true religiousness is another rendering of the same reality. In all this pairing of opposites, however, one must recognize enough light to choose the darkness. There has to be an active

82

election, a real rejection of the kind John is talking about. This means that superficial pulpit discussions of being a Christian (coming to that state, lapsing from it, returning to it) may not flow naturally from a proclamation of the Fourth Gospel, whereas profound reflection on one's existence as a human being may. John has in mind nothing less than the depth of selfhood in profound union of faith with others committed to Jesus as Son of man.

The immediate modern circumstances may be membership in the First Presbyterian Church, a matter not to be despised. From there, however, John takes the hearer to utter commitment to life in Jesus Christ, not death among the betrayers who do not believe. This speaks of membership in a worldwide communion, the great bulk of whose members are not known to each other. It speaks of some who are rejected by a God and a Christ of just judgment. This concept is so awesome that it eludes even those most earnestly devoted to the all-holy God. The profundities of the Fourth Gospel are such that they do not come trippingly from the tongue of the average shallow preacher (who is most of us). But the words sit there on the sacred page as an invitation to a wrestling-match of the spirit, literally an "agony." The congregation is blessed that has a preacher who loves them enough to do that for them: Wrestle with these profundities for the good of all.

John 5:30–40

The segment of chapter 5 that runs from verses 30 to 40 is a return to the testimony theme of 1:15–36 (John's witness); 40–51 (the witness of his new disciples); 2:11; 4:54 and 6:26 (the witness of the signs); and 3:11–12; 4:21–26 (Jesus' own witness to what he has seen in heaven). In the present pericope Jesus names those who have given testimony on his behalf: (1) the one who sent him (vv. 30–31); (2) John, whose testimony is more than human (vv. 33–35); (3) the works that he does, all Father-inspired (v. 36); (4) the Father himself (vv. 37–38); (5) the Scriptures which promise life (vv. 39–40). The catalogue is not fivefold so much as single. It is God who speaks on Jesus' behalf in a variety of ways, as Hebrews will also say (1:1, but subsequently throughout). Put another way, Jesus comes to give testimony to God (vv. 41–43). Jesus' assurance of sincerity is that he is totally devoid of the search for human glory (v.

83

41). His sole concern is that God be glorified. He then levels the accusation that quoters of the books of Moses against him are in a search for personal glory. They long to be hailed as the learned more than acknowledged as searchers for the truth (vv. 44–47). "If you believed Moses" [dative case] you would believe me" [uncharacteristically, also dative case], for he wrote of me" (v. 46). The Scriptures offer a witness to Jesus and it is being refused.

One sees the main lines of first-century argument from the Christian side: It is systematic, it is apologetic, it is accusatory. Those who believe in Jesus as the Son are assumed to be in the right. Those who resist such belief are in the wrong. As this applies to contemporaries we have the expression by the author of an aspiration, a hope (and an awful dread) rather than an accomplished fact.

John 7
Living Waters of the Spirit

The sequence of events in chapter 7 is not easy to follow. The first unit, verses 1–13, finds Jesus in Galilee previous to "going up" to Jerusalem for the Feast of Tabernacles (*Sukkoth* to the Jew, the mid-point of today's high holy days in fall). While the temple stood, torches were lighted on the seventh day of the feast. The priests went around the altar seven times with water drawn from the spring of Siloam. They then poured a libation into a bowl set on the altar (*M. Sukk.* 4.1, 9–10). Jesus goes up to the feast and is there teaching from the middle of the eight-day observance to the end (v. 14). He makes a bold public declaration about himself on the last day of the feast. It divides the crowd (vv. 37–43) and leads to a debate between officers of the peace sympathetic to him and "chief priests and Pharisees" who are hostile (vv. 45–52). In this succession of separate scenes, some familiar things and some new ones are said about who Jesus is and how people of good will should respond to him. There is no lengthy discourse of Jesus reported, only brief exchanges.

84

A long time need not be spent on problems of the sequence of chapter in the present text of John. Having held, however, that a probable transposition of chapters 5 and 6 accounts for the present order, we seem to be sustained in this by the *kai*-adversative with which verse 1 begins. No equivalent is given in any of the English translations, renaissance or modern, possibly because rendering it would not make logical sense. Why is a "but" needed to introduce Jesus' going about in Galilee if he is already there in Capernaum in the passage just before, ending at 6:71? It would make more sense to say, "He would not go about in Judea, because the *Ioudaioi* sought to kill him" (v. 1*b*) if he had just been in Judea and concluded it was unsafe to remain there. Place verse 1 after 5:47 (the English "but" in v. 47 is the postpositive *de*, not *kai*) and you have Jesus in Jerusalem for an unnamed feast deciding at the end of his discourse that it is not wise for him to go about there. Movement in Galilee, on the other hand, would be safe.

There is another curious fact about chapter 7. Verse 15 says that "the *Ioudaioi* marveled" (RSV adds "at it" for the sake of literary grace; the phrase does not appear in Greek). In the previous verse he "went up into the temple and taught" (14). They presumably marvel at the teaching he gave without having been learners from it (v. 15*b*). In verse 21 they marvel (the same verb) at his "one deed," not his teaching. But even an attentive armchair reader might have trouble recalling from the narrative which deed it was.

The passage (vv. 15–24) is concerned with keeping Moses' law and the widespread rabbinic view that circumcision on the sabbath was permitted if this were the eighth day after birth. The one work of healing turns out to be the one sabbath cure of this Gospel at 5:2–18. If verses 15–24 were placed directly after chapter 5, with its concluding debate about believing the writings of Moses, much comes clear. The references in the pericope from chapter 7 to Moses the lawgiver and seeking to kill Jesus (v. 19; cf. 5:46–47, 18), speaking on God's authority (vv. 17–18; cf. 5:43*a*), and seeking one's own glory (v. 18; cf. 5:41, 44) are all clarified. But does the removal of this pericope from its present place to the end of chapter 5 leave a gaping hole in chapter 7? Not at all. The transition from verse 14, "Jesus went up into the temple and taught," to verse 26, "Some of the people of Jerusalem therefore said," is quite smooth. The people's inquiry about who he is dovetails perfectly with his coming to the fore in Jerusalem in the middle of the festal week. There seems to be a clear case for rearrangement here.

85

John 7:1–14

That much said by way of preliminary, we can turn to this
chapter which has as its background the great harvest festival
of autumn. John must know the tradition of the non-acceptance
of Jesus by his near kin (cf. Mark 3:21, 31–32; 6:4), although the
only mention of them until now has been neutral (cf. 2:12).
Here, the brothers who "did not believe in him" (v. 5) propose
that he go to Judea so that his disciples there—not his Galilean
intimates—may see his works. Despite their encouragement to
"go public," these family members betray no belief in their
great one. Jesus is unreceptive to their urgings because, as he
says, his "time" *(kairos)* is not yet fulfilled (v. 8; cf. 2:4). But he
later goes—into the midst of a populace muttering and divided
over him (vv. 10–13) like the desert-wandering Israelites. We
begin to get here the clearest indication to date that the Evangelist is describing the reception given to teaching about Jesus
in John's home city more than he is the events of a half century
before. The verb "lead astray" of verse 12 is the precise one
used in the Hellenist Jewish world to describe a deceiver on the
unicity of Israel's LORD. We know it from the Matthew story of
the Pharisees' request to Pilate to set a guard at Jesus' tomb:
"that deceiver" (27:63 author's trans.). The charge against the
Johannine circle must have been the same, namely that in
preaching Jesus they led Israel astray. Jesus' protagonists, on the
other hand, call him "good" (v. 12). Both sides in the debate are
inhibited by the menacing presence of *"hoi Ioudaioi"* (vv. 11,
13, 15). Clearly this cannot mean Jewish people simply, since in
this narrative everyone is an ethnic Jew. We are back to our
mysterious *terminus technicus* describing a bloc of opponents
whom the earliest readers of the Gospel would recognize.

John 7:15–24 (originally following 5:47?)

The division which John reports is over Jesus' qualifications
as a learned person, someone schooled (v. 15). It probably goes
back to his lifetime. Whatever his "teaching" in the temple is
(vv. 16, 17), begun "about the middle of the feast" (v. 14), it will
not be aired in this seventh chapter. There is simply the declaration that anyone who wishes to do the will of God will be able

to distinguish between a teaching from God and one given merely on Jesus' authority (v. 17). But this has been the criterion throughout the Gospel. Jesus' disinterest in his own glory authenticates him as one in whom there is no falsehood; he seeks God's glory only (v. 18). The verses between 15 and 24 make sense, it has been pointed out in the overview to chapter 7 (p. 84), if the sabbath healing of 5:2–18 is still fresh in memory. Jesus' argument is the rabbinic one of "light and heavy." Later rhetoric in the West would call it *a fortiori* ("so much the stronger"): if the lesser be true, how much more the greater. If circumcision is permitted on the sabbath, how much more the healing of a whole body.

The rest of chapter 7 will be given to brief bits of revelatory discourse and the violent exchanges that follow from it.

John 7:25–31

With the pericope that runs from verse 15 to verse 24 identified as separated from its original moorings, we resume with the puzzlement of "some Jerusalemites" (v. 25) over the failure of the "authorities" to move against Jesus (v. 26). It follows logically upon verse 14 and is contrasted with the popular fears of verse 13 that keep people from discussing him openly. The speculation that Jesus may be the Christ (v. 26) springs at us rather suddenly. It has surfaced only among the Samaritans to date (cf. 4:25, 29, 42) and been settled in the affirmative, even though "Messiah" would not have been a term of their use. In that exchange John took the pains to equate "Christ" and "Messiah" for the reader a second time (4:25; cf. 1:41). Previously, too, the Baptist had denied that the title should be applied to him (1:20; 3:28). John is clearly on record that Jesus is "the Christ." As has been pointed out, he even uses the term "Jesus Christ" which must have been in vogue by his day (1:17). But he has not previously named this identification as something that could divide a crowd over Jesus to the point of leading to threats of killing (cf. 7:25). It sounds as if the Christ-claim has led to open violence in places of John's experience. A period of peace on the question, free of reprisals, must have led to wonder about the motives of the authorities. Have any of them become convinced (v. 26)? The popular notion is aired that the Messiah, when he comes, will be mysterious in his origins (v. 27b). Here the question of his origins is put in identical terms

87

with Pilate's challenge (19:9; cf. 9:29). To it is contrasted the prosaic character of Jesus' Galilean roots (v. 27a; cf. 1:45).

There seems to have been abroad the notion—the post-biblical Jewish writings in Greek contain it and, much later, Justin will refer to it—that the Messiah exists somewhere in hiding. His identity will not come to light, however, until Elijah first appears. John will shortly report the tradition that David's village is his expected place of origin (v. 42). Both of these speculations are put foward in the Gospel only to provide the framework for the true declaration which the Evangelist will make: that Jesus comes from God, the "true," who has sent him (vv. 28–29). All speculations on his human origins are thereby falsified, notably the dismissal of Jesus as a plausible candidate for the messianic role because he comes from Galilee (v. 41). Some translations render Jesus' bold proclamation in the midst of his teaching, about the crowd's knowledge of who and whence he is (v. 28b), as declarative but ironic (NEB, JB). Most prefer to read it as interrogative (RSV, NAB, TEV). It is an indifferent matter, since whether the temple onlookers are said to know his home place and parentage or are asked if they do, they are in any case on the wrong track. Jesus is sent from God, whom he knows because he comes from God. He does not come of his own accord (vv. 28cd–29). This is the truth about Jesus. Everything else is false. The entire Gospel exists in order to make such a statement.

John closes off the brief section with two familiar cachets: Any attempt to apprehend him had to fail "because his hour had not yet come" (v. 30; cf. 2:4); and, "many in the crowd believed in him," even in Jerusalem, because he passed the "signs" test which John has set identifying him as the Christ (v. 31; cf. 20:30–31).

John's stress on Jesus as the Christ is identical with his insistence elsewhere that he is God's only Son, the Word and Light of life. There are not two or multiple identities of Jesus. There is but one. This means that the Fourth Evangelist has altered the concept of Messiah, deserting not only Jewish understanding contemporaneous with Jesus and with the writing of the Gospel but also the various Synoptic understandings of "the Christ." Any Jew is right who says that the early Christians changed the content of the mythic symbol "Messiah." They certainly did, in the ways of the several New Testament Christologies. The Jews, likewise, changed the content of the symbol,

88

probably in the time before and after defeat in the war of 67–73. They demonstrably changed it, as we know from Mishnaic and Talmudic sources, after the defeat of Bar Kochba in 135 (cf. Jacob Neusner, *Messiah in Context*). It does not make sense for Jews or Christians to charge the other group with infidelity to tradition. "Messiah" did not have a firmly fixed meaning in any case, although warrior-king predominated. This gave way to two distinct conceptions of the ruler of the final age.

The Fourth Gospel provides testimony to some heated debates on the point during the late first century from one Christian viewpoint. The argumentation in favor of Jesus' being the Messiah is aprioristic ("We saw him. We believed in him"), despite its *a posteriori* appearance ("Would any Christ do more signs than this man has done"?). In the same way, the Jewish argumentation of the period after Jerusalem's fall began to hold that the days of Messiah would be a time of cosmic harmony and Jewish-gentile peace. That new conception followed the defeat by Rome because no leader had thrown off the oppressor's yoke, a fact put forward in evidence that the Messiah had not come.

Since two historical situations, the Jewish and the Christian, were in flux on the concept "Messiah," it is unwise to charge anyone in retrospect for having failed to recognize Jesus as such. John gives us the bitter exchanges on the question he was most familiar with. The faith in Jesus which John's circle helped contribute to the larger church can be known. The debates from his time which John reports are not so easily grasped. If it took the church the long, hard road from the Fourth Gospel to Nicaea to express its faith in Jesus as Christ and Son of God, the opponents of Jesus in John should not carelessly be charged with lack of faith in him. Preaching on a pericope from John is an exercise in awe and an immense labor of comprehension. It may never descend to cheap bullying or a demand of John's "Jews" that they comprehend at a hearing what the church required several centuries to take in.

John 7:32–36

Resuming the debate at verse 32, we find an alliance of "the chief priests and Pharisees" (5 times in John; 2 times in Matt.) sending officers to arrest Jesus. As this Gospel is plotted, all such efforts will fail until Jesus is turned over to a power given to Pilate from above (19:11), even though the appearance is otherwise (19:16). It is he who lays down his life that he may take it up again (10:17). Here, the move to apprehend Jesus by force serves merely as a backdrop to two points John wishes to make about him: The search for him is fruitless because his being is elsewhere than in the places he is being sought (the "where I am" of v. 34 equals his presence with the Father); secondly, there is the testimony of the officers to their failed mission ("No man ever spoke like this man," v. 46). All attempts to lay hold of him, in other words, will fail unless they start with some sense of his uniqueness as one sent from above.

Meantime, Jesus' immediate response about being on the human scene "a little longer" before he goes to the one who sent him (v. 33) anticipates the use of the same phrase to describe his limited earthly stay (cf. 13:33; 14:19; 16:16; 17, 18, 19). John never presents him as an ordinary human being formed in his mother's womb and fated to go into the grave. Jesus is always someone destined to go back after a brief interlude to the Father from whom he came. The query about going off to teach the Greeks of the diaspora (v. 35) could be rooted in a historical reminiscence. There were many Jews seeking proselytes among the gentiles in Jesus' day, a phenomenon that came to a near halt with the sack of Jerusalem. But it is unlikely that this accounts for the presence of the phrase here. In the Greek-speaking Jewish world of John, some Jews would have been much more at ease consigning to the pagan world the kind of thought the Gospel represented. It sounds like the echo of a proposal the author and his circle would probably have had hurled at them many times: "Tell it to the Greeks. They would love that sort of thing." The speculation about Jesus' going where he cannot be found is, in any case, an instance of the crowd's literal uncomprehending response to the John community's preaching of Jesus' return to the Father.

John 7:37–52

Only verses 37–39 of this chapter are employed as a Sunday proclamation. This brief pericope is proposed by the Common Lectionary as an alternate reading on Pentecost for Year A (1).

The tensions of the week of *Sukkoth* culminate on the last day (v. 37). As the Mishnah describes it, the day was one of unrelieved joy:

[The rites of] the *Lulab* [lit., palm-branch, but here mixed with myrtle and joined to a citron] and the Willow-branch [continue] six and sometimes seven days; the *Hallel* [Pss. 113—118] and the Rejoicing, eight days; the *Sukkah* [arbor] and the Water-libation, seven days; the Flute-playing, sometimes five and sometimes six days; (*M. Sukk.* 4.1). . . . This is the flute-playing at the [place or the act of the] Drawing-of-the water [Heb. term uncertain as to meaning], which overrides neither a Sabbath nor a Festival day. They have said: He that never has seen the joy of the Beth ha-She'ubah [the term above] has never in his life seen joy (*M. Sukk.* 5.1).

The water-libation ceremony of the seventh day provided the setting John needed for having Jesus proclaim in a revelatory tone that all who thirst should come to him to drink (v. 37*b*). There is a problem in the quotation found in 38*b*, which in the form provided does not occur in any biblical place despite the "as the scripture has said." It may be a targumic reframing of Psalm 78:16 or Zechariah 14:8, the latter a reading for the feast of *Sukkoth* which refers to a spring flowing out of Jerusalem's temple "on that day."

Slightly more complex is the question of whether the rivers of living water will flow out of the believer, as it at first appears, or out of Jesus the source, as one expects. Considerations of style and the absence of punctuation are not decisive. Even so, "Let the one who believes in me drink" (NAB's rendering, favored by scholars) rather than the familiar, "He who believes in me . . . 'Out of his heart . . .' " (RSV) does not solve the problem as much as it promises to. Only the sense of the passage in context can settle it. This seems to be that the believer will drink of the Spirit which derives from Jesus, under the figure of thirst-slaking waters (v. 37). After Jesus' glorification (cf. 2:22; 12:16) this gift of the water struck from the rock will be given in profusion—but not until then.

The by now well-known attribution to Jesus of prophet-hood and Christhood follow his pronouncement (vv. 40, 41). He has been termed the Moses-like prophet of Deuteronomy 18: 15, 18 before this (6:14; probably also at 1:45, and 4:19), and the Christ (1:41; 4:26), two titles which the Baptist refused for himself (1:20, 21). Here the popular division of verse 12 over the merits of Jesus becomes a split on two specific titles. The knowledge of his Galilean provenance is used to put an end to the discussion (vv. 41–42). But no satisfactory reason is given for why "some" wanted to arrest him (v. 44), any more than it was

91

earlier (vv. 30, 32). Nothing reported of Jesus' utterances thus far seems remotely like cause for detention by religious authorities. A possible explanation would be fear by the guardians of the Jewish community in his day that a highly acclaimed charismatic could bring on Roman reprisals. The talk of arrest has to be code language for a much later situation when division over Jesus' disciples and their teaching is thought to be totally destructive of fidelity to the Torah. The designations "prophet" and "messiah," innocuous enough in Jesus' lifetime, have taken on overtones of capital offense (cf. v. 19*b*) as Judaism tries to unify itself in the aftermath of the war (C.E. 67–73).

The testimony to Jesus' unique powers of speech (v. 46) by the officers deputed to arrest him is part of the witness pattern of this Gospel. It is also faith testimony by the partisan believer John. Hidden beneath it is the struggle among the learned of a later period. Nicodemus (v. 50) who was chided as a teacher in Israel was last heard from after being told about a Son of man who must be lifted up (3:9–15). He returns as a spokesman for the due process required by the Mosaic books (v. 51; cf. Deut. 1:16–17; 19:18). The opponents of Jesus deal with him by an argument *ad locum,* namely the implausibility of the northern province as a breeding-ground for prophets (v. 52). Chesterton's remark that any stigma can beat a dogma comes to mind. But the Gospel exchange rings of verisimilitude. When Jesus began to be taken seriously he had to be dismissed seriously. The argument in favor of the Judean, hence Davidic, origins of Israel's deliverer in the last age was a serious one. It cannot be dismissed by Christians as denoting bad faith. Indeed, the prologues to Matthew (1—2) and Luke (1—2) which provide Jesus with Davidic origins may indicate how seriously it was taken.

There is a poignant tale in the tractate of the Tosefta ("Addition" to the Mishnah) entitled *Sheḥitat Ḥullin* ("On the Slaughter of Animals for Food") at 2:22. It dates to some time around C.E. 200, after Judah the Patriarch had completed his work of compiling the Mishnah. This passage tells of a certain Rabbi Eliezer ben Damah who was bitten by a snake. Jacob of Kefar Sama came to heal him in the name of Jesus, son of Pantera (viz., of Nazareth, Pantera being the paramour of Miriam in a defamatory story about Jesus' parentage). Eliezer dies before the healing can take place. Rabbi Ishmael addresses to his corpse the consolatory words that he had died in peace because he has not broken down the hedge erected by the sages. A passage from Qoheleth 10:8 about snakes and walls, which is quoted, must have inspired the tale.

A second story follows. The same Eliezer was brought to a law court for *minut* (leading astray in matters of the LORD's oneness, the charge of v. 12 *plana,* "he is leading . . . astray"). The judge—who is called by the Greek term *hegemon*—sends him off with a Latin *"Dimissus"* because, in his grey hairs, he should have known better than to get involved in such a thing. As Eliezer leaves the court, still troubled at the charge, Rabbi Akiba (d. after 135) comes up to comfort him:

> He said to him, "Perhaps someone of the *minim* told you some-
> thing of *minut* which pleased you." He [Eliezer] said to him,
> "By heaven! You remind me. Once I was strolling in the camp
> of Sepphoris. I bumped into Jacob of Kefar Sikhin, and he told
> me a teaching of *minut* in the name of Jesus ben Pantiri, and
> it pleased me.
> (trans. in J. Neusner, *Messiah in Context,* pp. 62–63).

Eliezer then confesses the rightness of his arrest, giving a pious quotation from Proverbs 5:8, and is credited with teaching that one should avoid not only the disreputable but even the appearance of the disreputable. This brief tale conveys much about the dilemma of the sages who were caught between admiring the teaching of Jesus (it was their own teaching!) and keeping *Torah* intact by not admitting any breach in the hedge they had newly erected. Valid ideas versus systems-in-place is among the oldest of human dilemmas.

PREACHING ON THE ACCEPTANCE
AND NON-ACCEPTANCE OF JESUS

It is eminently clear by now how John goes about present-ing Jesus as someone to be believed in. Recording his appear-ances in Jerusalem in a festal setting (first at a Passover in 2:23, then at an unnamed feast, 5:1; a Passover, 6:4, and Tabernacles, 7:2, 14, 37)—hence as someone deeply committed to the wor-ship life of Israel—John's Jesus is someone who will be immedi-ately recognized by hearers of the Gospel. He speaks and acts identically with the Johannine circle. All the familiar current debates are there: on belief in one who is presented as flesh and blood to consume; as one who sets the sabbath law aside and is made equal with God who works at will; on a claimed son of David and Messiah who originates in Galilee. The most potent objection of all is that of Rabbi Ishmael, found in John in the

93

form: "Have any of the authorities or of the Pharisees believed in him" (v. 48)?

The homilist who exhorts listeners to heed the sublimities of the Fourth Gospel need feel no inhibition in presenting the Jesus Christ of faith who emerged there: a Son who does all that he sees the Father doing, someone from the Father who alone has seen God, a man whose origins are in deity and not in any identifiable earthly place. What homilists may not do is accuse "the Jews" or "the authorities" or "the Pharisees" in the Gospel of ill will at nineteen centuries' distance, no matter how much the Evangelist felt free to do so. John and his company evidently thought themselves badgered and beleaguered. Modern preachers do not. The first-century Christians, moreover, had not yet experienced the full rabbinic development, which came with pressure-cooker force in the decades after the siege of the city. The rabbis, or sages (who would not become *the* Rabbis," transmitters of oral torah as if it has the force of Sinai, until after the Patriarch Judah's day, c.e. 200), had missed the entire Christian development: in and out of Palestine, Synoptic and Johannine alike. The debates in John are a shouting match between the students of a *yeshiva* in Brooklyn and a Christian faculty of divinity in Manhattan or the Bronx. A poor example, in light of the centuries of Jewish and Christian history which have intervened? Not so poor. The main outlines of the dispute are still in place.

The Christology contained in John is a speculation which, on the evidence of the Mishnah, the rabbis were not remotely ready to entertain. But they had to entertain it, John insisted. He provides them with ripostes that give us the impression that they *were* entertaining it. They were probably doing nothing of the sort but using the language of the John community to reject its teaching. At the most, some might have admired from afar some "words" of Jesus in the Synoptics, like Eliezer.

As to preaching the Gospel of John in our day as if the hearers in the churches were those resisting it, that is another matter. They may be. At least they have had a lifetime's exposure to its terms.

PART THREE

Who Is Jesus?

JOHN 8—12

John 8
Jesus Bears Witness to Himself
Amidst Bitter Exchange

John 7:53—8:11 contains one of the most beloved stories of Jesus' ministry. It is at the same time doubtful from a textual standpoint. Some modern Bibles put the story of the woman taken in adultery in brackets. Others omit it entirely. It is missing from this place in the earliest manuscripts. The later manuscripts which place it here (in Greek, not until after A.D. 900) probably do so because of Jesus' saying at 8:15 that he judges no one. The reason may also lie in verse 26, where he says he has "much to judge" [i.e., condemn]. A few manuscripts place it at the end of John, others after Luke 21:38. This testifies both to its existence as an independent narrative and to the sense of copyists that it belonged with Jesus' teaching in the temple (cf. John 8:2) as part of his final eschatological warning. Eusebius says that Papias reproduced "the story about a woman falsely accused before the Lord of many sins" which is to be found in the Gospel to the Hebrews (*C.H.* 3.39.17). The tale clearly resembles the story of Susannah and the elders, a Greek addition to the Book of Daniel (chap. 13 in LXX; Daniel and Susanna of the Second Canon, chap. 1). Jesus, like the young Daniel, suspecting hypocrisy, will have "no part in the death [RSV, 'the blood'] of this woman" (Dan. 13:46; Dan. and Sus., 1:46). Unlike Daniel, he does not engage in a search for conflicting testimony. The motives of the accusers are more his concern.

Chapter 8 resumes at verse 12 without interruption from

95

7:52. In declaring himself to be the Light of the world and the Light of life on the feast of Tabernacles (John calls it *skenopegia* in 7:2, the "tent-pitching"), Jesus may again be making capital—as John tells it—of the ritual observance involved. *Mishnah Sukkah* 5. 2–4 describes the Court of the Women on the first day of the feast as being brightly lighted by golden bowls of oil set at the top of candlesticks that can only be reached by ladders. The wicks were made from the worn-out garments of the priests; four priestly youths replenished the oil supply. Not a courtyard of Jerusalem failed to reflect the water-drawing. Men danced with burning torches while the Levites played music and two priests blew trumpets at cock-crow. The description is stirring. The figure of Jesus as the world's Light, however, has so rich a background in Jewish—and pagan—religion (i.e., teaching as illumination) that it seems unwise to tie his declaration that he is the Light of the world (v. 12) too exclusively to this liturgy.

The light image for him has already appeared (in 1:5, 9; 3:19–21; 5:35) and will recur at 12:35–36. The saying given here, "I am the light of the world" (v. 12), is probably anticipated from 9:5; it will occur again, introduced by the adverb of comparison "as," in 12:46. The "I am" statement (we have already encountered the phrase without a predicate in 4:26 and frequently in the bread of life discourse) is used here merely to bring on the controversy about being a witness to oneself (vv. 13–18). The full development of Jesus as Light will not come until the next chapter. Still, chapter 8 gives the saying in its fullest form, going on to maintain that whoever follows Jesus will not walk in darkness but have the Light of life (v. 12). The latter phrase anticipates the double sense of the daylight *and* Jesus as illuminative, which will be spelled out in 12:35–36.

Testimony and the rules of evidence under the law of Moses are once again the theme of verses 12–20. The two witnesses required in the Scriptures have come forward: "I bear witness to myself, and the Father who sent me bears witness to me" (v. 18; cf. 5:31, 36–37). Verses 21–30, like the verses immediately preceding it (cf. 14c), are concerned with where Jesus comes from and whither he goes, namely from God and to God—the one who sent him—who is true (v. 26). Here, however, we encounter the use of "below" and "above" to supplement "of this world" and "not of this world" (v. 23) describing the spheres proper to Jesus and his opponents. The two adverbs also prepare the hearer for the course of Jesus' cosmic journeys, although later usage will feature his being sent into the world and going to the Father.

Verses 31–59 contain the heart of christological affirmation in this Gospel. To master it is to know what John means by freedom in Christ and enslavement to sin. It has the tragic appearance of being anti-Jewish because of John's anger at his opponents' reading of their own religious history. Their fidelity to tradition is infidelity to him, his fidelity to Jesus the supreme infidelity to them. The seeds of all diametrically opposed religious difference are here. Featured in the bitter exchanges of chapter 8 are Israel's parentage from God through Abraham, the innate freedom of the Jewish people, and Israel's perseverance in the truth of God. The Evangelist sees the heritage perfectly epitomized in the Son Jesus and betrayed in the hands of his opponents through adherence to "your law" (v. 17).

John 8:1–11

The Catholic Lectionary alone employs 8:1–11, on the Fifth Sunday of Lent in Year C (3). Its traditional place in the Tridentine missal was the previous day (paired with the Susanna story).

The coupling of "scribes and Pharisees" (v. 3) is not Johannine, nor does the Mount of Olives (v. 1) appear by name in the Fourth Gospel. In the books of Moses both male and female adulterers are to be put to death, but there is no mention in this passage of the apprehension of the woman's partner. Perversely, over the centuries, Jesus' denunciatory, "Let him who is without sin among you be the first to throw a stone at her" (v. 7*b*), has become a watchword of exculpation for the solidly guilty. The actual issue in the story is the far greater guilt of the accusers than the woman. Jesus is protecting her, not them, by charging them *all* with sin. None of them is innocent. Today's white collar criminals and politicians "on the take" fleece the citizens and then have the gall to quote Jesus. Hoping to draw attention away from themselves, they prove their kinship with the types he censures.

One can only regret that the manuscript evidence on this pericope is weak. It has a solid place in the Authorized and Douai-Rheims Versions but textual purism may be seeing to it that it is less and less preached in all its vigor (against hypocrisy, against sexism), while the caricature of it remains vigorous,

97

namely, leniency all around because of the universality of human weakness.

John 8:12–20

Is the Mosaic prescription which is cited in 8:17 (Deut. 17:6; 19:15) no longer the law for John, or is he simply disowning his opponents' reading of it? He must consider it binding or he would not be at such pains to show that Jesus fulfills it. Therefore, Jesus is cited as a true witness on his own behalf—or one who could be if he wished in conjunction with a second witness, God (vv. 14–16). The irony is that he who could judge justly, does not, while his opponents who cannot, do (vv. 15–16). They challenge him, equivalently, to produce his mysterious "Father" as witness, but are told that since they do not know (i.e., believe in) Jesus they cannot know the Father he speaks of.

The "Pharisees" of verse 13 deserve good marks for requiring more than one witness to Jesus' claim on his own behalf. The Mishnah would later promote general principles in this regard, for example, "Whoever is suspected in what concerns any matter may neither judge nor bear witness thereof" (*Bekhoroth*, "Firstlings," 4:10). This is what Jesus means by witness "according to the flesh" (v. 15), that is, one based on self-interest. But the initial assumption of the Pharisees is that, testifying on his own behalf, Jesus *in fact* lies about himself (v. 13). The Mishnah is severe, but just, on this point: "Witnesses become subject to the law against false witnesses only if they bear false witness about themselves (*Makkoth*, "Stripes, 4.1"). Jesus' first move is to deny their allegation that, because he has a stake in the matter, he necessarily gives false testimony (v. 13). He gives as his reason that he alone knows his origin and destiny, something his challengers cannot know.

Jesus then conforms to Mosaic precept and proposes the Father and himself as the valid deliverers of testimony regarding his person (vv. 16–18). The offer is found insufficient since he cannot produce the Father as one might bring forward a human witness (v. 19*a*). The Christian response of faith will always transcend the ordinary rules of evidence, being in another order. Since John's day the intuitive Christian reaction to challenge on Jesus' credentials—and to Christian proclamation apart from any challenge—is that God can be known in Jesus in a way that is like no other. Jesus is very much a man of earth but not of "this world" (v. 23), the realm "below." His human life has an intimate connection with godhead, the limitless reality which has as its proper sphere the "above." The vocabulary, whether it be first-century Hellenist Jewish or vaguely gnostic, need not put us off. The simplicity of the claim is what matters: "If you knew me you would know my Father also" (v. 19). Jesus is the one who in his own person manifests God fully. His opponents' incapacity to accept the kind of person he is poses a barrier to their taking in even a fragment of the awesome mystery of godhead.

The argument is not so much circular as correlative. True knowledge of Jesus is knowledge of the truthful God (v. 19), just as not having the love of God within oneself prevents one from receiving Jesus (5:42). At that point in the narrative the exchange is declared a stalemate. Jesus' immunity from capture is repeated (v. 20), even though no cause for such a move is evident. There is simply the laconic repetition that his hour has not yet come (cf. 2:4; 7:30).

The exact place of this teaching is given, the *gazophyla-kion* or Temple treasury, literally an offering-box (v. 20a). The detail may be the cachet of historicity. It is also mentioned in connection with the widow's mite in Mark 12:41.

John 8:21–30

Jesus' threat of departure (v. 21, the latter part repeated from 7:34b) anticipates what he will later tell his disciples (13: 46), but it is delivered here in a quite different spirit. It also echoes the speculation that he will go among the Greeks (7:35), but with the much darker suggestion that he will take his own life (v. 22). Who but a suicide can predict imminent departure to another sphere, his antagonists wonder. John is being ironical, but we cannot but speculate if such a tale were ever spread abroad about Jesus' end. It is *they* who will die in their sins unless they believe that *"I am,"* Jesus says (v. 24). They ask him who he is and he answers: "Even what I have told you from the beginning" (v. 25). Perhaps this highly idiomatic phrase should be rendered, "Why do I speak to you at all?" But John's Jesus does not respond here in pique or impatience. He speaks of himself throughout this Gospel as the Son who is the Word or Wisdom of God. Insofar, he is "in the beginning . . . with God" (1:1). He has heard enough from God, who is with him (v. 29a),

99

to act as humanity's judge but he forbears (v. 26). Only when the Son of man is lifted up from the earth—in the double sense of crucifixion-exaltation—will the terrible intimacy described by "I am" become clear (v. 28). Meanwhile, as in the Samaritan exchange of chapter 4, "many believed in him" (v. 30).

The Origin of "I am"

Where does the pregnant phrase, "I am" *(Ego eimi),* so characteristic of Jesus in John, come from? It occurs twenty-nine times in this Gospel, twenty-six of them spoken by Jesus. Clearly it has heavy theological significance for the author. (Could it have been a phrase of the earthly Jesus found once on his lips in Matt., twice each in Mark and Luke)? In John it occurs with seven different predicates, a number that may be significant: "I am . . . bread" (6:35, 41, 48, 51), "light" (8:12), "door" (10:7,9), "shepherd" (10:11,14), "resurrection and life" (11:25), "way, truth and life" (11:25 and "vine" (15:1,5). Schnackenburg speculates that the original seven might have been bread, water (see 4:14; 6:35; 7:38), shepherd, vine, light, life, and door, all symbols familiar to natives of Palestine and having a significance in Judaism. He further thinks that these basic seven were expanded in an abstract and somewhat artificial direction, but always connected with the life *(zōe)* which Jesus is and gives to believers. The unusual feature of the phrase is its absolute use without any addition, as here in chapter 8 (vv. 24, 28, 58). It appeared in this form in 6:20 when Jesus walked on the water and will again at 18:5, 6 and 8, the description of Jesus' arrest. In these cases it is the way he identifies himself, but clearly it is an expression of his authority, even his capacity to inspire awe. The use of "I am" in 8:24 and 28 is different (the same will be true in 13:19). There, the formula is a matter of believing in Jesus and knowing him in his whole being. The claim is totally emphatic, making the demand that Jesus be acknowledged as unique in his form of being. Its use seems to be different in 8:58, "before Abraham was, I am," but there it is not really about Jesus' priority in existence to the patriarch, although it is that; rather, as before, it highlights the absolute character of his existence.

The origins of the phrase are probably biblical, augmented by development in the post-Maccabean period. The Hebrew *ani hu* ("I am"; in its Septuagintal form *Ego eimi*) is a cue that some self-declaration of God will follow. It is especially charac-

100

teristic of the Second Isaiah, but the occurrences in the Pentateuch and the prophets are also important (see Gen. 28:13, 15; Exod. 3:14; 20:1–5; Isa. 45:5, 6, 18; 46:9). In those places the phrase stresses the divine uniqueness and majesty, likewise the LORD's loving choice of Israel. Importantly, one must ask if John intends by his use of it to attribute to Jesus divine being on a par with that of God. Exodus 3:14 in the Septuagint seems clearly to lie behind John 8:58 and Isaiah 43:10–11 to form the background of 8:24, 28. Both places provide parallels, as do no others, for the absolute use of "I am." While it is true that the Johannine "I am" phrases with a predicate match those in the Hebrew Scriptures calling the LORD Israel's savior (Isa. 43:11), keeper (Isa. 27:3), and healer (Exod. 15:26), namely by having Jesus do the saving work of God, it would be a mistake to see in "I am" used absolutely (8:24, 28, 58) a claim to identification with God.

Obviously Jesus' hearers could have taken it in that way and are reported as having done so (see 8:59; 10:31–33). But John is so clear in insisting on Jesus as God's revealer of the final age, one who comes from above and can speak of God only as he does (see 3:11; 8:26; 12:49), that it would be wrong to see a departure from that pattern in the absolute use of "I am." Here as elsewhere the Son is claiming total intimacy with the Father. He is uniquely commissioned to deliver a message from the One who sent him. He gives unique access to God, having been chosen to serve as the sole means of salvation to any who hear his voice. Jesus' "original and inexhaustible fulness" (Schnackenburg pp. 2, 88) is sufficient to account for this high christological title. While some few think that the "I-saying" goes back to Jesus, it is much more likely—both predicatively and absolutely—to derive from cultic usage in early liturgies, as a way to encompass claims made in behalf of the God of Israel as well as claims made on behalf of some favorite Hellenistic deity, like Isis. It is, in any case, a way to convey that Jesus is the unique bringer of salvation in his own person.

John 8:31–47

Have the Judean opponents of Jerusalem in Jesus' day become *hoi Ioudaioi* of the evangelist John's embattled career? It would seem so. The designation is surely that of a particular group within the larger framework of peoplehood. Some main-

101

tain that only an ardent Jew-hater, hence a non-Jew or a bitterly disaffected one, could have framed verse 44. The attribution of the parentage of *hoi Ioudaioi*—whatever the term may mean—to the devil is inconceivable, they say, as the work of a Jewish writer. A careful study of Jewish obloquy in matters of religious conviction, however, yields surprising parallels. The covenanters of Qumran could write against their targets in the Jerusalem temple, all Jews:

> Preachers of lies and prophets of deceit, they have schemed against me a devilish scheme, to exchange the Law engraved on my heart by you / for the smooth things they speak to Your people.... But You, O God / Despise all Satan's designs.... You will destroy in judgment all men of lies . . . ."
>
> *(Hymns, IV passim).*

The designation of Jesus' opponents in controversy in verse 31 as *hoi Ioudaioi* creates certain problems. In verse 30 we have been told that, "many believed in him *(eis auton)."* The verb "believed" is in perfect participial form, normally denoting completed past action. The pronoun has lost the governing preposition it had in the previous verse *(eis* = in). Many find it incredible that current believers in Jesus could receive the tongue-lashing from him that follows in this chapter, and so translate the participle "who *had* believed in him," assuming a different audience from the believers of verse 30. Some (RSV and NIV) even create a new paragraph; but Nestlé-Aland begins a paragraph with verse 30, thereby supposing that the audience of believers is the same. Some also find a weakening of commitment to him in the change from the accusative to the dative case *(eis auton* to *auto).* A common opinion is that verses 30–31a are a gloss, or that 31a alone is added as a corrective to 30; in any case, a transition has been supplied to the Johannine text to get from verse 29 to the lengthy polemic that follows.

It can reasonably be asked whether the final editor is distinguishing between putting some kind of credence in Jesus' teaching (marked by the dative) and abiding in his word (by the accusative). Another possibility is that some of the believers of John's day in the group he stigmatizes as *hoi Ioudaioi* have a wrong faith in Jesus that merits bitter correction by the Johannine community. They are not "truly" his disciples because

102

they have not persevered in his word (v. 31). This word is the relation between Jesus and the Father as John perceives it. They are "still slaves of sin" (v. 34), which here is not moral fault in general but the sin of boasting in peoplehood rather than committing themselves to the truth of Jesus' origins. They persecute the John group (v. 37: "you seek to kill me") because true faith in him ("my word") finds no hearing in their midst. It is a clear struggle for John between truth (v. 46) and falsehood (v. 44). God is the father of the faith community of the Evangelist; the devil is the father of those who oppose that community and the faith in Jesus it professes.

Since in the Evangelist's view Jesus and those who follow him are of God, they hear the utterances of God in a way that the opposition does not (v. 47). Instructed by the Father, Jesus speaks the truth (vv. 28, 45–46). This is a language his antagonists are incapable of. Truth or "the true" in this context is always the reality of God and the sonship of his prophet-witness Jesus. The latter faithfully speaks a word that describes what he has seen in the Father's presence (v. 38).

As has been suggested, it is likely that John is presenting some form of ongoing trial or testing at Jewish hands in the chapters that follow chapter four. The exchanges reported may derive from certain historical reminiscences of Jesus' lifetime. They will contain numerous echoes of Synoptic material (e.g., "Abraham is our father," v. 39 = Matt. 3:9 and Luke 3:8; reference to Jesus' having a demon, vv. 48–49 = Mark 3:22–30 and parallels; the claim of Jesus' superiority to Abraham, vv. 56–58 = his superiority to Jonah and Solomon in Matt. 12:39–42 and Luke 11:29–32). We can only be sure of a common tradition in church proclamation. Thus, when John insists on Jesus' importance relative to Abraham and the prophets, the Synoptic debate on David's reverence for his "Lord" who is nonetheless his son (Mark 12:35–37 and parallels) comes to mind. If each evangelist wrote up in final form the most persuasive arguments for Jesus he had been employing over several decades, we have an account in John of the polemic whereby his circle thought it had made the most telling points.

Therefore, while John is weaving traditional materials into a pattern of his own, he is doing it in an existential or life setting. Each new exchange has the ring of debate personally engaged in.

John 8:48–49

The *Ioudaioi* next level the charge at the John circle through Jesus: "You are a Samaritan and have a demon" (v. 48). He denies the second charge (a Synoptic echo; cf. Mark 3:22 and parallels) but disregards the first.

It has been conventional to find in the Samaritan accusation of verse 48 a piece of ordinary Jewish invective, the equivalent of demonic possession, as if the two were in apposition. We know that the Samaritans Dositheus and Simon Magus were dismissed by the Jews as demon-possessed. But if the John community is here acknowledging its Samaritan component freely, the failure of Jesus to respond to the taunt may be the key to the whole chapter. Recall the outcome of his two-day stay in Sychar: "And many more believed because of his word. They said to the woman . . . 'we know that this is indeed the Savior of the world' " (4:41–42).

God is the Imminent One of the later Samaritans, the "light of their life" who will achieve both their salvation and that of the world on a cosmic scale (cf. Marqah's *Teaching,* II, 3). According to their third-fourth century Aramaic prayer book, the Ta'eb ("Restorer") will come to bring final and irrevocable salvation to Israel for all time (cf. A.E. Cowley, I, 58). Does belief in a savior figure on terms other than those of the Davidic messiah of Judea persist in the Samaritan wing of the Johannine community? And are the members of the community at large being taunted for numbering Samaritans among them? The Johannine response is that Jesus honors God (v. 49), who in turn glorifies Jesus (v. 54). Jesus has God as his Father uniquely (vv. 18, 27–29). This is presented as a counterclaim to that of the *Ioudaioi* who say Abraham is their father. When they get the drift of the Johannine argument, they too claim divine parentage (v. 41*c*), but Jesus disallows it. He proposes love of himself ("me") as the one thing which ensures that a person is born of the Father (vv. 42–43).

Belief in God's word is the great matter at issue in chapter 8. John sees in the Moses-like champion of the true God, Jesus, the healer of an ancient schism. This man from Nazareth in Galilee (1:45; 7:27, 41, 52) would bring the people of the south and the north together, Samaritans included. The Jerusalemites found the idea preposterous. "Are you from Galilee too?" the Judeans asked Nicodemus (who, in fact, was). "Search and you will see that no prophet is to rise from Galilee" (7:52). And to Jesus: "You are a Samaritan and have a demon" (v. 48). They were no bastard breed, they said (cf. v. 41). The implication is clear. Davidic origins provided legitimacy, whereas it was evident that no one could vouch for the parentage of Samaritans and Galileans. There may even be an echo in the taunt of birth "from fornication" (v. 41) of the charge that Jesus had no identifiable father.

Does John Allude to Isaiah 43?

Knowing of John's allusive use of Scripture in preference to quoting or paraphrasing it, some have suggested a relation between this chapter and Isaiah 43. Aileen Guilding thinks it was the Scripture portion for the first sabbath of the feast of Tabernacles (*The Fourth Gospel and Jewish Worship*, p. 107). In this poem God looks to his son, the Jews of an undivided kingdom, with love:

> But now thus says the LORD,
> he who created you, O Jacob,
>   he who formed you, O Israel:
> "Fear not, for I have redeemed you;
>   I have called you by name, you are mine (v. 1).

> bring my sons from afar
>   and my daughters from the end of the earth
> every one who is called by my name,
>   whom I created for my glory, . . . (vv. 6,7).

> "You are my witnesses," says the LORD,
>   "and my servant whom I have chosen,
> that you may know and believe me
>   and understand that *I am* He" (v. 10, author's italics).

Then follows a review of the LORD's saving power from a drowning in the sea, to be thoroughly eclipsed by God's restoration from exile of

> the people whom I formed for myself
> that they might declare my praise (v. 21).

But Jacob did not call upon the LORD; Israel grew weary of him: 105

> Your first father sinned,
> [Jacob? the patriarchs collectively?]

and your mediators transgressed against me.
Therefore I profaned the princes of the sanctuary,
I delivered Jacob to utter destruction
and Israel to reviling (vv. 27,28).

John is not demonstrably interested in the key phrase in Isaiah, "See, I am doing something new" (v. 19; author's trans.), referring to the restoration from Babylonian exile, but in the ideas of witnessing to God, knowing and believing in him, understanding that only God or someone as close to him as the Son can say "I am." John wishes to proclaim the LORD's glory. All these things the Son who is Jesus (8:28, 36, 38) does admirably. What Jacob-Israel fails to do, Jesus achieves. You will die in your sins "unless you believe that *I am,*" Jesus says (8:24).

The whole eighth chapter is about who Jesus is. In a more basic sense it is about who God is: the one who is true, who sends a truthful speaker, who could say much in condemnation but does not, who says of himself "I am" and authorizes the one who is sent—who is "not alone" in judging (v. 16)—to say the same. The truth that sets free from all enslavement is the truth of God. Abiding in Jesus' word is that truth (vv. 31–32). The person, Jesus, is himself the word; man and message are one. Jesus resembles the rain and the snow that come down from the heavens:

"so shall my word be that goes forth from my mouth;
    it shall not return to me empty,
but it shall accomplish that which I purpose,
    and prosper in the thing for which I sent it" (Isa. 55:11).

"I do nothing on my own authority," says Jesus, "but speak thus as the Father taught me. And he who sent me is with me; he has not left me alone, for I always do what is pleasing to him" (8:28–29). The man who is the Word of God fulfills God's will. It cannot be otherwise, for an utterance is true to its utterer.

The Homilist and the Polemics of John 8

The easiest pulpit treatment to give this chapter is to castigate the lack of faith of Jesus' opponents in him. This gives short-term satisfaction because it places both preacher and hearer in a superior position. It loses sight of a number of things. One is that it took the gentile church four centuries to make fully explicit (at Chalcedon) its faith in who Jesus was in relation to the Father. The normal Sunday expositors of Christian faith are not likely to be familiar with the debates of those ages, hence may go on the assumption that the Evangelist's meaning is perfectly clear because they have done a little exegetical study. In fact, it was made clear as a matter of Christian faith only in a philosophical context other than the one of its composition. To trust the "assured results of modern scholarship" and expound these verses confidently obscures the fact that the sands have shifted so quickly in the last fifty years that they give less than complete assurance.

Even today, many authors assume that *hoi Ioudaioi* of chapter 8 are a known quantity, namely the leader class in the Jerusalem of Jesus' day. The present treatment takes the line that the Mosaic loyalists of John's day are intended—men who lived by the emerging *halakah* being spelled out by the sages. In the Evangelist's time they were probably a mixture of Jewish non-believers in Jesus and believers in him in a way the author found unacceptable. The best service that the present comments can offer is to sow seeds of uncertainty in the preacher's mind that the adversaries of Jesus in his lifetime are identifiable with certainty.

The chief concern of modern homilists must be with the modern adversaries of Jesus, starting with themselves. Who they are in the present century is a fairly accessible matter. They are not, first of all, today's Jews. Modern Jews, including the learned among them, have seldom heard Jesus discussed by Christians except in terms of the expectation that they should believe in him. On the Jewish side there is often the unquestioned assumption that the doctrine of the incarnation logically requires belief in two gods. Christian charges of Jewish unbelief have traditionally been a matter of vigor and virulence. Even quiet-toned pulpit references to "the Jews," as if they were the same persons as now-living Jews, partake in this spirit.

The opponents of Jesus who are unequivocally addressed by John 8 in the modern period are believers in him whose faith is flawed, or who once believed in him and have apostasized out of sloth or to pursue some advantage. There can be a mixture of ignorance and prejudice which is readily stirred to violence in such Christians. The Christology of today that merits the censure of John 8 is that of those who deny that Jesus truly has come from God as the bearer of divine truth or who, conversely, view him as a god walking the earth in a human body. Far more

107

numerous are those who have no quarrel with the ancient creeds but let their lives go totally untouched by the faith in Jesus Christ they profess. It is this inadequate faith which deserves censure. Then, as now, failure to hear the words of God stems from not being "of God" (v. 47). The formula sounds circular and, in a way, it is. The Johannine author, without going into the workings of what later came to be called divine grace, makes a basic demand of openness, good faith, or willingness to let God be God as the condition for recognizing Jesus for who he is.

To resist knowing Jesus is to be earthbound, to die in one's sins as the subject of judgment (vv. 21, 24, 28), not acknowledging that "I am." These condemnations are serious. They should not be delivered to one's Christian contemporaries lightly. They may not so much as be mentioned unless ministers of the word have labored hard among congregations to expose the Jesus who is the revelation of God. Proof-texts do nothing to show forth the one who is "from above" (v. 23). It is equally unhelpful to superimpose on first-century material the long and painfully developed faith of the church in Jesus and say naïvely, "It is all there in John." What is all there in John is a remarkable first-century Christology that is at base *theo*logy, an exposé of faith in God to which faith in Christ is related, not vice versa. A serious offense Christians commit is to put Jesus in God's place. This is done to the scandal of the Muslim and Jew and the confusion of the Christian. Some unbelievers tend to be at home with it, having made this confused Christology the basis for their rejecting Christianity and sometimes religion itself. They cannot accept the confusion and they give this as the reason for their unbelief.

John's Gospel is guilty of no such offense. His Jesus is a sacrament of God, at the same time the Son and Word, who is the humanly personal pledge of the bottomless well of deity. To know him is to know the Father, but the one is not the other under all aspects. "I have much to say about you and much to judge; but he who sent me is true, and I declare to the world what I have heard from him" (v. 26). Jesus' words are God's Word. He is himself that Word. True discipleship of him is a matter of abiding in that Word (v. 31).

108

The interesting thing in all this is that Jesus' *logos* ("word") and *rhemata* ("words," i.e., "sayings") of chapter 8 are never spelled out in detail. He speaks about speaking, he utters words about his word, but he never says *what* he says, only *that* he says. The frustration of the reader or hearer, however, is not total. Jesus' spoken word is identifiable as his person. Conveying this is something that the preacher does more by being than uttering. The case with expositors and with all Christians is the same as with Jesus himself. The difference is that only he is from above. He is the unique sacrament of God. But all who hear his words and abide by them give to those who experience their presence something of the reality ("truth") of God.

In Jesus' words, being in bondage is the opposite possibility to being free: being slaves to convention, to church allegiance, to colonial stock or frontier stock, or being self-made or whatever our boast may be. Only the Son of the house who is supremely free can set free those who claim a tie with him (vv. 35–36). To live in sin and be its slave is to claim another God than the true God, to live by another word than the true word which is the man Jesus. "If God were your Father, you would love me, for I proceeded and came forth from God" (v. 42). Jesus stands before the believer. His presence calls for love. The one who loves abides in him and knows the Father as one's own father. Parentage of another sort is attributed to the devil, the father of lies (v. 44). Satan as the countervailing force to God is absolutely necessary in Hebrew antithesis. There are those who refuse to hear; there is truth and there are lies. Only a God of truth and the deceit of the human race personified, the devil, can account for this opposition. "The one [He, RSV] who is of God hears the words of God; the reason why you do not hear them is that you are not of God" (v. 47).

John 8:50–59

The Lectionary of the Tridentine missal used 8:46–59 on what used to be called "Passion Sunday" (the second before Easter). At present no lectionary proposes any of John 8:12–59 for reading on a Sunday.

The God who is One seeks the glory of Jesus and is the judge in the same act (v. 50). He delivers from death all who are true to Jesus' word (v. 51). Fidelity to this word is freedom, light, and life.

The ultimate tragedy for the Christian would be to claim God as one's God and not know this God (vv. 54–55). Unthinkable? John supposes it to be a distinct possibility and warns against it in every line. The clear path to God-knowledge is seeing Jesus' day and rejoicing in it (v. 56). The jubilant cry of Christians is that they—they alone—are walking on this path. They see and know Jesus, therefore they see and know God. The claim is perilous. It can be perverted from a faith claim— and it is that, for he is the one way for those who know him—to a boast. Seeing one's own glory under the guise of promoting the praise of God can turn the whole venture to ashes. To claim that God's revelation in Christ is superior to every other way whereby God is self-revealed can be an empty exercise if a claim for the glory of Christianity is made because the claimants happen to call themselves Christians.

If genius is to madness near allied, faith is separated from frenzy by a paper-thin wedge. At this, "they picked up stones to throw at Jesus" (v. 59). Who did this? People who believed either too much or too little about Jesus, who in any case did not abide in his word. Their caricature of Jesus failed them. He was either God in a human body or the preacher of a God who would save them from pain and loss or a prophet like Moses, but one who had nothing special in common with God. Whatever their terms were he would not save them on these terms, this Jesus-who-never-was; and so they turned on him.

There is the possibility from the Christian side that one can make up a Jesus who is a weapon, a club with which to reduce others to silence. Normally it is the theological "right" which sins in that way, believing without ever quite saying it: "One nature only and that nature divine." The Arian left is no more without its burden, speaking of a great one in Jesus, the exemplar of deity but not in any sense deity in its human knowability. Jesus was right to speak in God's name, it maintains, to proclaim the word of his Father, for he is the "firstborn of all creatures." This supremely rational Christianity is fit for our times: It has about it no superstitious elements. Yet the Johannine Jesus had said, before ever Arius came to be:

> Truly, truly, I say to you
> before Abraham was, I am (v. 58).

This is not merely the Johannine difference. It is the Jesus difference, and was perceived as such on some terms—if not precisely those of divine preexistence—by all the witnesses from the apostolic age, the authors of the New Testament.

110

Jesus' claim that he knows Abraham and keeps his covenant (v. 55) is clearly meant by John to be a link of fidelity with the first of the patriarchs. Abraham's "rejoicing" has a long history in Jewish midrash. It accounts for his laughter when he heard that his wife would bear a son (Gen. 17:17), and his delight on the occasion of the weaning of his son marked by a great feast (21:8). Here in John the Christian midrash has Abraham looking down the ages and seeing the offspring of Isaac who would cause him great joy. The "on that day" of Abraham's cutting the covenant (Gen. 15:18) becomes "my [i.e., Jesus'] day" (v. 56). "You are not yet fifty" (v. 57), comes the challenge—not mature enough to have had visions of Israel's founding father. In his response about existing before Abraham, Jesus says nothing blasphemous. He speaks of himself in the hearing of *hoi Ioudaioi* as the revealer of God who is the timeless *logos* and Son. There is no claim by Jesus through the use of the title at the bush, "I am" (Exod. 3:14), to be the God of Israel, only to be before Abraham was. But it is understood as the impugning of the Name. Otherwise the taking up of stones in punishment of blasphemy (v. 59) would be meaningless.

Just as the whole chapter argues who Jesus is as related to God in the terms proper to the Evangelist's lifetime, so it concludes with the conviction of John's opponents that Jesus' followers are putting him in God's place. It is helpful to recall here the unfortunate Elisha ben Abuya (ca. A.D. 90–150, hence the contemporary of Rabbi Akiba). He is referred to anonymously as "Another" in the Babylonian Talmud because, in promoting the angel Metatron ("Beside the Throne") to a high place in heaven, he was accused of saying: "Perhaps there are two divinities" (*Hag.* 15a). In the Jerusalem Talmud there is no record of such an offense (see *Hag.* 2, 1); but that collection does call Elisha an apostate and informer. If it was possible in later Jewish life to hint at duality in deity and be forever reviled for it, the Christian claim on Jesus' behalf would surely linger in memory as blasphemous.

Jesus' going out of the temple precincts to hide (v. 59) is meant to be a mysterious slipping of human bonds until his hour. This regular withdrawal on his part is encountered in the Synoptics and was probably part of the historical tradition. The paradox of Jesus was that he was a solitary much on the public scene, an activist who was a committed anchorite. All four evangelists portray him as a hidden one revealed, a disclosed one sequestered. There is no Jesus of the Gospels but a Jesus whose epiphany is secret, who is a perfectly public enigma.

111

John 9
A Blind Man Sees

The Lutheran Lectionary proposes John 9 for the Third Sunday of Lent in Year A, but the others have it on the Fourth Sunday, not far from its place on Wednesday of that week in the early Roman church. It was used as one of the three "scrutinies" imposed during Lent, at first investigations of the motives of adult candidates for baptism, later become exorcisms, even of infants. It is important to remember how John was first read out publicly in the West, namely which pericopes were employed on which occasions as especially befitting them. Baptism was, of course an "enlightenment" (see Justin, 1 Apology, 61), hence Gospel passages which spoke of darkness or blindness were put in the service of this "coming into the light."

Jesus had come up to Jerusalem for the feast of Tabernacles (7:10). Nothing in the subsequent two chapters (8—9) indicates a change of locale. For all we know, the various debates reported in all these chapters are situated in Jerusalem, specifically in the temple area (7:14, 28). In a fitting symbolism, Jesus has declared himself to be the light of the world at the feast of Tabernacles (8:12). This claim is repeated at 9:5, an argument for the continuity of the locale—but the same phrase will also occur in 12:46 at a Passover feast. His cryptic declaration that he is "going away to him who sent me" (7:33) will lead inevitably, he has said, to a search for him (7:34). This prompts speculation that he means to kill himself (8:22) or go off to the diaspora to teach the Greeks (*tous Hellenas,* 7:35). The talk of suicide is the kind of *reductio ad absurdum* that the Johannine irony revels in: Symbolic utterance of Jesus is run into the ground by his literal-minded hearers. Jesus' departure to the lands where Jews were scattered is no less ironical, perhaps even more so if in a different way. For it conveys the reality of the Evangelist's day that Jesus' influence is greater in distant parts and among gentiles than in the homeland that did not receive him (cf. 4:44.)

There is no change of feast or season indicated from 7:2 until 10:22–23, when the laconic remark is made: "It was winter." This places Jesus in Jerusalem again, walking on Solomon's portico at the feast of *Ḥanukkah* (John calls it *eg-*

kainia, "dedication"). The interval from Tabernacles in early autumn to December must have occurred, but John has no interest in chronology as such. His sole concern is with the calendar of feasts.

The actual healing story with which chapter 9 begins—it is an afterthought that this is a sabbath miracle (v. 14), as in 5:9–10—is reported in verses 1, 6–7 in terms quite like those of the Synoptic Gospels on blindness (cf. Mark 10:46–52 with parallels in Matt. 9:27–31; Matt. 20:29–34; and Luke 18:35–43). In all of the latter, except Matthew 9, the parabolic nature of sight is featured; those cured "follow" Jesus in the sense of becoming his followers. In a similar story of Mark 8:23, the Johannine detail of spittle occurs (cf. vv. 6, 15). As the John 9 narrative unfolds, it becomes clear that the man's sight is the spiritual seeing characteristic of this Gospel. Blindness from birth is probably not meant as a factual detail (as it may have been in the tradition) but a contrast with the new vision which is itself a birth. The key verse of the chapter is 39: "For judgment I came into this world, that those who do not see may see, and that those who see may become blind."

Great delicacy is required in preaching on this chapter effectively because the world of the first century was not alerted to the physically handicapped in the same way ours is. Using the blind and the leprous as examples of the morally culpable or the spiritually insensitive may have been usual in those days. It is intolerable today. At the same time, the confusion over physical impairment and moral fault characteristic of that age still lingers. This means that this major theme of John 9 can be put to pulpit use with ease only by the exercise of consummate skill.

The narrative has received excellent treatment in J. Louis Martyn's *History and Theology of the Fourth Gospel.* In summary, Martyn suggests that the chapter be divided into the miracle story (vv. 1–7) and a dramatic expansion of it (vv. 8–41), with the participants in the first portion being Jesus, his disciples, and the blind man, and in the second—a drama in six scenes—the respective participants: (1) the blind man and his neighbors (vv. 8–12); (2) the blind man and the Pharisees (vv. 13–17; (3) the Pharisees (in vv. 18 and 22, *hoi Ioudaioi*) and the blind man's parents (vv. 18–23); (4) the Pharisees and the blind man (vv. 24–34); (5) Jesus and the blind man (vv. 35–38); (6) Jesus and the Pharisees (vv. 39–41).

INTERPRETATION

Synoptic healing miracles regularly conclude with a confirmation of the wonder such as the healed persons' demonstrating their health or the onlookers' commenting on the cure in amazement. Verses 8–9 seem to fulfill this function except that they introduce new characters, who converse not with Jesus but with the person healed (vv. 10–12). This is not characteristic of Synoptic narratives and is our clue that a multi-person drama of a non-synoptic type has begun. The trial nature of the inquest of the blind man and his parents by the Pharisees (vv. 13, 15, 16; *hoi Ioudaioi*, vv. 18, 22) and the possibly juridical action they take in ejecting him from the synagogue (vv. 22, 34) have been observed by many. The similarities in the way the drama is constructed to 5:1–18 (the healing of the lame man) and 18:28—19:16 (the trial before Pilate) are so evident that few will deny the literary skill of the Evangelist, whatever their commitment to a theory of his dependence on sources.

Jesus says early in this chapter, *"We must work the works of him who sent me, while it is day"* (v. 4), an indication that the Evangelist has his contemporaries in mind as the doers of works, not just Jesus. Martyn sees in the darkened world from which Jesus has departed (vv. 4b–5) a night which is brightened by the works of his disciples (v. 4a and 14:22). Jesus goes back to the Father who sent him (cf. 7:33; 12:35; 13:33; 14:19; 16:16–17) but continues to be a powerful presence, "the light of the world" (v. 5), through the works performed by his followers.

In this chapter as elsewhere, the drama seems to be played out on two levels of history, namely during Jesus' lifetime and in the Johannine church where Jesus' presence is still being felt. The following six scenes are thus distinguishable at two levels. The second one (in parentheses) comprises Martyn's hypothesis:

Scene 1. a street in Jerusalem near the temple (in the Jewish quarter of John's city) (vv. 1–7)

Scene 2. near the man's home (the Jewish quarter?) (vv. 8–12)

Scene 3. the Sanhedrin of Jerusalem? (a meeting of the *Gerousia* or ruling body of Jewish elders in John's city?) (vv. 13–17)

Scene 4. the same courtroom (vv. 18–23)

Scene 5. the same courtroom (vv. 24–34)

Scene 6. a street (near the meeting place of the *Gerousia?*) (vv. 35–38)

114

John 9:1–7

Jesus healed a man of his sightlessness in his lifetime, applying a mud paste to his eyes in doing so (v. 6). John reiterates the claim that Jesus is the world's light (v. 5; cf. 8:12) as a natural complement to the necessity of working the works of God (v. 4; cf. 5:17; 6:28–29). The community of believers enlightens a darkened world by its belief in Jesus, which is the one true work of God (see 6:29). John finds significance in the name of the pool at the south end of the city from which the libations of Tabernacles are drawn: Siloam (*Shiloah*, "sent," from the verb, "to send"). He refers to Jesus as the one sent to give light to the blind, both physically and in figure (v. 5; cf. 8:12).

The response of Jesus to the question about the man's blindness is important in the search for a relation between human suffering and human causality. Jesus refuses to look for a culprit. The man was born blind "that the works of God might be made manifest in him" (v. 3), an answer reminiscent of the God who "is working still, and I am working" (5:17). This statement of verse 3 and that of Luke 13:2–3 (that these Galileans were no worse sinners than all other Galileans because they suffered as they did) show that we can conclude from sin to suffering but not from suffering to sin. God will overcome the initiative of finitude: all those secondary causes in nature that go into making an imperfect newborn child, for example, or are part of the carelessness of a surgeon in an operation. God is greater than all suffering because God overcomes it in solidarity with our salvation. This is the meaning of the phrase "manifesting the works" in the man blind from birth. It is neither a glib response about human pain nor an assurance that a miracle impends. It is a statement that God will overcome the man's impairment in a way and at a time known to God.

The "deeds of him who sent me" about which Jesus speaks (v. 4) are deeds of light, termed by Schillebeeckx "the divine positivity." No one can work when the night comes on. Night is the time of negativity, either the initiative of the finitude of all creation or of active resistance—diabolic or human—to the divine will.

John 9:8–12

The witnesses are divided as to what has happened and to whom it happened. Familiar as they are with the man cured, their testimony differs. Thus, the Evangelist underscores the reality of the miraculous change ("I am the man," v. 9) and the possibility of diametric opposition as to whether a cure (or conversion) took place on the basis of the same data. The question of the man's familiars concerning Jesus, "Where is he?" (v. 12), is significant in light of previous inquiries as to Jesus' whereabouts (7:32–36; 13:33). It must be remembered that in relation to the present scene in the Johannine community Jesus is an absentee. Challenge as to the whereabouts of the one so often proclaimed must have been a commonplace in the early days. The literally correct answer of a person who is not yet a believer is, "I do not know" (v. 12). Believers were convinced they knew.

The sensitive question in this section is: "How were your eyes opened?" Two third-century figures in the Talmud, a certain Jacob (T. *Hullin,* 22) and the grandson of Rabbi Jehoshua ben Levi (J. *Sabbath* 14*d*), are reported as having been healed in the name of Yeshua ben Pantera (Yeshu Pandera), an uncomplimentary reference to the Jesus revered by Christians. People in authority interfered. They said: "It is not permitted. . . . It were better for him had he died." John 9 tells of a courageous little Jew who keeps telling the truth and will not be silenced by intimidation. There is no mention in John as there is in Acts of healing "in the name of Jesus." The recounting by the blind man of how it happened (v. 11), however, identifies Jesus as a still-powerful presence in the midst of authoritative figures who maintain, "It is not permitted."

John 9:13–17

Some of these "Pharisees" have a predictable scruple over the sabbath healing. More significantly, they are divided like the man's neighbors (v. 9) over what has taken place (v. 16; cf. 7:43), probably reflecting the division over Jesus in John's milieu. Who are these Pharisees/Jews? Martyn assigns them the dual role of Jerusalem's highest body in Jesus' day, the Sanhe-

116

drin, and that of a local court at the time of the writing. A less formal body in both cases, however, would seem to meet the terms equally. The only justification for introducing the Sanhedrin would be the conviction that the tradition from the Synoptics on Jesus' final hearing is being played out here. Remembered opposition to Jesus by the learned in his lifetime would seem to fit the facts just as well.

In any case, the inquiry shifts from how Jesus did the cure (v. 15) to who he is (v. 17). The blind man's first answer is that he is a prophet. This had been the perception of the Samaritan woman (4:19). Jesus is a prophet of deeds like Elijah and Elisha. Later in the chapter he will be described as "from God" (v. 33) and "the Son of man" (v. 35).

John 9:18–23

In the courtroom supposition which underlies the hypothesis suggested above, the man's parents are summoned as witnesses (v. 18). They refuse to give testimony about how he can see or who opened his eyes and refer the questioners to their son, who is of age. Their affectation of total ignorance regarding the cure conveys the fear within a family in the late first century when one of its members shows sympathy for the Jesus movement. The Evangelist speaks to the audience directly in verses 22–23, explaining as the play itself could not that *hoi Ioudaioi* have agreed on a sanction for any who acknowledge Jesus to be Christ. The parents presumably know that anything which sounds like a faith statement from them will mean being rendered *aposynagogoi* like their son (v. 22). This word will occur again at 12:42 and 16:2. It has no other incidence in the New Testament or any Jewish or Christian literature. Coupled with the phrase in verse 34, "they cast him out" (something which Jesus using the same verb in 6:37 says he will never do), the term leads many to think it a technical one for formal separation from the Jewish body of believers. Other possibilities are less drastic: temporary expulsion from the synagogue building, from the synagogue gathering, or from participating in the life of the local synagogue. W.D. Davies has distinguished himself by theorizing that the twelfth prayer of the daily Eighteen, the one against deviants from true faith in one God *(minim)*, was framed to catch crypto-Christians in the Jewish community who presumably would not read out publicly a curse against

117

fellow-believers. Popular as the supposition has become, there is insufficient evidence to sustain it.

There are nineteen invocations of the daily *Amidah,* the prayer said in silence and standing, despite its title *Shemoneh Esre,* "the Eighteen." The twelfth is more properly a malediction. Its authorship is attributed to Samuel the Small at Yavneh in the time of Gamaliel II (ca. A.D. 90). Samuel is said to have arisen and presented ("composed"? "revised"?) a prayer against apostates—the *notsrim* and the *minim*—and to have forgotten it the following year despite two or three hours spent in trying to recall it (B. *Berakhot* 28B–29A). An attempted reconstruction of the prayer against apostates reads:

> . . . may there be no hope for them; may the kingdom of arrogance be speedily uprooted; may the *notsrim* [Nazarenes, i.e., Christians] and the *minim* [in the 1st century, deviant Jews; by the 2d and 3d centuries in Galilee, non-Jewish sectarians] perish immediately; let them be blotted out of the book of life in order that they not be inscribed with the righteous. . . . [Then follows a variant reading:] For the apostates let there be no hope unless they turn back to your covenant.

It is noteworthy that the *notsrim* are a different group from the *minim* and not included under them. Also, in the last phrase there is hope for the return of recalcitrant apostates. This is not the situation envisioned in theories of a final separation of Christians from Jews as reflected in John's Gospel. The expression of the possibility of repentance will become a High Holy Days theme in later times. Coupled with the phrase "the book of life," which like repentance is confined to the days from Rosh ha Shana to Yom Kippur, it suggests that originally the Birkath ha Minim (ironically: "Blessing on Deviants") was recited only once a year and not daily as now. If this were true, it would account for Samuel the Small having forgotten a prayer that he had composed only a year before.

The other major flaw in the theory that the prayer was a test to catch Christians is that no first century data that we have on forms of the "ban" fit a final-expulsion situation. Any such excommunication practice came later. Other phrases of the prayer, moreover, could just as well be construed as tests of other groups: Thus the second, which is about resurrection, could have been a test for Sadducees; and the fourteenth, on the restoration of Jerusalem, could have been used against Samaritans.

118

All in all, while the Johannine term *aposynagogos* appears to describe an exclusion technique of some sort, there is not sufficient evidence to correlate it with the twelfth "benediction" of the *Amidah;* this latter would seem to have come from some later period and be a blanket condemnation by a beleaguered people of its many enemies. These would have included the Christians who were well separated from Jewish unity by the time they merited the doubtful honor of inclusion in that "benediction."

Consequently, Christian thought is unwise to suppose that the opposition to Jesus reflected in the term *aposynagogos* had already, by the time of John's Gospel, taken the form of administering a public test of loyalty to Judaism.

The affirmation that Jesus is a prophet surfaces in verse 17, a spontaneous confession of awe at his power like that of the Samaritan woman (4:19). The Pharisees are briefly replaced (vv. 13, 15, 16) by *hoi Ioudaioi* (vv. 18, 22), probably indicating popular opposition to the Jesus party rather than the protagonists of ritual purity (cf. 7:32, 45, 47–48; 8:13), especially as it touches the sabbath (v. 14). The man's parents are intimidated by the Pharisees (v. 22), for the good reason that confessing belief in Jesus bears with it a serious adverse sanction. Why acknowledging Jesus "to be Christ" (there is no article in the oldest Greek manuscripts) should have brought about active separation from the assembled community (v. 22) is not clear. Many were hailed hopefully as Messiah in the days between the death of Herod the Great (4 B.C.) and the Bar Kochba revolt (A.D. 135). In those circumstances such a negative sanction was unthinkable. Jesus' status as a crucified Jew could not have made the difference. It would have identified him as not the Messiah but nothing worse, just as Rabbi Akiba's candidate Bar Kochba was clearly shown not to be the Messiah on the expected terms. (Both of the latter were executed in the unsuccessful uprising under Hadrian.) The title *Christos,* distinctive of Jesus' Greek-speaking followers, and all its connotations seems to make the difference. In the Johannine milieu it is the watchword which invites vigorous reprisal.

It appears evident from the tenor of the dramatic expansion of verses 8–41 that we are no longer in the Jerusalem of Jesus' day but in the tense Jewish quarter of some diaspora city. The lines have been drawn between the Jesus people and those who oppose them. Everyone concerned seems to be Jewish, but

119

they are divided bitterly over the claims Jesus' disciples are making on his behalf. Believers in him are in a state of extreme vulnerability. They are being got at through family members and economic boycotting techniques. Justin, recalling the situation in Samaria a few decades later, would write in his *Dialogue with Trypho:*

> So far as you and all others have it in your power, each Christian has been driven out not only from his own property, but even from the whole world; for you permit no Christian to live (110).

However exaggerated that last phrase, the passage does speak of economic reprisals and violence. Hence we should not be surprised at the kind of ostracism testified to in the Fourth Gospel. The Dead Sea community was very strict in its *Community Rule:* "All who are not reckoned in his covenant are to be separated, both they and all they have" (1QS, v. 18).

John 9:24–34

The terms of the late first century debate, as viewed by believers in Jesus, have been made somewhat clear from chapter 8. There are the disciples of Jesus, "the Son" who makes free, and those who claim sonship of Abraham, a Jewish bloc in opposition, undoubtedly the majority, which takes its stand on peoplehood. The Pharisees seem to be a second group of opponents (cf. 7:32; 8:13), but they are characterized as divided among themselves (cf. v. 16). Jesus is considered to be a "sinner" by *hoi Ioudaioi,* the larger group, hence someone whose prayers to God are, by definition, not heard (vv. 24, 31). Those who consider themselves disciples of Moses (v. 28), not of "this man" (v. 29), are taunted by the blind man who asks with heavy irony whether they care to become his disciples (v. 27). The man just cured is happy to place his new condition above Pharisee tradition (v. 25).

The story is masterfully told and gives the impression that the Johannine author has been party to this sort of polemic many times over. The objectors imply that Jesus cannot be devout or do God's will because he is not a disciple of Moses, meaning a disciple on their terms, nor can anyone be sure of his origins (v. 29; cf. 3:2, 11, 31–34; 6:38, 41; 7:27; 8:19). But the believers in him retort through their spokesman, God has done the unheard of, he has given sight to a person blind from birth

120

through this "sinner" (vv. 30–31). Their axiom is that "Against a fact there is no argument." The heated exchange ends in an impasse. The one who defends Jesus must be impugned as a sinner and cast out (v. 34). There is no room in the assembly for both protagonists of Moses and followers of Jesus, for whom such clearly impossible wonders are claimed. Interestingly, the question of sabbath offense, which looks as though it has been an afterthought for John, does not enter into the debate. Whatever the Evangelist's milieu, its *Pharisaioi* and *Ioudaioi* (if John means to distinguish between them) are portrayed as determined to argue on another front than non-observance, namely, whether it is the power of God manifested through Jesus or some other force.

John at that point reintroduces Jesus into the narrative and brings things down to a case of belief in "the Son of man" (v. 35)—the title which he uses of Jesus—without further qualification. He does this for the ninth time now and without any apparent relation to its Synoptic contexts. Jesus is to be believed in (v. 36) once he has been "seen," so the vocabulary of this Gospel (v. 37). The Greek word for "said," in verse 38 *(ephe)*, occurs in only one other place in John and the word for "worshiped" *(prosekynesen)*, occurs nowhere else. The manuscript witness to verses 38 and 39*a* is likewise weak, either because it was inserted or because the copyists who omitted it found the idea of worshiping Jesus totally uncharacteristic of John (although redolent of Synoptic passages like Matt. 14:33). They may also have found the man's response protesting his belief needless and an interruption of the story's flow from verse 37 to 39*b*.

Judgment or division *(krima)* is described as Jesus' work in the world,

> that those who do not see may see,
> and that those who see may become blind (v. 39).

As everywhere in this Gospel, Jesus does not take the initiative in judgment so much as let people pass judgment on him and hence on themselves.

This chapter is unique in its narrative power and delineation of the work of Jesus. Sabbath observance via the emerging oral law is something the author knows about, but it is not of central importance. True discipleship of Moses is. John experiences daily its being proposed in some Jewish circles as the

121

matter of highest value. Belief in Jesus is thought to be incompatible with it. The Gospel writer is clearly of another mind. He does not disbelieve in Torah, written or oral, nor does he think it unimportant in illumining the human scene. He thinks it has been succeeded, however, by the revealer of God who possesses and is himself the Light of life (see v. 5; 8:12). Jesus is the Light that judges and saves the world. He is also a blinding Light—not to those who admit their blindness, for to these he gives sight—but to these who proclaim that they see and in their boast of vision are blind (see v. 41.) Discipleship of Moses in itself does not seem to be castigated here, only such as sets itself up in opposition to acceptance of Jesus as the world's Light. Any other discipleship than this one, if persisted in, will merit the Evangelist's censure.

PREACHING ON THE TESTIMONY TO JESUS OF THE MAN BORN BLIND AND ON DIVISION OVER JESUS

The preacher's concern with the various texts of this chapter—which is best read publicly without interruption—must at one level be the same as the people's concern. At another level, the preacher may have to struggle hard to see that pulpit and pew alike are in tune with John's concern. The problem of unjust suffering, as it is widely perceived, is of paramount importance to any congregation. On a given Sunday some hearers will have it as their major problem with God, either because of recent trauma in their lives or because they have it as a lifetime concern. The exchange of verses 2–3 on whose sin caused the blindness, once heard by congregations, may block out any other hearing of this chapter, including Jesus' response in verse 4. The paradox is that chapter 9 is both about human affliction and not about it. It is not about ordinary suffering or about God's injustice, since it ends fairly soon in a miraculous intervention, a matter outside the experience of almost everyone. The story *is* about ordinary suffering in that it deals with it as a mystery and not a problem ("It was . . . that the works of God might be made manifest in him," v. 3). John proposes that God's way is to transcend suffering by overcoming it at the level of belief in Jesus. Such belief is called "sight"—seeing what is truly there whether blindness or other physical infirmity continues. John does not write about a flawless universe or about one shot-through with miracle. He writes about the God who has sent the Son Jesus and rendered deity eminently knowable through him.

If people wish to hear a homiletic reflection on the mystery of suffering, they should. It is one of the most absorbing questions in life. They should not be allowed, however, to remain forever on a plateau of their own choosing. They must be brought forward into the Johannine development, and that can be done only by a homilist who has pondered long and hard the mystery of God's manifestation in Jesus. The one thing that will not do is to indulge in fulminations about blindness and sight that are likely to be diametrically opposed to the sense of the Gospel. Jesus, through John, is talking about openness to God's initiative. That much is sure. He is not doing this in a simplistic way that equates conformity in a religious tradition to faith and non-association with the religious community to non-faith. Taking a stand on Jesus, and on Jesus in his relation to God, is by all means the matter at issue. What needs to be examined is how Jesus as the Christ is the world's Light. This can include inquiry into how cleaving to a teaching that is perceived to be at variance with Jesus' teaching—whether it be Moses' law in John's day or aspects of the Protestant principle or Catholicity or Orthodoxy—can be a blindness that is clung to. Such inquiry can be a fairly painful business. By no means is the repudiation of an entire tradition envisioned here, for each is in its way faithful to God. It is the little blindnesses that cry out for examination, and these should be fearlessly explored.

Jesus is the Light of the world when faith in him has nothing to do with partisan loyalty or long-held prejudice, when he is let be a prophet, a truthful speaker for God. There is a widespread assumption among Christians that the various forms of Christianity acknowledge Jesus as the Light of the world while Judaism does not. But this is the very matter that needs examining. What precisely is the faith stance praised in John 9? What is the resistance to faith that merits its censure?

"And who is he, sir, that I may believe in him?" (v. 36). Asking the question is more than half way to having the answer. "You have seen him, and it is he who speaks to you" (v. 37). "I who speak to you am he" (4:26). The Jesus in whom faith is required reveals himself and reveals God through him in the word spoken in the community. No Johannine Messiah or Son is the Light of the world except the one known through the Johannine company of "that man's disciples" (v. 28). These are identified as much by who they are *not* as by who they *are*. They are not disciples by the mere fact of rejecting others as the

123

disciples of Moses. Even less are they those who reject faith in Jesus as coming from God. Either rejection can tell those who indulge in it something about themselves. The true believers in God are not the angry or the arrogant or the smugly isolated on a plateau of religious rightness. John is convinced that their identity consists in their common belief in the Son.

A theology of paranoia, a church with an "enemies list," is fraught with peril. Yet the Evangelist is sure that cleaving to Jesus by "knowing" him—his term for right faith—will bring in its train rejection and family division. The profession of complete trust in Jesus will be followed by pain and loss. Such pain in our day is acute. It is not always felt over leaving all to follow Jesus, a course which all four evangelists commend. People leave the churches, the synagogues, the enlightened secularism of their childhood and go in new directions. Some of these moves seem to others bizarre, like all examples of full commitment. Following the truth as one perceives it, at whatever cost, is something which casual onlookers can never comprehend.

Any total dedication to what is perceived to be the truth is suspected of being wrong. The truth, never before a matter of passionate concern, comes to be defined by the casual onlooker as the familiar, even the familial. Any departure from it as thus defined comes to be taken as fanaticism or, at the least, a repudiation of family tradition. Nowhere do the Gospels describe Jesus as an apostle of self-determination against all the odds, a person in revolt against his family and the religion of his people for its own sake. They do speak of him as knowing the Father's will, telling what he has seen, dividing the world into the seeing and the blind.

The first tentative step in walking by the world's Light while it is day is walking by whatever light one has. Christ is not necessarily the first light one sees. He may be such in the assurances enshrined in the verbal formulas of childhood but then may be literally extinguished, engulfed, by the smothering certitudes of a family or an ill-informed religious community that barely comprehends him. Searchers for the true Light may spend some time, even years, in what believers in Jesus Christ identify as theological darkness. If they are truly searchers, they should be respected as such.

124

The pulpit, therefore, must never ring with denunciation of Judaism, ancient or modern—the infallible sign of the preacher's ignorance of both—or of other traditions that are truly concerned to know the divine. It must ring at times with acknowledging the pain of separation that accompanies going where the Light leads one. For the preacher to be convincing, the preacher must know something of this pain.

"As for this man, we do not know where he comes from" (v. 29*b*). Where, indeed, is he from? The Messiah was to have been known in his origins, or completely unknown, depending on to whom one talked. "Give God the praise" (v. 24)—"Tell the truth and shame the devil," as our modern phrase puts it. "We know that this man is a sinner" (v. 24) "Whether he is a sinner, I do not know; one thing I know, that though I was blind, now I see" (v. 25). That is the irrefutable logic of experience. It is the logic that people who are converts to any cause go on. "I was there. It happened to me."

What happens to persons who experience Jesus? In one sense, nothing. In another sense, everything. The God of light and truth reveals to them the fullness of deity itself in a human being.

John 10
Shepherd and Sheep: A Hanukkah Lesson

In chapter 9 Jesus found the man who was ejected from the assembly (vv. 34–35) and opened up to him the possibility of belief in himself: Jesus. This community outsider can become an insider, the Gospel maintains.

John begins his next chapter, ten, with a meditation spoken as if by Jesus uninterruptedly from his accusation of guilt in 9:41: "but now that you say, 'We see,' your guilt remains." John calls the first reflection a *paroimia* ("figure," v. 6). This is the closest Jesus will come in this Gospel to telling a *parabole,* as the Synoptic writers call it. At least one more of these figures will follow immediately, possibly two (vv. 7–18). In verses 2–5 Jesus praises the solicitous behavior of the shepherd for his sheep as contrasted with that of the thief and the robber (the second word, *lestes,* v. 8, is used to describe a highwayman and, in Josephus, an armed insurgent in the war against Rome; cf. 18: 40; Mark 15:27). The Evangelist has Jesus speak in the second instance of a "good shepherd" (vv. 11, 14), deserting the third

125

person usage of verses 2–5 for the first person, "I" (vv. 11–18).

Verse 7 (repeated in v. 9) is the third of Jesus' figurative "I am" sayings involving a predicate (cf. 6:35 with 41, 48, 51; 8:12). The other two have said of Jesus that he is bread and light. These "I am" sayings will continue: in verses 11, 14 ("good shepherd"); 11:25 ("resurrection and life"); 14:6 ("way and truth and life"); 15:1, 5 ("true vine," "vine"). They are clearly faith statements of the Johannine community about Jesus and derive from the properties attributed by Wisdom to herself in the biblical "Writings," the Wisdom literature. As was mentioned early in chapter 1, there may be some influence as to form from the declarations of the goddess Isis about herself, a staple of Hellenist religion.

The words of Jesus result, as before, in a sharp division of his presumably Jerusalem hearers concerning him (vv. 19–21). This split continued in the Jewish circles of the Evangelist's experience, one supposes. Some find it impossible to believe in him and they dismiss his claims as those of a man possessed (v. 20). Other Jews, like the man blind from birth, maintain that healings of this sort cannot be the work of the devil but must come from God (v. 21; cf. 9:31–33). The attributing of demon-possessions or madness to Jesus (v. 20) is John's way of reporting what is elsewhere called blasphemy against the Holy Spirit (cf. Mark 3:28–30 and parallels). This polemic must have been carried on countless times between members of the emerging Jesus communities and their opponents.

The second part of chapter 10 (vv. 22–39) takes place on the occasion of a feast other than Booths, namely Dedication or *Hanukkah.* The concluding portion (vv. 40–42) describes Jesus as in hiding beyond the Jordan. Not only should the first two segments that make up verses 1–21 be dealt with separately in preaching, but the homilist must learn how to keep the attractive "good shepherd" and "sheepgate" images within the total Johannine context. There is always the danger of letting them flourish independently. They have so often been applied to the church life of later centuries, to pastoral care, and in this century to the ecumenical question that they have come to have a life of their own. Such momentum may be centrifugal, namely away from Christ the center and the judgment passed on him by believers. This is necessarily a judgment of the hearers on themselves. This is not the same as saying that the Evangelist is interested only in individual judgments. The ancient world

126

knew about personal responsibility, to be sure. The separation of individuals from their families over Jesus of Nazareth stalks the pages of the New Testament. Still, the divisions spoken of are communal rather than individual. Jesus was presumably concerned for persons taken singly, but the author of John has as his greater concern a group of believers which finds itself cut off from a larger faith group. The John community is not a "sect" of Judaism or Christianity in the modern sociological sense. It does, however, experience all the pain of not being at one with the larger social entity, the Jewish people. It will not follow a stranger, namely someone who tries to lead it in a direction the group cannot go.

There is, unfortunately, sufficient material in these middle chapters of John to bolster the contemporary self-justification of one church group against all others in the matter of fidelity to Christ (let us say, illustratively, the autocephalous churches of Eastern Orthodoxy against the Roman Church, or the latter against the Protestant communions, or a small Christian group against anything that is larger in size). The game of picking one's "thieves and robbers," one's "other sheep not of this fold," is an old one. It may also very well be fruitless. All Christians worthy of the name must have the minimum conviction that their church or congregation is fully allied with Jesus in his work of bringing salvation to the world. They must at the same time decide whether they treasure him as a principle of unity or a principle of division; if both, then they must face squarely the paradox he represents. For he would have all to be one in him, according to John, but separated from the world. If one spirit prevails over the other, the two being the spirits of unity and division, this will determine how congregations read the Fourth Gospel and how they proclaim it in their midst. The contradictory stance makes possible a hailing of "unity" in word while causing it to be a watchword of division in deed.

No Christian confession or group should indulge lightly in declaring others "outside the fold." Their being of the same fold with all who bear the Christian name should be a matter of hope and prayer. If the Spirit of unity, which is the divine Spirit, is the creator of unity, the attempts at fidelity to this Spirit should be task enough for believers. They should continue at the work of belief under the Spirit's guidance, letting this Spirit achieve what unity it will.

The shepherd figure has traditionally been taken over by

127

the clergy and applied to themselves. A *pastor* in Latin is literally a "feeder" of stock, usually an itinerant who follows the animals as they graze. Various paraphernalia of grazing have likewise been adopted by the clergy, for example the shepherd's crook which has become the crozier of a bishop. Yet close inspection of the herding and grazing texts of the Hebrew Bible reveals that what is being illustrated is political rule, not spiritual care in the modern sense. Kingship in a theocracy could either protect or threaten the religious life of a people. But rule or kingship and its exercise, not religious life, was paramount in the biblical shepherding texts (cf. Num. 27:16–18 concerning Joshua; Jer. 10:21; 23:1, 4; Ezek. 34:1–10). Hence, when texts from Ezekiel and Jeremiah on sheep and shepherds are read out, preachers will be right to remind hearers of threats to civil and religious liberty posed by administrations, régimes, office-holders, and unjust laws. In doing so, they should remember that the Christian flock was originally the Israelite people as a political/religious entity. Spiritualizing the Bible in the sense of giving it an exclusively religious meaning is a sure way to misinterpret it. Biblical teaching in both testaments is always concerned with the whole life of a people.

Jesus' description of himself as the noble (*kalos*, not *agathos*) shepherd in John (like the N.T. use of so many biblical figures) was an attribution to him of a symbol of the God of Israel. In New Testament faith, Jesus is the human repository of all the powers and functions of Israel's LORD. The portrait of Jesus as apolitical, which has been the commonest reading of the Gospels, has altered sharply the biblical figure of the LORD as shepherd. It has made Jesus interested in our individual welfare—which he is—but not in our corporate destiny, in which he is far more interested!

John 10:1–7a

The Gospel reading in all the lectionaries on the Fourth Sunday of Easter in Year A (1) is verses 1–10.

There are two contrasts at work in John's first figurative juxtaposition. One is between the shepherd and thieves and robbers (vv. 1–2), the other between the shepherd and a stranger (v. 5; later in the verse the word becomes "strangers"). A minor character, the gatekeeper (v. 3), seems to be a sub-shepherd of sorts. If the two comparisons or figures of speech had first existed separately as verses 1–3a and 3b–5 and then been joined—one about a thief versus a true shepherd, the other about a familiar leader versus a stranger—the difficulty we experience would largely vanish. It is vain to look for a neat allegory here, namely Jesus as the shepherd, God as the gate-keeper, the enclosed area the place of safety in religious belief, and so on. There is simply the development of the shepherding or grazing theme in various ways, in which the terms of legal and illegal activity in tending sheep are presumed to be well known to the hearer. The first story is one of peaceful entry (v. 2) by a legitimate shepherd, the second one of leading out (v. 3c) by a stranger (v. 5). The stranger becomes a "hireling" later in verse 12, a paid individual who has no personal care for the sheep. The "stranger" of verse 5 is probably a "rustler," in the vocabulary of the old west, "another" who has no business leading a flock that is not his. He will not be recognized by the sheep and his voice will not be heeded.

Allegorical possibilities inevitably suggest themselves (e.g., teachers of John's day whose teaching about Jesus as the Christ and Son of God is deemed false) but we do not have the key to the allegory. The Evangelist deplores his hearers' incomprehension regarding these simplest of his figures: "This figure Jesus used with them, but they did not understand what he was saying to them" (v. 6). They failed to understand because the illustrative speech, while it is crystal-clear to the teller, is nothing of the sort to his religious opponents.

Is the distinction that John had in mind clear to us at this late date? Yes, in the sense that we know that right faith in Jesus is the thing at issue throughout the Fourth Gospel. John's people possess it; the unidentified others against whom he is writing do not. We are unsure, however, what exactly this faith consists in. At the broadest this faith is discipleship of Jesus that sees in him the prophet of the last age. This is put in contrast with being disciples of Moses, which others view as being mutually exclusive of discipleship of Jesus. At its narrowest, Johannine faith is faith in Jesus as the Word become flesh. John disagrees strongly with the view abroad in his place and time that following Moses is incompatible with following Jesus. Had his adversaries viewed the lawgiver and his symbolic function correctly, early chapters of this Gospel maintain, their problem with Jesus would disappear (cf. 3:14; 5:45; 6:32; 7:22). They are being challenged by John to see Jesus as the fulfillment of all that is given

129

in the law. A psalm quoted in verse 34 ("I said, 'You are gods,' " Ps. 82:6) understands that this echo of the Torah refers to Jesus. (Cf. the comment on this verse in section 10:22–42 below.) By definition the opponents are not able to do as they are challenged because they do not have the Evangelist's faith. This does not keep him from accusing them of bad faith. They should have recognized Jesus when he appeared because a sufficient number of witnesses, including God himself, have testified in Jesus' favor.

John 10:7b–18

Verses 11–18 (Episcopal, 11–16) occur on the Fourth Sunday of Easter in Year B (2), the "Good Shepherd Sunday" of some medieval service books, although in others the reading occurred on the Second Sunday of Easter.

Quite apart from John's gift of inspiration as the church conceives it, he injects an authoritative tone into his "I am" speeches that invites the believer to identify with Jesus. The preacher as believer, therefore, accepting the invitation, can become gate and shepherd, while those in real or fancied opposition to the Gospel can fall easily into the roles of thief and hireling. A mammoth effort of self-discipline is required to keep preaching on this second *paroimia* of the door, or second (7b–10) and third (of the good shepherd who lays down his life for his sheep, 11–18), within the bounds of John's theory of salvation while staying clear of strident censure. The identification of any Christian with Jesus and his cause must be humble and tentative. When it is totally self-assured, danger lurks, specifically the danger of claiming the fullness of Johannine belief in Jesus Christ to which the disciple can only aspire.

The Evangelist means to pay faith tribute to Jesus with the words he puts on his lips. Hence, it is always in order for Christians to praise the Savior for his breathtaking generosity in the act of saving (cf. vv. 10b–11; 15b; 17–18; for the title see 4:42). The danger is that shepherds who are doing the preaching will identify themselves with the "noble shepherd" at all points. It is good, even essential, to make Jesus' cause one's own, but making one's cause that of Jesus is a risky business. Pulpit rhetoric regarding these texts, therefore, must be subjected to heavy self-scrutiny by the preacher.

130

Were the "all" who preceded Jesus as thieves and robbers (v. 8)—probably teachers of Mosaic Torah in another spirit than

John—ineffective? If the sheep did not heed them, why does John bother to speak so strongly against them? Is the wolf who will come later (v. 12) a worse threat to them than the hireling? The wolf destroys them whereas the hireling merely lets it happen (cf. Matt. 10:16; Acts 20:29). Again, the dangers of allegorical interpretation are evident. One may hold in a general way that those who pose a threat to the sheep are a variety of messianic pretenders and false teachers who came after Jesus, those whom Jesus least resembles. He knows his sheep by name (v. 3). The false shepherds are cowardly; they turn and run and let the wolf destroy (v. 12). The real difference is that just as Jesus has an intimate knowledge of his sheep and they of him (v. 14) so he knows the Father and the Father knows him (v. 15; cf. Matt. 11:27 = Luke 10:22). No such claim can be made of any other shepherd. Others may risk and even give their lives for their charges, although the Evangelist seems to know of no such case. None but Jesus is so intimate with God as he is or able to take life up again having laid it down freely (vv. 17–18). To do so is the subject of a divine command (v. 18). No one else has been similarly charged.

As regards the identity of "this fold" and which persons will in time make up the "one flock" (v. 16), one possibility is that those in the sheepfold are all who believe in Jesus on John's terms, the other sheep being those who do not believe in him on any terms. Jesus thus expresses the hope—and indirectly charges his disciples to work (as in 4:35–38)—that others, the present non-believers in him, may hear his voice (v. 16). Again, since the present "fold" *(aule)* is probably a Jewish-gentile mixture, the non-Jewish wave of the future may be meant. So C.K. Barrett: "John was written in the context of the Gentile mission" *(The Gospel according to St. John,* p. 376). R.E. Brown thought in his commentary (1966) that this consideration was present at the time the Gospel was written and should not be discounted as a possible cryptic meaning of Jesus in his lifetime (I, 396). By the time of *The Community of the Beloved Disciple* he finds that, "The hirelings are shepherds of the sheep, which means leaders of Christian groups, perhaps of Jewish Christian churches" (p. 78). As part of this there is "the Johannine thesis that Judaism has been replaced by Christianity"; hence these Jewish Christians are being charged by John with not having distanced their flocks sufficiently from "the Jews" who are taking them back to the synagogue.

131

Whatever theory is held, it is stated that the other sheep "will heed my voice" (v. 16). Clearly this is a prophecy. Unlike those who are addressed later in the chapter in the words, "But you do not believe, because you do not belong to my sheep" (v. 26), the group here envisioned will resemble those who now believe: "My sheep hear my voice . . ." (v. 27).

The view Jesus has of these "other sheep" is therefore not only benign but hopeful. They do not know him but they will. This could designate the Jews of Judaism, but little in John makes us think he has any influx of such future believers in mind. It could also mean non-Jews. This theory has against it John's relative disregard of the gentiles (only *Hellenes* in 12:20, as most students of John think the term means). The text, "the children of God who are scattered abroad . . . and not the nation only" of 11:52 is more supportive of such a notion. Yet the Gospel is played out on a small stage, not the worldwide one which was later thought to be its concern. If the Evangelist's major interest is in ethnic Jews and Samaritans, it is from these that the new believers are to come; but if 11:52 (with 12:20) betrays a major interest in gentiles, then the new believers are to come from them. The Gospel seems to provide only enough clues to support some version of the Brown hypothesis: that the "other sheep . . . not of this fold" (v. 16) are ethnic Jewish believers in Jesus who have a faith in him which John cannot approve.

It is at least suggested in this chapter of John that Jesus' self-sacrifice will prove to be life-giving. Verses 17–18 do not state this. They only give his self-sacrifice as the reason for the Father's love for him. In the real world of shepherding, laying down one's life for one's sheep would seem purposeless unless the marauders had first been rendered ineffective. Otherwise, with the shepherd dead, the sheep would be more vulnerable than before. Clearly, belief in Jesus' death as having improved the lot of the sheep who follow him underlies this passage. Only in 15:12–13 is it said that the commandment of mutual love requires dying for one's friends. The command to love one another as Jesus loved his disciples has been given in 13:34, but the corollary of self-sacrifice is not spelled out there. It comes for the first time two chapters later (viz., in 15:12–13). Here in chapter 10 we have the first hint of the power of Jesus' self-sacrifice to achieve a transcendent good for many.

John 10:19–21

The violence of the response to the figures Jesus employs about gates, shepherds, and wolves to which this chapter testifies (vv. 19–21) goes back to the healing of the blind man. Talk of "having a demon" (10:20; cf. 7:20; 8:48) corresponds to being "a sinner" in that narrative (9:24–25). The polemic of the Evangelist's day must have been fierce to give us the report contained in the three verses, 19–21. Their mention of opening the eyes of the blind indicates an editorial hand uneasy that the narrative of chapter 9 has not been brought to a satisfactory conclusion.

John 10:22–42

Verses 22–30 (Catholic Lectionary, 27–30) provide the Gospel reading for the Fourth Sunday of Easter in Year C (3). The pericope is well lodged in the Christian consciousness. Needless to say, regular readers of the Bible know it best of all. They may also be those most prone to interpret it individually rather than in the communal or ecclesial sense in which the Evangelist conceived it.

In the new setting of Solomon's Porch—a public arcade at the south end of the second temple area—at the joyous December feast of *Hanukkah* ("Dedication"), the debate as to Jesus' identity continues. It has been called the messianic secret of John. This Evangelist has used the transliterated title *messias* twice before, explaining it to non-Jews, who may not know Hebrew, as the equivalent of *christos,* "the anointed" (1:41; 4:25, 29). Using this term, Andrew expressed his early faith in Jesus, and the Samaritan woman the hope of her people and her own dawning faith. At the beginning of the feast of Tabernacles (cf. 7:2), a discussion of Jesus' identity arose that was centered on the Greek title *ho christos* (7:26–27, 31, 41–42). There the emphasis was on the unknown character of that person's origins, other than that he would be Davidic and therefore a Bethlehemite. Also featured were the signs he might perform relative to those of Jesus. When John refers to Jesus as the Son of God (5:25) and the Son of man (5:27), or to the Father as "the one who sent me" (4:34; 5:30 and *passim*), he does not introduce the element of secrecy. It is only in relation to the Messiah that this occurs.

133

INTERPRETATION

The question put to Jesus in verse 24 resembles that of his Jewish inquest in Luke 22:67 and the Marcan inquiry by night (14:53–65). It is asked in a tone of impatience and even vexation. The *Ioudaioi* gathered around him (v. 24) wish to see an end to the confusion about him. It is a stand-off. He has told them who he is and they do not believe (v. 25). Verses 26–30 repeat the content of the shepherd-sheep figures that have gone before: "You do not believe, because you do not belong to my sheep" (v. 26). This sentence, which seems explanatory, explains nothing; it only describes the state of affairs. Verses 28–29 provide a little enlightenment. Jesus' sheep are the Father's gift to him, hence the mystery of divine choice seems to be the reason why some believe and some do not. There is no rescinding the gift of eternal life nor snatching of the elect from the hand of Jesus (v. 28) any more than from the hand of God (v. 29). The two have it in common that they will not release what the one has given to the other.

Again, in expounding this text, wariness is the homilist's wisest posture. Declaring that the mystery of divine election is a fact makes better sense than attempting to explain it. It is well to follow John in praising God for the gift by which Jesus' sheep are his sheep. Accounting for the refusal of any to believe, either in John's day or ours, is relatively fruitless, especially if John thinks that the absence of belief is an eschatological mystery. It is likewise foolish to proceed from this text to lectures on the incapacity of the once "saved" to be "lost." All that we can say from this passage with certitude is that deity is far more powerful than humanity. The homilist who fully understands, "I and the Father are one" (v. 30), is the only one qualified to explain the entire pericope. This verse is at least a rephrasing of verse 15*a,* which said that Jesus' commitment to his sheep to the point of giving his life was like the knowledge he and his Father have of each other. Jesus, for John, is the human embodiment of the divine Word. The relation in which he and the Father stand to each other is best understood by his relation to the believers in him whom the Father has given him. He and the Father act together in love and obedience, the latter the Son's obedience to the Father. Jesus' sheep are in a relation of oneness to him, their shepherd, like his to God.

134 The *prima facie* meaning of "I and the Father are one" in its Johannine context may well be the functional one that Father and Son work in perfect unity. But its popular reception

over the Christian ages as an ontic claim (i.e., of unity in being) finds support in the next verses (31–33). The attempt to stone Jesus for blasphemy corresponds to nothing in the Mishnah on the penalty of stoning or the requirements for blasphemy. (Of these, but one is cited: that the Name [YHWH] be spoken, *Sanhedrin* 7.5) The John passage, like many in the Synoptics, testifies to heated passions over claims and counterclaims in the first century.

The whole setting has a violent, extra-legal flavor. Yet A.E. Harvey maintains in *Jesus on Trial* that this is the third in a series of confrontations in which competent judges bring a charge against Jesus, find him guilty of a capital offense, and then suffer the indignity of having him elude their grasp (v. 39). The first two instances of this phenomenon, Harvey thinks, are 5:9*b*–18 and 7:37–44, culminating in 8:59. In each, Jesus' identity as Messiah—or the claim that is heard, in which he makes himself equal to God—is the matter at issue. In chapter ten, as before (cf. 5:20, 36; 7:3, 21; 9:3, 4), Jesus cites the works he does in the Father's name as evidence in his own behalf (vv. 25, 32, 37–38). For Harvey, this is his defense in his trial. "Your Torah" (v. 34) is another.

How can "I am the Son of God" (v. 36) be blasphemy, Jesus asks, if Psalm 82:6 does not hesitate to call "sons of God" those to whom the word of God came (v. 35)? In context the psalm verse seems to make the Israelites the equals of the angels of the heavenly court (*elohim,* the "gods" of Ps. 82:1) and "sons of the Most High" through having received Torah. Their injustices to the poor, however, render them mortal like the earth's princes (Ps. 82:2, 7). The polemical point seems to be that this is the strongest Old Testament citation John can find for attributing deity to humans. If all Israel is rendered godlike by receiving Torah, why should the special consecration and sending of Jesus by God be objected to (v. 36)? At that point the objections to the Johannine community are laid bare. Its angry opponents are reading much more into "I am the Son of God," as well they may. The works that testify to Jesus, the community contends, will convey that the Father is in him and he in the Father (v. 38). This is considerably more than the psalm verse calls for, on any reading.

Jesus escapes arrest yet another time (v. 39). It is not his hour. He flees across the Jordan presumably to Perean Bethany, "the place where John had been baptizing earlier" (v. 40; cf.

135

1:28). With this safe refuge of Jesus, his next to last (cf. 11:54), the Evangelist makes his final comment on the Baptist. Although John never performed a sign—Jesus alone does "signs" and "works" in this Gospel, as do his disciples—the Baptist testified to the truth of all that Jesus said (v. 41). This is the ultimate deemphasis of John the Baptist in the Four Gospels, yet it is meant to be, from John's perspective, the ultimate praise. The Baptist could have risen no higher than to be the supreme human witness to Jesus in a cloud of witnesses divine and human.

The conclusion of chapter 10 brings to an end the middle section of the Gospel (chaps. 7–10). The setting is Jerusalem, the Judean capital. The identity of Jesus is the question faced. The claims he makes on his own behalf are magisterial, lordly. The response from those who do not believe in him is bitter.

A Reflection: How Close Is Jesus to God?

It is necessary here to identify the claims made for Jesus by the Johannine community and to ask how faithfully the church of subsequent ages has continued in the same vein. This is not to ask whether the church has been faithful to John's spirit. Christians hold it as a doctrine of faith that the truths they profess have their origin in the New Testament. The question is always, What relation does the developed faith of a later period bear to the faith of the various New Testament communities, specifically this one? The Gospel of John appears to affirm on every page, and in this middle section in particular, that the Jesus whom it calls "the Son" is known to God uniquely. Likewise, Jesus knows God as no human being does. Each one is in the other as if by perfect interpenetration.

Are Son and Father merely creature and creator for the Evangelist, an obviously divine Father and an exalted but no more than human Son? Is the affirmation about the Word early in the Gospel required to make us think otherwise? It is barely possible to maintain this, although there is already an infinite imbalance posed by speaking of God and any creature in mutual relation. The initial poem about God and that expression of God who is the Word become flesh makes the matter simpler. Yet the subsequent silences of the Gospel on Jesus' "Wordhood" make it more complex. To be sure, Jesus has omniscient knowledge which could have been given him, a creature, by an all-illumining Creator.

136

The Word is on the side of godhead, not creaturehood. This point has been maintained above on exegetical, not merely doctrinal, grounds. The case has further been made that the Word, who as flesh is "Jesus son of Joseph from Nazareth" (1:45), is necessarily the Son of God of the rest of the Gospel. This one and undivided person was "present to God in [or 'from'] the beginning" (1:2). Subsequent Christian tradition has always made this case for the identity of the Son with the Word and has seen in Jesus as Son, throughout John, a divine Son of a heavenly Father. One good reason is that the Evangelist is thought to have said as much elsewhere: "This was why *hoi Ioudaioi* sought all the more to kill him, because he not only broke the sabbath but also called God his own *(idion)* Father, making himself equal with God" (5:18). The intimate knowledge the Son has of the Father (cf. 10:15*a*, 38*b*) can only confirm the correctness of this perception. No mere creature could know God in the same way that God knows the creature.

Yet close examination of the entire Fourth Gospel after the prologue, notably the middle section, shows that the explicit equation of Word and Son is never featured. It may be deduced, but it will be a deduction in every case but two: namely, Jesus' claim, "before Abraham was, I am" (8:58) and his prayer to the Father for glory "in thy own presence with the glory I had with thee before the world was made" (17:5). For the rest, Jesus is someone who is sent by God (cf. 8:42), who reveres his Father (8:49) and keeps his word (8:55*d*), that Father who is greater than all in what he has given to Jesus (10:29). Whatever is attributable to God is attributable to Jesus. But the relation in which Jesus stands to God is one of perfect reflection or imaging by a man in his humanity. Jesus is God as fully expressed as is possible within human limits. There is no question of "seeing God" in the biblical sense when one sees Jesus, "He who has seen me has seen the Father" (14:9*b*) notwithstanding. Yet to see Jesus and to know him is to see and know God because Jesus sees (8:38) and knows (8:55) the Father and tells the world what he has heard from him (8:26).

In a word, even if no preexistence of Jesus with God were stated or suggested in this Gospel—and it is—there is a presentation of him as one who is divine in his humanness in another way. That way is the thoroughgoing inherence of deity in humanity, described as being totally unlike the ordinary presence of God to human creatures. This presence is an intimacy so close

137

that it neither intimidates nor reduces the human to silence but evokes a response that is adequate to the call. Jesus speaks of God in John's Gospel in the way of a complete intimate. Unlike Moses or the prophets, he knows God in a way it is not given to humans to know God. The constant preaching of Jesus by the Evangelist must have resulted in the charge in John's lifetime that eliminated all nuance: "He makes himself equal to God." Indeed, it was concluded that all speech about Jesus like the Johannine is blasphemous because it derogates from the divine majesty.

The resistance of Jews, Muslims, and Unitarian Christians to the message of the Fourth Gospel is in this vein. Often disinterested in Johannine nuance, the resistance to the notion of Jesus' godhead speaks of "a second god." But even though Saint Justin Martyr could use such a phrase (*Dialogue with Trypho*, 56), neither John nor the Jesus about whom any New Testament writer reports knows of such another. There is the one God who is Father, he alone, and a Word through whom God expresses godhead before time began. The Word becomes a Son in time through human birth. God is self-expressed in him as God is expressed in no other. Fully human, the Jesus of chapters 7—10 is also fully divine without threat to the unity of God. As to God and Word, they are one in the indivisible unity of godhead. Regarding Father and Son, they are two in a different sense: indivisible godhead and the one who does always what pleases the God who is Father (8:29). To be sure, the Arian challenge was required to state the above with such clarity, but it accords perfectly with the Gospel text before us. When later some claimed that in Jesus Christ there were not two wills, but only a divine will, it was condemned as heresy (III Const., 681).

PREACHING ON THE CHRISTOLOGY OF JESUS AS GOOD SHEPHERD

The homilist is not permitted a single shallow move regarding the contents of chapter 10. The temptations are many. One can find oneself reconstructing a pastoral setting never experienced, complete with murderous brigands setting upon a hapless shepherd who falls in all too willingly with their plan to kill him. Again, the hireling can be excoriated in the pulpit for his lack of concern, the chief evidence of which is that he works for pay; and so on. Actually, the brief tales of shepherding speak adequately for themselves. They need little exposition beyond a deft hint about what to listen for: the juxtaposition of the straightforward statement and symbolism; and the two contrasts, one between the good shepherd and thieves and robbers and the other between the good shepherd and hirelings. "The only unity in the discourse is Christological; Jesus draws to himself every epithet which the picture of sheep and shepherd suggests" (Barrett, p. 372).

The christological motif is at least twofold: the unparalleled intimacy between Jesus and the Father and the effect of his laying down his life freely for his sheep. The latter is the more attractive sermon topic. One should realize, however, that it is nowhere said in the chapter just how Jesus' sacrifice achieves a marvelous benefit for his sheep. When he gives them everlasting life it is as a result of their following him (v. 28), not because he has died for them. John's soteriology is strangely muted.

The mystery of divine election stalks chapter 10. The Father commands Jesus to lay down his life (v. 18); the divine plan, moreover, cannot be thwarted (vv. 28–29). Those who refuse to believe do so because they are not Jesus' sheep (v. 26); hence belief is essentially a matter of the divine choice.

Compounding the christological matter is the God-Jesus relation. The hungry sheep in congregations may wish to hear a helpful comment on, "I and the Father are one." It can easily be Chalcedonian. Will it also be Johannine? If the text is interpreted in the realm of moral unanimity, will it then be Johannine? "The Father is in me and I in him." The church fathers used a figure from the dance, *perichoresis,* to convey this reality found in the Fourth Gospel (in Latin, "circumincession"). Have such terms any place in the pulpit? Yes, if the pedagogy is good; no, if they are terms lightly thrown off without careful attention to the Johannine text. No foray into the deep waters of deity and humanity in mysterious conjunction should be attempted unless the homilist has read and reread, pondered and prayed over the Gospel texts—in Greek if the homilist is able. No other approach but one made in humility will give a listening people satisfaction.

Hearers may not understand John, but they understand all too well the times when John is approached confidently, brashly, without the necessary study or prayer.

139

John 11
Lazarus Lives

Jesus has spoken of himself in chapter 10 as the ensurer of safekeeping (v. 9), the giver of everlasting life (v. 28). He had been far more explicit, however, in 5:21, 25, 28–29:

> For as the Father raises the dead and gives them life,
> so also the Son gives life to whom he will. . . .
>
> "Truly, truly, I say to you, the hour is coming and now is,
> when the dead will hear the voice of the Son of God,
> and those who hear will live. . . .
> Do not marvel at this;
> for the hour is coming
> when all who are in the tombs
> will hear his voice and come forth, ...

We have in chapter 11 a realistic narrative that shows Jesus doing that, summoning the dead from the grave by the sound of his voice. The passage in chapter 5 seems clearly intended to proclaim Jesus as a life-giver to the dead in other than literal, apocalyptic terms (cf. v. 25, "and now is"). The raising of Lazarus may be the same kind of writing, namely a wholly symbolic tale. But it would be out of character for John to engage in his familiar symbolism by spinning a tale of resuscitation which had no historical basis whatever in the tradition. It is much more likely that he proceeds from a historical reminiscence of the raising of a dead man to a set of observations about new life in another sense.

The account at first seems relatively straightforward. But it is not long before we know that other things are going on than ordinary illness and death and extraordinary restoration to life. The Evangelist intersperses Jesus' activities with brief examples of the oracular speech he has made us familiar with. The brevity, with its seemingly conversational character, should not deceive us. At verse 4 John has Jesus say that Lazarus' illness is "for the sake of the glory of God," much as the blind man's affliction was explained in 9:3. This phrase connotes revealing God's activity while not eliciting praise for the divine deed of power—

140

although that is not ruled out. Verses 9–10 are proverbial speech about walking safely in the daylight hours, which echo 9:4. Their symbolic reference to Jesus as the true light during his "twelve-hour" season of activity cannot be missed. A word of Jesus in verses 25–26 declares him to be both resurrection and life. To believe in him is to have assurance that one will come forth to—indeed, already possesses—a life that conveys something of the glory of the new age. This is an elaboration of 6:57, but with the added note ("though he die") of a life restored on new terms after its loss. Finally, Jesus prays to his Father in verses 41–42 in a way that is reminiscent in its address of the prayer found in Q: Luke 10:21–22=Matthew 11:25–27 (even though different verbs are used). In both prayers Jesus expresses thanks or praise to God: in the Synoptics for what God has revealed to babes and hidden from the wise and understanding, in John for God's having heard his prayer over Lazarus for the sake of the crowd (RSV, "the people," v. 42). Interestingly, the Q prayer contains the statement that no one knows the Son except the Father and no one knows the Father except the Son and any to whom the Son chooses to reveal him. This bears a resemblance to the briefer 10:15*a* of John (cf. v. 38*b;* 14:11*a*).

Overall, the story of Lazarus' resuscitation does not take the form of a Synoptic-style miracle (it has, in fact, no Synoptic parallel), nor even a Johannine miracle of healing. Normally in John such an account is reported briskly as a prelude to an extended soliloquy. Sometimes, by way of exception, none follows (cf. 2:11; 4:54). Here, as in the non-miraculous exchanges with Nicodemus and the Samaritan woman, Jesus' reflections on the meaning of his sign are shared slowly, as also in chapter 9.

John 11:1–16

The Fifth Sunday of Lent in Year A (1) features 11:1–53 in the Lutheran Lectionary; (1–16), 17–45 is provided in The Common Lectionary and 1–44 (or 1–45) in the remaining three, with shorter edited versions proposed by the Catholic and the Lutheran.

The story begins with an identification of the three Bethany family members through reference to the *next* chapter (v. 2; cf. 12:3). This argues for displacement, or else familiarity on the part of John's hearers with a Synoptic story like that of the anointing at Bethany (cf. Matt. 26:6–13=Mark 14:3–9=Luke 7:36–50). In the first three Gospels no family members are named but, in conflated details, Simon the leper, a Pharisee, is

141

the host and the woman is a repentant, weeping sinner. This last portrayal has contributed to making Mary of Bethany both the Magdalene and a sinner in the popular expositions of the Gospels which have prevailed. There is no warrant for such an identification. John's vocabulary of the anointing, incidentally, most resembles Luke's.

Jesus does not go when he is first summoned from where he is staying in Perean Bethany (cf. 10:40; 1:28) to Judean Bethany, the family's home (v. 1). After a conscious delay, which goes unexplained (possibly to heighten the power of the sign, since v. 50 seems to say that Lazarus is already dead), Jesus suggests a return to Judea (v. 7). The region spells trouble to the disciples because of the hostility to Jesus of elements in Jerusalem (v. 8; cf. 8:59; 10:31). The fact that Lazarus is described as "he whom you love" (v. 3) makes some students of the Gospel think of him as "the disciple whom Jesus loved" (13:23; 19:26; 20:2; 21:7, 20). It seems unlikely, however, that Jesus' special love would be confined to one person. It is equally unlikely if the never later-named friend were Lazarus that that fact would not have been mentioned. This has not prohibited speculation that Lazarus revivified is the beloved disciple, but there does not seem to be sufficient warrant for it in John.

Jesus utters a cryptic word about sleep and death (vv. 11–15) which is not unlike the usage in the story of Jairus' daughter (Mark 5:9 and par.) The Synoptics quite apart, it is the sort of juxtaposition of literal and symbolic that John delights in. His disciples decide to accompany him boldly despite the danger, Thomas taking the lead (v. 16). They have Jesus' assurance, after all, that the perilous journey is in the interests of their faith (v. 14; cf. 4:40; 12:28–30).

John 11:17–44

On their arrival at Bethany, which is accurately located (v. 18), Lazarus is found to be already dead four days. The colloquy between Jesus and Martha (vv. 21–27) may take place at the edge of the village in the vicinity of the tomb (cf. v. 31). The *Ioudaioi*, the inhabitants of Judean Bethany who are the sisters' neighbors, observe their movements (v. 31). In this conversation she laments Jesus' tardiness, for he could have saved her brother from death by the power of his prayer (v. 21). This power is no less now that Lazarus is dead (v. 22). They exchange conventional Pharisee certitudes about the resurrection of the dead, augmented by Jesus' asking her if she believes that faith in him can bring the dead to life. This is the great concern of the narrative. She says she believes it because he is "the Christ, the Son of God, he who is coming into the world" (v. 27). There has been no faith statement so nearly complete, by a Johannine standard, up to this point in the Gospel.

The characteristics of Martha and Mary in this tale are not unlike those encountered in Luke 10:38–42. In both, Martha is the more aggressive, Mary the more passive yet ultimately more demonstrative of the two (vv. 32, 33; cf. Luke 10:39). Mary echoes her sister's sentiment that had Jesus been there Lazarus would not have died (v. 32; cf. v. 21). The Judean townsfolk who accompany her to the tomb weep with her in familiar Semitic fashion (v. 33). It has taken the tragic events in the Middle East—the piercing cries at the funerals of loved ones brought into family homes by television—to tell us something of Orien- tal' expressions of grief. As part of this, Jesus is reported as "deeply moved in spirit" and "troubled" (v. 33). These two verbs, one of them found in the Synoptics, might well have been found in the earliest Aramaic telling of the tale. The note of indignation and anger is not absent—perhaps at the victory of Satan and sin represented by death, in the Jewish under- standing of it.

The brief exchange between Jesus and Martha about removing the stone sealing the tomb is extremely practical from her point of view (vv. 39–40). She mentions the stench of a man four days dead, probably to highlight the reality of his death. It is a prelude to what Jesus calls the display of "the glory of God . . . if you (sing.) would believe" (v. 40). Several people are required to remove the stone. Jesus looks upward and utters his prayer of thanks, beginning "Father." Then comes his per- emptory command to the dead man to come out. Lazarus emerges swathed in burial cloths. Jesus commands the bystand- ers to untie him and let him go free. It is told with the restraint if not the brevity of miracle accounts in the Synoptics. The high point, of course, is the word of Jesus in verse 25, which explains all:

> I am the resurrection and the life;
> he who believes in me,
> though he die, yet shall he live,
> and whoever believes in me shall never die.

Jesus, in obedient dependence on the Father, can give life to whom he will (vv. 25*b*–26). The life is that which the Gospel features throughout. It is not simply a physical being alive but having as a gift from Jesus the life which he has from his Father. This is not the old life which is promised to Lazarus but a new life, *aionios*—the life of the final eon.

If the life is in another order, is the death equally so ("though he die." v. 25)? Probably. But real death like the death of Lazarus is its symbol.

The purpose of the miraculous restoration to life is not that the family should be reunited in happiness, much as Jesus would have reveled in that family joy. It is that Martha should "see the glory of God" (v. 40) once she had believed and that many of the *Ioudaioi* would likewise believe in Jesus (v. 45).

John 11:45–53

If the Johannine plot of the Sanhedrin (vv. 45–53) does not occur for the Fifth Sunday of Lent in Year A (1), as in the Lutheran Lectionary, it is not read elsewhere.

The chapter concludes with John's account of heightened efforts on the part of "the chief priests and Pharisees" of the council (v. 47) to apprehend and kill Jesus. The Jewish populace that came to know of Lazarus' resuscitation, as previously, was divided by this sign over whether to believe (vv. 45–46). The Jewish leaders are described as unanimous in their fear of Roman reprisals, as if Jesus' many signs could have the most dire effects on them politically (v. 47). Temple and peoplehood are both at risk (v. 48). The high priest that fateful year speaks more truth than he realizes, in the kind of ironical twist which John loves (v. 51). One man must die lest the whole nation perish. The statement can be read with equal force politically or theologically. Caiaphas in virtue of his office (hence "not of his own accord") enunciates a truth not only with respect to the nation. It likewise touches the "children of God who are scattered abroad" (v. 52), the company known to God alone of those who would believe in Jesus. John calls the Jews an *ethnos;* he does not put in contrast with it the ordinary noun for scattered Jews, *diaspora,* preferring another participle. He means non-Jews indisputably for the first time in his Gospel, Samaritans excepted. This is the Fourth Gospel's clearest show of awareness of the salvation of the gentiles.

144

While Jesus withdraws to Ephraim near the desert with his disciples (v. 54; probably modern Ain Samniya, 25 miles northeast of Jerusalem), the gathering Passover crowd is curious as to his whereabouts (v. 56). The word goes out that if he is spied he should be taken (v. 57).

John places this story toward the end of his "book of signs," if such there was (cf. v. 47), for the double purpose, it would seem, of a prelude to Jesus' resurrection by the power of God and an explanation of the Sanhedrin's motive in finally apprehending him. The tradition of Mark (11:18)—which Luke (19:47–48) follows but Matthew ignores—situates the plot against Jesus in the leaders' fear of Jesus after his cleansing of the temple. Mark makes a connection between Jesus' action on that occasion (joined to a citation of a conflated Isa. 56:7 and Jer. 7:11) and the decision of his adversaries. He also remarks the people's astonishment at Jesus' teaching. Luke makes this teaching the sole cause of the chief priests' and scribes' search for a way to destroy him. The entire process of the Evangelists' alleging a historical motive, however, is rendered doubtful by the clue Mark planted early in his narrative, putting his readers on notice about a plot against Jesus' life. (Cf. Mark 3:6=Matt. 12:14=Luke 6:11; in Luke the intent to destroy him is softened.) In Mark the plot is clearly a literary device which the other two seem to modify when they doubt its historical likelihood.

John at an early point in his narrative (2:13–22) has proposed a motive for Jesus' symbolic action of driving out the money-changers, namely to declare himself the end-time temple or *locus* of Jewish worship. In a diptych, John first presents the historical reminiscence of the antipathy aroused (vv. 13–17), then the only reasonable motive for Jesus' action since all imputations of venality and illegality fall to the ground. The money-changers were in fact providing an essential service *if* this mode of worship were to continue.

John, then, appears to employ the raising of Lazarus as the immediate cause of a plot against Jesus' life chiefly for symbolic reasons and only remotely for historical. Certainly none of the evangelists was privy to the thoughts or discussions of the religious leaders. John's speculation, through the high priest's "prophecy," that the death of one was preferable to the death of many (v. 50), is more insightful than anything in the Synoptics. He does not put it forward to exculpate the priestly leader-

145

ship. That is a matter in which he has no interest. The high priest's suggestion is a piece of political wisdom which has behind it the thoroughly admissible morality of the lesser evil. Christians are not wrong to see in Jesus an innocent sufferer, but they might ponder more deeply the theological wisdom of Caiaphas' utterance without taking it as fact and viewing him as supremely cynical. John could only have guessed at the high priest's thought processes decades after the event. He probably had no concern for them except insofar as they contributed to his narrative. Caiaphas' remark is a calculation in the political order, and a sound one, but only insofar as it contributes to a theological reflection of John. Saving "the whole nation" *(holon to ethnos)* from perishing could well have been the political goal which brought about—unintentionally on Caiaphas' part— one man's dying "for the people" *(hyper tou laou,* v. 50). John's use of human occurrences to fulfill the divine purpose throughout his Gospel strongly suggests it.

John 11:54–57

The movement of Jesus to Bethany (vv. 54–57) is not read in any lectionary on Sunday. But Protestants and Catholics alike cherish preaching on this narrative on the occasion of death and burial.

The *dénouement* of the chapter is brief and its few details familiar. Jesus withdraws not for safety but for solitude; even more, to keep to the schedule appointed by his Father (v. 54; cf. 6:15; 10:40). The Jerusalem crowds ask anxiously if he will appear (v. 56) as before (cf. 7:11). And the "chief priests and the Pharisees—an unlikely historical coalition—take practical steps to apprehend him (v. 57) according to the counsel they had taken to destroy him (v. 53).

A Retrospective View of the Origins of the Lazarus Narrative

The historical character of the Lazarus story is not an easy matter to solve. It may be impossible. How could the Synoptics have passed it up if it had anything like the influence on Jesus' arrest that John proposes (v. 53)? We know of the selection exercised by the various evangelists, more indeed than we know of the traditional materials from which they chose. We also know that they came upon narratives and sayings in various

146

stages of development. Could John's chapter 11 be another form of Luke's parable of the poor beggar Lazarus? That other Lazarus was *not* raised from the dead to warn the rich man's brothers, despite the despairing man's entreaty. Or, in reverse, could the beggar of the parable have acquired his name (no other character in all of Jesus' stories has one) under the influence of a familiar narrative about a man who *had* come back from the dead without convincing many thereby to believe in Jesus? The obvious third possibility is that an unrecovered reminiscence from Jesus' lifetime was floating around which received the form it has before it became a parable about remorse in Luke and a resuscitation story in John.

Our chief concern here is the story John tells us, the use he makes of it, and the use a modern preacher can make of it. Obviously the tale of Lazarus' restoration to life at Jesus' word of command is meant to illustrate the power Jesus claims he has with God. But his is not the power merely to raise from the dead—as if that were not enough. It is the power to give new life. The account is also a parable of Jesus' own return to the glory with the Father. This glory is the power of God manifested for all to see (cf. vv. 4, 40). It is a gift of glory, as we shall discover, that the Father and Son can bestow on each other (cf. 17:5–6). This same gift is one that the Son gives to believers from the Father in order to achieve unity among them (17:22–23). Basically this glory is the Father's gift to the Son before the world began, which those whom the Father gave him can behold (*theorosin,* v. 24) in the consummation that lies ahead.

If the chapter is a prelude to the later discussion of the divine glory by Jesus at the supper table, it is also about Jesus' total inner-directedness in going about the work of salvation (vv. 6–7, 15) and proceeding to his death. The Father alone determines the hour. Jesus the giver of life is not one to have his own life taken from him without his willing it. His withdrawal to Ephraim after performing the life-giving sign (v. 54) cannot be construed as cowardice. He will knowingly return to Judean Bethany as Passover draws near (12:1). If the human journey is to be carried on in the Light which is Christ—clearly the meaning of the insertion at verses 7–10, which otherwise does not touch the Lazarus story—then he himself can take no false steps, either of delay seemingly to no purpose or walking into his enemies' trap.

147

PREACHING ON THE RAISING OF LAZARUS

Chapter eleven abounds in details that have their own interest which it would be fatal to feature at length in a pulpit exposition of the text. Thus, there is the relative position of the two sisters. Mary is first to the fore, then Martha—who in verse 27 makes the powerful statement of faith in Jesus under three titles, "the Christ, the Son of God, he who is coming into the world"—then Mary again, in weeping solidarity with her towns-folk. This portion bristles with questions of the original source(s) and the redactor's hand. Jesus' use of the Johannine technique of foils for his utterances is present (e.g., v. 12), likewise his employment of the Thomas-tradition (v. 16). Here Thomas is a man of courage, not a doubter, but in any case not Jesus' twin as he will be in the Syriac tradition to which the *Acts of Thomas* belongs. Lazarus' death as a matter of four days probably reflects Jewish belief that a person's shade hovered near the tomb for three days before consignment to *sheol.* Jesus' anger is likewise interesting (*enebrimesato* with *to pneumati* clearly added, v. 33). Is it anger at death? Probably so. It can scarcely be at the professional mourners, so much a part of the ritual of passing. It would be heartless for Jesus to be angered by Mary's reproachful grief.

To dwell on any of these features in a homily could be pedantic in light of the weightier questions addressed. These questions surely include the power Jesus' prayer has with the Father; the nature of the divine glory *(doxa)* which is such that Father and Son possess it equally, yet, as will be made clear, it can be shared with believers; the fact that who believes and who does not believe is a matter of the Father's choice; and the profound difference between Jesus as the resurrection and the conventional Pharisee faith in resurrection on the last day. Life from Jesus to those who believe in him is life in a way quite different from the life he gave back to Lazarus.

Or is it?

The restored life of a dead man could be an egregiously bad "sign" if what is anticipated is life in an entirely different order, unless it is seen precisely as a sign and not as the reality. Does John mean to portray Lazarus as having been loosed from the bondage of the old eon and launched on the risen life of the new age? His presence at the banquet in Bethany in 12:2b suggests his resumption of the old life. But the world's literature is rich

148

in speculation that he could never go back to it, that he lived out his days in a daze at the vision of new life he had been shown. Is this not John's intention, namely to tell the story of one who, by anticipation, has received in its fullness the life Jesus came to give?

Another possibility already hinted at is that John has taken one resuscitation story among several and made it into a parable; hence, that to address questions to it like the historical ones above is the supreme irrelevance.

Several pitfalls can be avoided in preaching on this pericope and a few directions can be suggested in which to go. One pitfall would be to turn it into a tale of human sentiment. These sentiments are present, and John wishes them to be, but only in the service of his message of the divine glory. This is not a simple story of human grief or of Jesus' compassion for a beloved friend—much as it is these. It tells of a Jesus impatient with ordinary human responses to death, even those of the noblest Jewish piety, in light of the life available through him. The narrative is at the same time not meant to be a disquisition on the equality of Father and the Son with "glory," a term equivalent to the divine nature, possessed equally. Subsequent christological debate would make it such, but that is not what John meant by glory. Any preacher going down that path must distinguish between the *doxa* that is uncreated grace, deity itself, and that which is created grace capable of being shared with humans. But John has no such clear distinction in mind. The "glory" of the Fourth Gospel is a divine property that is sharable on some terms with human beings. It may point forward to the Chalcedonian settlement (and that of II Arausicanum [Orange] on grace), but the later development is by no means all there.

Lastly, and most challengingly, the story does not say simply that to believe in Jesus is to be sure of being raised on the last day as Lazarus was from the Bethany tomb. There has been much comfort offered and received in this vein, but such an interpretation is precisely the one that the Evangelist will not permit. Martha hinted at this as the meaning of Jesus' statement (v. 23) in verse 24, a possible anticipation in her lifetime of the final judgment, and Jesus rejected it outright. In doing so he made her one more victim of John's literary ruse. She holds what any right-thinking person of the time might hold: that all the just will be raised at the last day. But the life and the

149

resurrection which Jesus is, John maintains, is quite different in kind. Jewish future eschatology is not here being denied. The present life of the final age is not being put in place of the life to come. Lazarus lived to die again and await the hope of resurrection on the last day, as countless commentators have observed. John's point is that Jesus as resurrection, Jesus as life, is in another order. For both the living Martha and Mary and the dead Lazarus, before and after his restoration to his family, living with the life Jesus came to give is qualitatively different from being alive in the body. Chesterton catches something of this in "The Convert":

> After one moment when I bowed my head
> And the whole world turned over and came upright
> And I came out where the old road shone white,
> I walked the ways, and heard what all men said. . . .
> They rattle reason out through many a sieve
> That stores the sand and lets the gold go free:
> And all these things are less than dust to me
> Because my name is Lazarus and I live.

The eleventh chapter of John is the *tour de force* it is, an example of high risk on the author's part, because it allows the hearer to deduce from it the very opposite of what he intends to convey.

That is the genius of John throughout. Notice, though, that he plays fair, populating his pages with adenoidal literalists, some of them Jesus' best friends. Here he has them draw all the wrong conclusions: "I know that he will rise again in the resurrection at the last day." Jesus says, in effect: "Well, we Pharisaic Jews all know that. But I who am resurrection and life speak of the very life that I am. Whoever lives and believes in me shall never die to this life."

This chapter does nothing to establish Jesus as a wonder-worker doing deeds in virtue of his own power. It does, however, establish a thought fundamental to this Gospel, "that God is seen in the self-effacement of Jesus" (Barrett). This is especially important to keep to the fore at funerals. Often survivors of the dead person, in their grief, are not ready to hear about what the powerful Jesus might have done, but did not do, on their behalf. Being told that he will do it on the last day may not comfort them but only compound their grief. The passage and any homilies drawn from it have to console or else John 11 should not be featured. Its chief consolation is that the everlasting life which Jesus gives is basically the same on both sides of the grave. "Life is changed, not taken away" is profoundly a statement about Johannine life. The resurrection of the just at the end of time is but a result, an outcome for John. It comes of *life.*

John 12
Jesus, Anointed for Burial,
Enters Jerusalem to Face His Hour

The Judean Passover mentioned in 11:55 and 12:1 is the third one clearly spelled out in this Gospel (cf. 2:13, 23; 6:4). The unspecified feast of 5:1 may be a fourth. This calendar observance in John is, in any case, the source of a "three-year ministry" for Jesus. The Synoptics are not interested in chronology except for specifying brief intervals—which even then may be symbolic—until the last days of his life. There, too, the references to time tend to be obscure.

The Evangelist John devotes this chapter to a balance sheet of support for Jesus by believers in him, as a result of the sign of Lazarus or the other signs that had preceded it, and of those in opposition to him. It concludes the first half of the Gospel. The second half (chaps. 13–21) can be called with an equal fittingness "The Book of the Passion'" or "The Book of Glory." The opposition to Jesus is quite specific. The chief priests (cf. 11:57, "and the Pharisees") plan to kill Jesus and Lazarus too (12:10–11). Jesus' entry into the city as a festal pilgrim is recorded somewhat as in the Synoptics (vv. 12–19=Mark 11:1*a*, 8–10; Matt. 21:1*a*, 8–9; Luke 19:28, 37–38). An approach is made to Jesus through Philip by "some *Hellēnes*" who wish to "see" him (vv. 20–21). Jesus in response discourses on the arrival of his "hour" from which he will not shrink, even though his soul is troubled at the prospect (vv. 23–28). There is an exchange with a crowd of bystanders who hear a voice from the heavens "for your sake" (vv. 28*b*–30), as Jesus explains it. Now is the time for judgment on the world, in which this world's prince will be driven out (vv. 31–32). Jesus will draw all to himself when lifted up from the earth, an intimation of how he

151

is to die (vv. 32–33). A repetition of the debate on how to recognize the Christ ("this Son of man") ensues, Jesus answering in the familiar terms of "belief in the light" (vv. 34–36). The failure of some to believe despite the many signs worked in their presence is put down to the "blinding text" of Isaiah (6:9–10; cf. vv. 37–41 here). An interesting assignment of culpability follows: Many even of the authorities have come to believe in Jesus but refuse to admit it for fear of the Pharisees, who would see to it that they became *aposynagōgai,* somehow "out of the assembly" (vv. 42–43). The chapter closes with Jesus' proclamation of himself as the world's light. To believe in him is to believe in the one who sent him. Jesus does not condemn the world, he came in fact to save it. Rejection of Jesus or his words brings condemnation by a judge, namely the very word Jesus has spoken (v. 48). No one should be surprised at the sentence of the last day since Jesus has said only what the Father who sent him has commanded him to say (vv. 44–50).

In an important sense there is nothing new here, only a summation of what has gone before. There are some important narrative elements, however, and the preacher must decide whether to follow the easier course and feature them or explore Jesus' speeches for the treasures they may yield.

We have asked above whether John might have had in mind a week-long preparation for Jesus' first sign at Cana, matching another week in preparation for his last sign: his resurrection from the dead ("six days before the Passover," 12:1). It is a possibility, but as we pointed out the plotting of the days in the first week is a knotty task. At the beginning of John 12, we probably have a time reference from John's source, which he left undisturbed. The death of Jesus occurs in this Gospel on the Friday that is the preparation day for the Passover sabbath. Six days before it would yield the previous sabbath, but to this John attaches no special significance. Clearly, though, he has in mind the sacrificial symbolism of the Passover lamb.

John 12:1–11

The details in John's anointing story seem most to resemble those of Mark (14:3–9), not Luke (7:36–50), who has the house of a Pharisee as the setting—although nothing can be clearly affirmed about John's sources in the Synoptic Gospels or *their* sources. John has Jesus anointed before he enters Jerusalem, not

152

after, as in Mark. John has just told the story of Lazarus' raising, derived from a source other than Mark, and attempts to correlate the two stories by the linking sentence of verses 1–2. This reiterates the Bethany locale without declaring that the dinner took place in the Lazarus family home. John is at pains to use the story Mark uses (wherever he knows it from) of popular indignation at the waste of ointment (Mark 14:4) in order to highlight Judas' greed. Knowing of the tradition of betrayal for a set price, he concludes that money was Judas' motive, possibly because he cannot imagine another. There may exist a historical reminiscence that Judas was charged with the common purse (v. 6), but accounting for his otherwise incredible action by avarice seems to be the Evangelist's motive. It does not appear wise for the preacher to develop this theme. Whatever actually prompted the betrayer is lost to history. Reviling him can be a waste of time (cf. 6:70; 13:2, 27) when the point at issue is Jesus' symbolic anointing in preparation for his burial (v. 7).

Does John wish to feature Jesus' anointing as the Messiah? It would seem so, because Jesus enters the city hailed as the King of Israel (v. 13; cf. 1:41, 49). Yet Luke also calls him a king (19:38) without a previous anointing, and Mark speaks of "the reign of our father David" (11:10); hence if John intends the anointing as a symbol of kingship, it is because he already finds it in the tradition.

It is not clear why John has Mary anoint Jesus' feet as in Luke and not his head as in Mark, except perhaps to avoid the implication of messianism. The nard is described as *pistikes,* often rendered "genuine" as if the word were a cognate of *pistos* (also in Mark). It is probably a rendering of the Aramaic for the pistachio nut. Jesus' suggestion about "keeping" (v. 7) the ointment she is already using is thoroughly obscure and may derive from John's fidelity to Mark, or Mark's source. There it makes sense because there is no subsequent anointing, unlike the case later in John where Joseph and Nicodemus perform an elaborate one.

Jesus' much-quoted "The poor you always have with you" (v. 8) is, of course, from the Hebrew Scriptures (Deut. 15:11). It has paradoxically become a watchword of callousness. In its context in Deuteronomy it is followed by: "Therefore I command you, you shall open wide your hand to your brother, to the needy and the poor, in the land." Talmudic sources praise the care of the dead above almsgiving. This may lie behind the

153

original saying attributed to Jesus (Mark 14:7), but his favoring a good work done to him above care of the poor—quite uncharacteristic of what we can deduce of the historical Jesus—is in the genre of Q sayings about "a greater than Jonah [or] Solomon here" (Matt. 12:38–42=Luke 11:29–32).

The "great crowd" that flocked to see the revived Lazarus (vv. 9, 12) was made up of Judeans (vv. 9, 11), the same populace that quite naturally accompanied the sisters in their mourning (cf. 11:7, 19, 31, 36). In this case their going over to Jesus and believing in him on account of Lazarus (v. 11) is seen as triggering a priestly plot to kill them both (v. 10). As with Judas' motivations, historicity is impossible to trace here. If verse 11 represents a historical reminiscence, it is an important case of some "Jews" believing in Jesus toward the close of his ministry. The other cases of Jewish or Judean belief have been 2:23; 7:31; 8:31; 10:42; 11:45 and the favorable view of some in 7:12, 40–41. Historical or not, the Johannine record is not one of unrelieved opposition to Jesus by "the Jews" but of a people divided over him.

John 12:12–19

Jesus' entry into Jerusalem is composed of traditional materials, such as the jubilant procession with branches which John does little to put his special stamp on (vv. 12–19; cf. Mark 11:1–11; Matt. 21:8–11; Luke 19:29–38). An exception might be his unique use of the title "king of Israel" (v. 13; cf. 1:49). This he could be introducing as a prelude to his development of Jesus' true kingship (18:33–40; 19:1–6, 12–16), in contrast to the capital charge that he was a royal pretender (19:19). The entire Synoptic search for an ass is set aside; Jesus finds his own (v. 14). John wishes only to employ the Zechariah quotation about the Jews as a peaceful nation of donkey drovers, not devotees of steeds and chariots (v. 15; cf. Zech. 9:9). Chapters 9—14 of that prophetic book are hard to date, but if chapter 9 is postexilic, it is the last we hear in the Bible of a meek and humble redeemer figure. John resembles Matthew in using the quotation; the others refer only to riding on the foal of an unspecified animal.

154

More important than these details are what John makes of the demonstration in Jesus' favor. His disciples could not comprehend these things at the time, he says (v. 16; cf. 2:22; 13:17), but when he was glorified they did. The Evangelist is, throughout, the expositor to the reader of the terms of belief in Jesus and of the time at which disciples came to profess it. A puzzle remains as to what the crowds were celebrating about Jesus if not even his intimates understood the significance of the events. Probably the Evangelist means the true nature of Jesus' role as king, which only the gift of the Spirit (7:39) would make clear. John makes those who saw the Lazarus event the chief witnesses to Jesus (v. 17), the group that accompanied him being met as it were by a crowd already in the city (v. 18). The Pharisees express their helplessness at his popularity. Abelard, banished in the twelfth century from the Abbey of Saint Denis in Paris to Quincey where a troop of students followed him, wrote immodestly of himself: "Look, the world has gone after him!" Those deluded Christians of the ages who have seen in Gospel phrases a reference to themselves have been put down as vain (the case of Abelard) or mad.

John 12:20–22

The sole use made of this chapter by the Sunday lectionaries is verses 20–23, the passage on the grain of wheat that must die. It is spoken in response to the transmitted message of Philip and Andrew about the Greeks who wished to see Jesus. All four lectionaries proclaim it on the Fifth Sunday of Lent in Year B (2).

The Evangelist undoubtedly sets "the Pharisees" (now alone, v. 19; in v. 10 the chief priests had stood alone) in contrast with the representatives of "the Greeks." The elect resist Jesus' word, the non-elect express curiosity about it. Some think that Greek-speaking Jews of the diaspora are the questioners here, since there is no other gentile presence in the Fourth Gospel. Most, however, suppose that John is telegraphing to the many non-Jews in his community his awareness that they simply were not a presence in Jesus' earthly days. "Seeing" him—in Johannine vocabulary "believing in" him—is to come later. Meantime, if the two Galilean disciples with Greek names, Philip and Andrew, do manage to convey the message to Jesus, it is responded to by his death and glorification, not in any other recorded way. These must occur before belief in the fullness of Jesus' word can take place.

155

John 12:23–36

When Jesus answers Philip and Andrew he does so in a recasting of a word found in the Synoptic Gospels (v. 25 = Matt. 16:25) and the reversal of one found in the Gethsemane story (v. 27 = Luke 22:42). In the latter he soliloquizes more than addresses God directly and hears the divine voice from the sky, rather than being strengthened by an angel as in Luke (22:43). The self-effacement of Jesus, necessary if the saving plan of God is to work, deserves the homilist's most careful reflection. Verses 23–28 are a masterpiece of Johannine treatment of traditional material. They stress the glory that God will bestow on Jesus if he perseveres and does not ask for release. His "hour" can end in the bestowal of honor on those who serve him if he serves the Father by going to his death (v. 25c). The seed must die, one's life must be spurned ("hated"), the servant must follow Jesus to the extremity where he is (vv. 24–26b) if earthly exile is to end in glory.

These just-cited lines of John are indeed the masterful development of a theme. Preachers should preach regularly on the apparent failure the Gospel invites to, ending in death. A message of "success" has to contain large elements of a siren song of "this world." Those who preach need to be a living gospel of self-abnegation (by dying to the world)) if they are to speak on the subject with any conviction. When Saul Bellow made his acceptance speech of a Nobel Prize in literature he quoted Jesus in Luke's Gospel: "Woe to you when all speak well of you" (6:26), a salutary caution for preachers. The more successful they are accounted—in or out of the pulpit—the less they may be living the gospel. Their failure to live it may be the price at which their success is bought. In true Johannine fashion, the Christian's hour of glory is identical with the hour of obedience, pain, and servanthood. The adage has it, "No cross, no crown." In John, cross and crown are one.

Judgment has come upon this world and its ruler is driven out when life is not clung to on the world's terms. When the needs of the poor are given lip service and military might or political dominance receive primary attention, life is held onto in the way Jesus reprobates. Following Jesus is, from first to last, a matter of "letting go."

Modern acquisitive life is a matter of "hanging on." Being told to follow the injunction of Jesus, to let go, to die, to go into the earth so as to bear much fruit, creates consternation. Those who see in it the germ of a counsel for the good of nations have to be laughed out of court. Imagine a world without cutthroat economic competition, without the profit motive as the highest motive. To lose selfhood through losing the possessions that define selfhood is not the world's way. It can lead to being buried alive, much harder than being dead and being heard from no more. If an instructive voice is to be heard from some quarter, the heavens seem the least likely. From what quarter will assurance come, spoken for our sakes' rather than for Jesus' sake, when he heard:

> I have glorified [my name]
> and will glorify it again (v. 28).

The inscription that best sums up defeated glories and kingdoms past is the sand-covered, "My name is Ozymandias, king of kings." Israel thought it had a better champion: "I am concerned about you and about the way you are being treated in Egypt" (cf. Exod. 3:16). This was the God who asked: "Who makes man dumb, or deaf, or seeing, or blind? Is it not I, the LORD?" (Exod. 4:11, author's trans.). The voice came of old to Moses at the bush. Later it was spoken on Sinai and reiterated through the prophets. In Jesus' days, says John, it was spoken from the heavens. John means it to be but one voice in a chorus of testimony. The prevailing witness is the word of God spoken to Jesus and through Jesus. It is this that must be obeyed.

Ultimately the Fourth Gospel is a book of testimony to the faithfulness of God. It seems to be about Jesus, Son of God and Son of man, King of Israel, Messiah descended from David who is the "son of Joseph" and "his mother." Close inspection, however, shows it to be a book about Israel's God and the "glory" of this God who shows power on behalf of those the Gospel calls *huioi*, "offspring" (1:12). Jesus is very important in this Gospel, but he is subordinate. Although he can be seen as co-equal with Father and Spirit by deductive conclusion, he is primarily the one sent as revealer of the Father. Whoever knows Jesus knows much about God. Jesus stands at the end of a long list of what the Bible calls "signs" *(othoth)*. There are many signs worked by Jesus in John, but he is the great sign and he points to God. If he is "glorified" (v. 23) or his followers are "honored" (v. 26),

157

this has nothing to do with worldly recognition. It is strictly in the realm of manifestation of divine power. Human helplessness or humiliation is not the key to showing forth God's glory, even though Saint Paul said something very like this. A strong God does not require a weak creature. A strong creature glorifies God best. For a human being that means an obedient one, and Jesus was that. Obedience was his stance before God. He paid its price.

Insubordination and arrogance bring signs of success. Acquiesence in the divine plan brings signs of failure. Novelty placards behind the counter in small-town stores sometimes say: "This is a non-profit operation. We don't intend it. It just works out that way." God is not committed to human failure in matters the world describes as success. For the obedient it just works out that way. Obedient men and women, like Jesus, long to be delivered from "this hour." But they know that if the obedience is perfect there is no ultimate earthly deliverance. The choice is between pain and the glorification of God's name (cf. v. 28). Jesus has been given the strength that he needs to endure. Heavenly voices speak and signs are performed but they are not for his sake. They are for ours (v. 30). These works of power tell us that in all things God is to be glorified.

"Now is the judgment of this world," Jesus says (v. 31), a final, annihilating judgment (cf. 14:30; 16:11). This world's ruler is coming but only to be judged, namely in Jesus' crucifixion. Julian of Norwich wrote in the fourteenth century that Jesus said to her: "But all shall be well and all manner of thing shall be well. . . . For since I have made well the greatest harm, it is my will that you know thereby that I shall make well all that is less." The worst is over. Judgment has been passed—adversely—on the prince of evil.

Julian said, however:

> Though he showed me that his passion is the overcoming of the fiend, God showed that the fiend has now the same malice that he had before the Incarnation. . . . He may never do so great evil as he wills, for his might is all locked in God's hand. Also I saw our Lord scorning his malice and setting him at naught, and he wills that we do the same.

158

Such is the very teaching of John's Gospel. The power of the ruler of this world is broken. Yet he, or "this world," may be readmitted at any time. Whenever faith in God's work in

Jesus fails, the ruler is readmitted. Faith in the cross is the world's great exorcism. Anything else, whatever its flamboyance, is powerless.

When John uses the verb "lifted up" (see the comments on 3:14 in section 3:13–21), he is studiedly ambivalent in his reference to the raising of the victim in crucifixion and Jesus' exaltation in glory. His verbs for "glorify" (v. 28) and "lift up" (v. 32) occur in the Septuagint in close proximity in a passage regarding the LORD's "man of suffering":

> Behold, my servant shall prosper,
> he shall be exalted and lifted up . . . (Isa. 52:13).

A difference is that John knows this much of the crucified Jesus: in his adversity is his prosperity. The phrase "from the earth" (v. 32) is as explicit in poetry as the explanation of verse 33 will be in prose: "by what death he was to die." The maddening feature of John's exegesis—in this case the first verse enlarged by the second—is that in his asides to the reader he often explains the passages that least need it while those that cry out for it go unglossed. Jesus draws "all" (the male and female plural form) to himself (v. 32), just as the Father draws all who come to Jesus (6:44); "for whatever [the Father] does, that the Son does likewise" (5:19).

Much has been written on the extent of salvation envisioned by the Fourth Gospel. Does it affect the community and all who think like it or is the scope wider—perhaps all who will ever live? Verse 32 should convince anyone that the author's outlook is cosmic. With the impediment of the ruler's grip on the world removed by God's final, adverse judgment in the crucifixion, there is nothing to keep Jesus from his work of drawing all in the universe to himself. The link between judgment ("now shall the ruler of this world be cast out") and attraction is clear: "and I . . . shall draw all to myself" (vv. 31–32).

The statement in the Hebrew Scriptures, epitomized by John as "the law" (v. 34), that best supports the statement that "the Messiah is to remain forever" occurs in Psalm 89:35*b*–36*a*:

> I will not lie to David.
> His line shall endure for ever . . . (cf. Ezek. 37:25).

As has been stated earlier, the messianic expectation of the times was very much in flux. John however confines himself to the prevailing hope of Jesus' day which lasted until the Bar

Kochba revolt. By 160 Justin has Trypho expecting the Messiah in terms of Daniel 7 (*Dialogue,* 32). How can the Son of man be lifted up, in the sense of his earthly activity be terminated, yet the messianic dream be realized? (See v. 34, referring back to 23 but more to 24 with its talk of dying.) John assigns to the crowd an honest difficulty arising from the claim made by Jesus. Evidently "the Son of man" has no implications of the Messiah for the people in this Gospel. The objectors use the term as if it did nothing to modify the notion of death and failure, an idea which did not occur in any messianic context in Judaism at this date.

Actually, the crowd does not respond exactly to what Jesus has said but to the total proclamation of the Fourth Gospel. They object to the claim that he must be lifted up. But this necessity is not stated in verse 32, rather in Jesus' expression of what is required by God after the pattern of the Mosaic serpent in John 3:14. Their puzzlement regarding the identity of the Son of man is an extension of all the uncertainties and speculations in John as to who Jesus is (see 1:20–21, 25; 6:14; 7:40–41; 10:25). The term "Son of man" is John's term. The questioners here and elsewhere cannot assign it any satisfactory meaning, even though they see that it means the Messiah. The whole Gospel makes it its project to bring home the identity of the two in one person.

Jesus' answer is less than satisfactory as a response to their difficulty. It sums up his work much as verses 31–32 have done. The summary employs the verb for "walk" figuratively in a context of light and darkness. This is the case in the two previous figurative uses of *peripatein,* 8:12 and 11:9–10. The "little longer" (v. 35; cf. 16:16–19) is here the duration of Jesus' life, a phrase which most resembles the "twelve hours in the day" of 11:9*ab,* even though the absence of light is described as *in* the one who stumbles (11:9*c*). The phrases "believe in the light" and "sons of light" occur for the only time in John in verse 36. The occurrence of the latter in I Thessalonians 5:5; Luke 16:8 and Qumran identify it as a commonplace. Overall the Light is simply Jesus, as elsewhere in this Gospel. Darkness equals the absence of belief in him (cf. v. 46).

160 Preaching on this figurative language is safest when it progresses immediately from the conditions of light and darkness (viz., knowledge and ignorance of a right relation to God) to the faith act or its withholding that gives the figure meaning. God

illumines us by presenting Jesus to us as the object of our faith. Still, the divine action is nothing like switching a light on and off in a room. Neither is God the creator of darkness quite in the same sense as of light. God makes the light, we the darkness. There is no light in us unless we let ourselves be illumined.

Few in our time think of daylight as the condition of travel in safety. The electric switch is both ubiquitous and arbitrary in its use. This means that the figure of light and darkness needs careful thought if it is to be preached on effectively. The key to effectiveness may well be the use we make of the light in its *modern* figurative sense: keeping whole populations in the darkness of ignorance, not letting ourselves be enlightened out of laziness or prejudice. Jesus presents himself in John as the condition of all human sight, all knowledge, all progress in learning.

His hidings of himself are significant (v. 36; cf. 8:59 which uses the same verb; also 10:39–40; 11:54). They can be put down to his desire of not being apprehended until his hour, but his hiddenness is more like that of the heavenly bodies: a powerful reminder that he will not long be on the scene to ensure safe movement. With the moon's natural eclipse by the clouds the ancient world was literally imperiled except on clear, moonlit nights.

Jesus' public ministry in John is at an end, in any case, as he "hid himself from them" (v. 36).

John 12:37–43

The summary nature of this chapter is indicated by verse 37 and the two quotations from Isaiah which follow it, even as 20:30–31 recapitulate the entire work before chapter 21 is added. Jesus did many signs in their presence but "they" refused to believe. They should have believed as a result of the signs. Many evidently did. This compilation of signs has been made to bring about faith in the lives of many (cf. 20:31.) The quoted Isaiah 53:1, in context, is an exclamation, a marveling about what God has accomplished through a chosen servant. It really says nothing about disbelief (cf. v. 38*a*). The use to which Paul puts the verse in Romans 10:16 is so like that in verse 38 that an early anthology of texts used in Christian preaching is suggested: testimonies to faith in Jesus. This impression is bolstered by the immediate occurrence of Isaiah 6:9–10, which

161

various New Testament authors employ no less than six times. The text from Isaiah 53:1 occurs in both John and Romans in its exact LXX form (neither writer knowing the work of the other). Paul elsewhere (Rom. 11:7–8; II Cor. 3:14; 4:4) and John, on the other hand—and possibly Mark (followed by Luke 8:10)—use a non-LXX version of 6:9–10, while Matthew (13:14–15) and Acts (28:25–27) quote it in a form identical with the Sinaiticus text of LXX except for different introductions.

The verse that comes after the quotation (v. 41) sees the account of Isaiah's vision of the LORD in the temple (6:1) as a vision of Jesus' glory. The unknown Greek text of Isaiah 6 common to John and Paul implies a "judicial blinding" by God (the phrase is Dodd's). In using his version to account for disbelief in Jesus, with its omission of ears and hearing, John adds a phrase about the numbing of hearts not found in LXX but seemingly implied in Mark 3:5; 6:52; 8:17. At all events, an early church theory to account for the non-acceptance of Jesus is at work here, in which the divine activity is named as the first cause of the unspeakable mystery.

John has written throughout of the division of the population over Jesus. Here (v. 42) he has "many even of the authorities" believing in him while "the Pharisees" threaten them with separation from the synagogue. They thus intimidate the rulers as they had the blind man's parents (9:22). John's vocabulary regarding power classes in Jesus' day may be questioned on historical grounds, but he should at least be credited with knowing that in his day the Pharisees have emerged as clear opponents of the Jesus party. John is bitter in assigning the reason: "They loved the praise of men more than the praise of God [through the power shown in Jesus]" (v. 43).

John 12:44–50

It is not clear how Jesus could have made the proclamation from his place in hiding with which this chapter ends. The Evangelist is using the device to sum up both the chapter and the public ministry, reiterating some of the Gospel's main themes. Just as the entry into Jerusalem employed traditional materials, so here we find in verse 44 an echo of Matthew 10:40 ("believes in me" in place of "receives me"); in verse 47 the substance of Matthew 7:24–27 = Luke 6:47–49 without the parabolic elements of the house in the wind and the rain (also

Mark 8:38); in verse 48 the content of Luke 10:16 about rejecting Jesus, plus a certain elaboration. Important, however, are
not so much the sources—if indeed they are sources—but the
unequivocal statements of Jesus that he has come as the world's
light (v. 46), hence not to condemn it but to save it (v. 47). His
mission is thus identical with the work of the God of Israel as
the Hebrew Scriptures and Judaism see it. His words are the
words of God (v. 48), he speaks only what he has been commanded (v. 49). This is the stance of the prophets, of course, but
it much more reflects the position of Jesus' contemporaries on
needed fidelity to Torah or Wisdom (which was an oblique way
to speak of Mosaic teaching). For those contemporaries, keeping Torah or rejecting it would certainly determine one's fate
on the last day, the day of final judgment.

The new element here, and it was shockingly new to the
contemporaries of the evangelists, is the assumption that the
word of God uttered on Sinai and contained in Torah has been
equaled and surpassed in the words of Jesus. John's Gospel portrays Jesus as God's spokesman in a way that the Synoptics had
muted. The relationship of Jesus to God is unmistakable here.
He speaks what he has heard, teaches what he has been taught.
Jesus' fidelity to the Father should result in a like fidelity to him,
the result of which will be "everlasting life," the life of the final
age (v. 50).

C. K. Barrett provides an excellent insight into what is
going on as this chapter comes to a close:

> It is particularly striking that John ends his final summary of the
> public ministry on this note [vv. 49f.]. Jesus is not a figure of
> independent greatness; he is the Word of God, or he is nothing
> at all. In the first part of the gospel, which here closes, Jesus
> lives in complete obedience to the Father; in the second part
> he will die in the same obedience (p. 435).

The preacher's task is clear: not to make Jesus a "mere
man" (the charge endlessly leveled against those who understand the Gospels slightly, even John's) but to make him what
he is: God's Word to us enfleshed as the Galilean Jew, Jesus.

PART FOUR

The Prelude and Then the Hour

JOHN 13—19

John 13
Jesus' Last Discourse

The first thirty verses of chapter 13, including a lengthy utterance of Jesus, are largely narrative. In the final verses, eight in all, Jesus enunciates the new commandment of mutual love and engages in an exchange with Peter in which he predicts Peter's denial. These last verses act as a bridge to Jesus' four chapters (14—17) of scarcely interrupted discourse material.

Editors of Bibles and commentaries, as has been pointed out, tend to set chapters 13—21 apart as "The Book of Glory." These chapters might be called "The Book of the Great Sign," a complement to the favored (and not wholly accurate) designation of the first part as "The Book of Signs" (chaps. 1—12). Again, the first half of the last part (13:31—17:26) might fittingly be called "The Book of Jesus' Hour," since a good portion of it is a reflective prelude to that "hour."

Jesus, according to John, has been located in Judea since early in chapter 7, first at the feast of *Sukkoth* (Booths, 7:2,10), then *Ḥanukkah* (Dedication, 10:22), and finally six days before *Pesaḥ* (Passover, 12:1). He makes brief departures from Jerusalem and Bethany for safety's sake (10:39–40; 12:36). Now the action is brought up to "before the feast of the Passover" (v. 1), which turns out to be the night before the *eve* of the feast. Since, as in the other Gospels, John has Jesus die on a Friday

(19:31), the events of chapters 13—17 are required to occur on the previous night (cf. 18:1), unless there was an unspecified interval between 18:12 and 13. The supper for which Jesus and the disciples are gathered cannot be a Passover meal in John because it precedes any such observance by twenty-four hours. This feast is being kept throughout Jerusalem as Jesus lies in the tomb (19:38–42).

Jesus knows that his hour to "depart out of this world to the Father" is upon him—Luke had called it his *exodos* (9:31)—and so he gathers with his friends in a display of love (v. 1). As a group they are called his disciples (16:17, 29). Four are designated by name; a fifth described only as the disciple "whom Jesus loved" makes his initial appearance in this chapter (v. 23). The response to Jesus' proof of love in washing his disciples' feet is the act of betrayal by Judas. Later, in the traitor's absence, Jesus gives them the new commandment of love patterned on his love for them. It will be a talisman by which all will recognize them as his disciples (v. 35). The chapter ends with Peter's swearing everlasting fidelity to Jesus, in a narrative taken from the tradition (Mark 14:29–31 = Matt. 26:33–35). Jesus predicts in response that a threefold denial by Peter will precede the morning cockcrow. In brief, John wishes to tell the familiar tales of Judas' treachery and Peter's weakness but not in the setting of a cultic meal, rather, in a warmhearted act of love.

Many have sought to deduce what John means to do by omitting the memorial of Jesus in bread and wine, putting in its place the solicitous deed of washing his disciples' feet. Unfortunately, most of these attempts are rooted in the authors' previous view of sacraments (a term which did not exist in N.T. times). The Greek-speaking churches came to employ the word *mysterion*, "secret" or "mystery," for what the Latin tongue would later call *sacramentum,* from the sacred oath of a soldier to defend the Empire. If one is an anti-ritualist, it is easy to say that John inserted an act of personal concern at this point in the narrative to replace a rite which by definition is impersonal. Defenders of the sacrament concept are prone to say that John chose to dwell lovingly on the "bread come down from heaven" in chapter 6 instead of here. Jesus, the "true" heavenly bread, was the eucharistic food the Johannine communities were partaking of in the Evangelist's day.

166

Neither the pro- nor anti-sacrament people can propose

enough positive data from this Gospel to support their contention fully. As much depends on what the Evangelist does not say as upon what he does say. Meanwhile, the mystery remains. Why, exactly, does he not tell the story of the institution of the Eucharist at this point where the others do? And is there any reference to the rite of baptism in Jesus' discussion with Simon Peter of those who, being bathed, are washed clean?

John wishes to go deeply in chapter 6 into the full implications of Jesus as the bread of life whose flesh must be eaten and whose blood must be drunk. He is also at pains to use chapter 13 to explore the loving interrelation among disciples that must characterize them if they are to claim Jesus as their teacher. John may have supposed that a routine presentation of the tradition on Jesus' words about the food and drink at the supper might not accomplish this purpose. Again, while Mark (14:12) followed by Matthew (26:17) and Luke (22:8) describe Jesus' final meal as a Passover—thereby placing it at the onset of 15 Nisan (i.e., after sundown of 14)—John has the crucifixion take place on the Day of Preparation, the afternoon of Friday 14 Nisan; hence the meal occurs before it. Both seem to be operating symbolically, and if historically, only incidentally so. Thus, since Jesus is the church's Passover (or "Pasch," in what the Greek language did with the Hebrew term; cf. I Cor. 5:7), the Synoptic authors had to have the last meal of his life a Passover meal. With an equally compelling logic, John, who was convinced that Jesus was the Lamb of God (1:29; 19:36), needed to have him sacrificed at the very time the slaughter was being done at the temple in readiness for the blood-offering on the day of 15 Nisan, namely Friday afternoon 14 Nisan. Perhaps that is why he relocates the discussion of the Eucharist.

Frequently it is said that John has the best of it, chronologically speaking, because the Synoptic accounts contain impossible offenses against what Mishnaic law later taught concerning capital sentence at night and execution during the Passover. But these difficulties can be overcome if the law was not yet in place or if we have a case of what the Mishnah calls the "rebellious elder" (cf. *Sanhedrin* 11:2,4). The difficulties in John are, overall, no less.

It seems to be a draw between John and the Synoptics on the dating of Jesus' final days. None of the Gospels nor all of them together supply enough firm historical data to help us

specify Jesus' death day other than on a Friday close to Passover. This obscurity accounts for the problem of naming the
year of Jesus' death, with A.D. 30 suggested by many as the
greatest likelihood, A.D. 33 the second, and so on. In all such
schemes, John (as in the first one just mentioned) or the Synoptics has to be decided upon as the more historically dependable.
There does not, however, seem to be any compelling reason to
consider John such. He writes in his religiously symbolic way
and in this is like Mark and the others.

John 13:1–11

The first verse is probably intended as a preface to the
entire "Book of Glory," not just this chapter. The events about
to be described happen "before the Passover," a matter of theological importance for an evangelist who will describe Jesus as
the Passover lamb of whom not a bone would be broken (19:36).
"His own who were [still] in the world" recalls the usage in
10:3,4,12 more than 1:11, where the term "his own" is different.
John uses the same word for Jesus' transfer from one sphere to
another (v. 1, "to depart") that he has employed in 5:24: "he
does not come into judgment, but has *passed* from death to life"
(author's italic). The cognate verb describing ascent to the heavens or the Father (3:13; 6:62; 20:17) might have been better
than the one used, but there was no need to retain the verb of
upward movement in every case. Simple change of place is
being described: from the sphere of the ruler of this world
(12:31) to be glorified with God (vv. 31–32).

Jesus loves his disciples in this world "to the end"—here
probably "to the outer limit," although "until the time of final
consummation" cannot be ruled out. The devil instigates
Judas' treachery (v. 2; cf. 6:70–71; as Satan he does the same in
Luke 22:3). Little is made of this except perhaps that Jesus
proceeds with his affectionate service when nothing can be
done to reverse the diabolical decision taken. Jesus knows of
his betrayal (cf. 6:70–71), but he is even clearer about his uni-
versal mission decreed by the Father with whom he will soon
be united in glory (v. 3). The menial act of footwashing takes
place "during supper" (v. 2), no setting of the meal having
been indicated. John has no special historical interest as he
recounts his parable of love in action. The footwashing is a

168

humble service probably meant to point to Jesus' death (see his answer to Peter in v. 7). It is a service among equals in a company where no one's social status stands out, although Jesus' eminence as Teacher and Lord cannot be forgotten (cf. vv. 13–16). It shares in that act of "service which is full of inner authority" (Schnackenburg). Since John is convinced that the resurrection will show forth Jesus' glory, it is a memorable symbolic act and intended to be such.

Simon Peter's demurrer (v. 6) is countered with the by now familiar response of Jesus—really of John—that "afterward [he] will understand." Clearly John is creating a symbol out of hospitality's task of washing dusty feet. Peter's heated remonstrance (cf. Mark 8:32) has to do with his sense of the fitting. He no more understands the posture of the Son of God as humanity's servant here than in the Synoptics' Caesarea Philippi. His quick turnabout asking for a complete washing is in line with his impetuous "all or nothing" character. Here it serves as the "straight line" in Johannine dialogue to elicit Jesus' response. Peter receives an explanation in stages, verses 7, 8*b* and 10. Jesus says in verse 10 that his one symbolic act is sufficient. Further washings are pointless once the deed that symbolizes his death as a servant is accepted.

The introduction of the phrase "except for his feet" into verse 10, while intended to clarify—taking its cue perhaps from the words for bathing and washing—distinguishes between the feet and all other parts. It occurs in most manuscripts but not the fourth century Sinaiticus, the Vulgate or most Latin versions. The addition has led to a frantic search over the centuries for sacramental signification as distinct from ancient lavatory customs among houseguests—and no little polemic against multiple-baptizing Christian sects. The meaning is simpler. Submission to a cleansing at Jesus' hands—with total purification as the intent—is the proper disposition for partaking in the sacrificial drama to follow. Being bathed by Jesus means being symbolically taken into the event of the cross. It is likewise a model of service for the disciples. Preachers are right to feature the latter signification because the Gospel so instructs them (vv. 14–15), but they may not overlook the primary one (vv. 7, 8*b*, 10). In popular exposition, it is evident that Jesus' deed of service has won the day. But one must be washed by Jesus to have a part in him.

169

John 13:12–20

With Jesus' resumption of his reclining posture—the Greek mode of eating adopted by Jews at Passover—he makes clear that what he has done must be replicated in the lives of his disciples (cf. v. 35; v. 16 closely resembles Matt. 10:24–25a and v. 20 Matt. 10:40). This passage is as explicit as this Gospel will get in explaining its many symbolisms: "For I have given you an example, that you also should do as I have done to you" (v. 15). Verse 17 (cf. 12:47a) also contains the first of John's two beatitudes. The other is spoken to Thomas in praise of believers who do not see (cf. 20:29).

John 13:21–30

There is an unexpected return from the theme of discipleship to that of the traitor. John exonerates Jesus of ignorance, as it were, in his choice of Judas (v. 18). That choice was made "that the scripture may be fulfilled," in this case Psalm 41:9, which speaks of the treachery of a friend. The prophecy made now can only be understood later (v. 19; for "that you may believe that I am [he]," see commentary on 8:24 in conjunction with Isa. 43:10). The claim Jesus makes is so like that of the LORD in Isaiah that it may have prompted verse 20, which in John is an expression of the intimacy Jesus shares with God.

Jesus is "troubled in spirit" over his imminent betrayal as he had been when faced with Lazarus' death (v. 21; cf. 11:33). He predicts the betrayal with the aid of his solemn formula, the initial double "Amen." This leads into the narrative of Simon Peter's attempt to learn the traitor's identity by asking the beloved disciple who was nearest to Jesus, and being given the sign of the morsel (v. 26; cf. Matt. 26:23) dipped and handed to Judas. The placement of the disciples identifies the one Jesus loved as having a position superior to Peter's. Nowhere in John is he situated with reference to the Twelve, an indication that for this Gospel his importance is in another order than theirs. The disciple's failure to take action when apprised of Judas' perfidy ("It is he to whom I shall give this morsel. . . . What you are going to do, do quickly") is inexplicable. We can only assume from verse 28 ("Now no one at the table knew why he said this to him") that John means that the beloved sees the sign but is

170

no more able to interpret it than the rest. Once again the Satanic influence is invoked (v. 27), perhaps to exculpate all but Judas. A prosaic motive for the traitor's departure is assigned (v. 29) and he, having eaten the morsel, leaves the celebrating company. In one of the most telling lines of all literature John says laconically: "and it was night" (v. 30).

The figure of Judas is immensely attractive in popular preaching. He is the favored one who turns on his friend, the table companion who acts against one whose only deeds were love. How to account for it? In a culture like ours, where human motivations are of paramount importance, this question can make even the world's salvation look insignificant. The latter is cosmic and therefore daunting, but the microcosm of the human heart is the stuff of drama. The Evangelist, it should be noted, does not linger on the betrayal. He discredits the traitor by calling him a thief (12:6) without naming avarice as Judas' motive for handing Jesus over. In the apprehension of Jesus in the garden, John omits the kiss of Judas as the identifying sign. In sum, he is content to specify diabolical influence as the compelling motive. But once this flight to the preternatural has been taken, the pulpit dramatist feels cheated. The amateur psychologist is at home with the ordinary run of human motives: a bit of Shakespeare, a bit of Freud, a counseling course just completed. John situates the struggle on higher ground: the all-holy God challenged by the ruler of this world through a contemptible weakling. John should be let have his way.

Few can handle the successful influence of an angelic creature on a free human will, but the Johannine record should stand as it is. John assigns ultimate responsibility for the entire drama of salvation to the work of providence. That is more mysterious still, for as Dame Juliana said, the fiend's might is all locked in God's hand. Many a thinker has run afoul of the problem of the sovereign will of God, chiefly by misprizing human capacity at the expense of divine. The pulpit expositor of John's Gospel must think long and hard before launching onto the deep waters of God's inexorable achievement of will without interfering with the free wills of creatures. Yet launch the preacher must, for no easy handle is provided which situates Judas' behavior exclusively in his love for gain. Nowhere are we told why Satan's promptings were attractive to him in his free choice to betray his friend. We can only speculate. Much of the speculation will be based on our own betrayals of friendship.

171

John 13:31–38

This portion of the chapter (vv. 31–38) supplies the only Sunday reading found in the lectionaries. All employ the "new commandment" passage (vv. 31–35) on the Fifth Sunday of Easter of Year C (3). This means that certain congregations are relatively assured that the passage will be explored in their hearing once every three years. In cases where preachers rely on the Spirit's assistance in making their choices, certain congregations may hear it more often.

With his false friend departed, Jesus sees his hour approaching. The mutual glory of Father and Son is imminent (vv. 31–32), brought on by the Son's act of obedience. Jesus' discourse at the supper begins with the claim that now the glory of the Son of man is revealed (v. 31) in what he intends to do. The footwashing is the sign. Glory will overtake him "at once" (v. 32)—that is, in his resurrection, but indeed as soon as his crucifixion for those who have the faith to see it.

The tender form of address, "children," occurs here for the only time (v. 33). The context is imminent separation, a repetition of what had been said in 7:33 and 8:21. The reference to Jesus' speech addressed to the Judean crowds may be the Evangelist's way of telling his contemporaries: "You are no more ready to face death, to be glorified with Jesus now, than the people of Jerusalem who were mystified by him in his lifetime. Mutual love is the only key to the door of being united with him" (see v. 34). Simon Peter obliges Jesus by his opaqueness, since in every Johannine dialogue someone must respond with a kind of uncomprehending "What?" Peter grows vehement about his intentions, promising solidarity in death. He is told of the instability and cowardice that will shortly lead to denying the one he calls "Lord." It may well be asked whether Peter if he had not failed but lived up to his boast—that is, stayed with Jesus until he too was arrested and crucified—would have "followed [Jesus] now" (v. 36) in the sense intended by John? Surely not. For while John knows of the disciples' failure and Peter's in particular, and while he is exhorting his congregation to follow Jesus in the communal love that is their distinguishing sign, he is aware that Jesus' going to the Father is an event of *his* now, not anyone else's. All who come after him must come later. The distinction is one between the present age and the new age. Disciples, even courageous ones unlike Peter, are called to enter into the new age at a different time and in different circumstances than Jesus. He must go first. They can follow him afterward.

The Gospel of John takes place in its entirety on a borderland which is twofold. On one side is the world of remembered event or history: supper preparations, a courtesy performed by Jesus girt in a towel, human perfidy, failure of nerve. On the other side is the world beyond: the "being with the Father" of which the Son so eloquently speaks. In the world which the Gospel describes no one has yet traveled. Hemmed in between the two—the borderline of history on the one side and the glory of the Father on the other—is the pincer-existence of the life between. It is the life of John's community. Yet, ever since Jesus' resurrection, it is "everlasting life." It is the life of Christians now, a frustrating combination of being and becoming, of following Jesus as a disciple, not yet having faced the "later on" when they shall come after him where he is.

The early allegorists of Alexandria, men like the Gnostic Valentinus, were surely onto something when they read the Fourth Gospel appreciatively and concluded that it was "pneumatic," filled with the Spirit. It could not have been as prosaic as the other three, they thought. They were wrong in their estimate of the Synoptic Gospels as mere chronicles but right to see the Fourth Evangelist outrunning them in his raid on "the Great Code" of the Jewish Scriptures. For John not only employed the Bible, which he knew, as his arsenal of imagery but forged another arensal of his own. It is a fairly simple one. The journeyings of Jesus, his teachings, and his miracles all stand for a few unseen realities. These are his relation to his Father as Son, his predestined call to go back to where he was before, his mission to share a measure of the glory that was his, a glory that is otherwise called light and life.

The later Gnostics were impatient with what the Catholic Alexandrians, more anchored to the earth-bound community, never forgot: that Jesus like them was a man of space and time. But the expositor of John may never forget in pulpit preaching that the work is mystical or symbolic at every stage. Although it recounts a human history, it never becomes mere history. It is at every point a chapter of the human history of God through the Word with a peculiar people called "believers in him." That Word is Jesus the only Son.

173

John 14—17
Jesus' Prayer for Those the Father Has Given Him

Any division attempted within chapters 14—16 proves artificial, whereas chapter 17 stands apart as a prayer of Jesus addressed to God. Indeed, the progression from the end of chapter 13 to the beginning of chapter 18 is so natural that it is revealed as the original sequence, with the, "Rise, let us go hence," of 14:31*b* once having been the conclusion of the narrative at 13:38. Chapters 14—16 may well have come as a reflection on the prayer of chapter 17. The style of the four chapters is repetitive, whole verses and pericopes appearing more than once or surfacing in a slightly different form from their appearance earlier in the Gospel.

Chapter 14 has Jesus speak of his return to the Father while he promises to do for his disciples anything they ask in his name. The only condition is that out of love they keep his commands. In his absence he will send them another Counselor *(parakletos)*, the Spirit of truth. And he will come back to them. Fidelity to his word is the proof of their love while he is away. He gives peace as his farewell gift to his friends, not this world's peace but the kind that negates distress and fear.

Chapter 15 begins with the allegory of the vine and its branches under the vintner's watchful eye—respectively Jesus, his disciples, and the Father. The pruning process is described as necessary for an increased yield. Disciples and Master live in the same relation to each other as vine and branches. They are two but there is one life. Jesus lives in God's love; his friends live in his love. They are his friends, not servants (literally "slaves") because he has shared with them all he has heard from his Father. They should expect the world's hatred if they remain faithful to him, even as he is faithful to the one who sent him. For disciples to love one another is to incur the world's hate and harassment because they do not belong to this world.

In chapter 16 this harassment is spelled out. The disciples should not be surprised at it. Jesus has forewarned them. It is right for him to go back to the one who sent him despite the grief of his friends. Otherwise the Counselor who must convict the world of sin and judgment and condemnation will not come. This Spirit of truth will guide them into all truth, having received from Jesus what the Spirit declares to them. Grief will mark his friends in the "little while" of his absence, but their sorrow will turn to a joy that no one can take from them. Petitions made to the Father in his name will be answered and will give them the fullness of joy. The disciples finally say what Jesus longs to hear: They believe that he has truly come from God. Though they now believe, they will be scattered, Jesus says, leaving him alone, except for the Father who is always with him. The disciples may suffer in the world, but they must take heart. He has overcome the world.

Chapter 17 is Jesus' prayer to God for all humanity, but especially those the Father has given him. Jesus has glorified God by his life and now asks that God give him glory in return. He prays for his friends and for all who will believe in him through their word. His prayer is that they be sanctified in truth, that they be one as Father and Son are one, that they be "in us" as the sign the world needs in order to believe that God did indeed send him. Jesus wishes to lose none that the Father has given him but bring all to be with him where he is.

Authority in the Fourth Gospel

By this time it should be apparent that the community of John's Gospel has no organization or structure beyond that of mutual love. Leaders, discipline, accountability in the ordinary sense are not mentioned. We cannot discover the leadership pattern, if indeed there was one. Up till now "the disciple whom Jesus loved" has appeared but once (13:23). Subsequent references to him (19:26; 20:3–8?; 21:7, 20) show that he is the apostolic authority to whom the community looks in a special way. He outranks Peter in chapters 13—20 of the original version, understanding Jesus better than Peter does. In chapter 21, as we shall see, the pastoral role and authority of Peter over all the church is underlined, after he has been thrice subjected to the Johannine criterion of love (21:15–17). Previous to 13:23, however, there has been no authority figure of any kind, even though the Twelve are mentioned once (6:70–71). We can only conclude that, "Johannine theology was opposed to authority in teaching and discipline being invested in the ministry. . . . For

175

these communities, a direct and personal bond with Jesus was determinative for Johannine ecclesiology or the doctrine of the church" (E. Schillebeeckx, *Ministry,* p. 25).

Presbyters begin to appear in II John 1 and III John 1. This fact testifies to change in at least one Johannine community. At the time chapters 1—20 of the present Gospel were edited, however, the Counselor is viewed as the only teacher (14:26; 16:13). All human teachers including the beloved disciple are witnesses of the tradition interpreted by this Counselor (19:35; 21:24). When that disciple dies, his followers continue to transmit the teaching they have from him. To do so is to carry on the work of the Counselor who will be with them always (14:16). It is never thought a bad thing for the Johannine church that Jesus went away. He would return upon his glorification in the person of the Counselor (16:7), teaching as it were through another. This Spirit of truth bears witness along with the witness of the Johannine believers (15:26–27).

All these ideas occur in the four chapters under consideration. Paramount among them is the living presence of Jesus in every Christian, thanks to the indwelling of the Counselor. This presence is conveyed in the picture of the vine and the branches, that is, a direct and personal bond with Jesus (a theme which marks the whole of the Fourth Gospel). The bond remains the basis for all church authority in the John tradition. When, therefore, preachers of all the churches examine these texts to prepare to speak about them, they realize that the Church Catholic that emerged from the various apostolic churches accepted the continuing presence of Jesus and the indwelling Spirit-Counselor as part of their heritage. No extant Christian communion is exclusively Johannine, but there is none that is not Johannine in its warp and woof. The mutual love of Christians and their acceptance of the love of which Jesus gave proof by laying down his life (15:13) is the great public symbol of faith. Where it is lacking there is no Christianity, only a parched husk of forms and formulas.

If things are going awry in a Christian group—from smallest local assembly to worldwide church—it is proper to appeal to the "charter of love" which this final discourse constitutes. In the church there is no higher recourse under God than to Jesus in the Spirit. One must recall, however, that a bond of personal love did not prove adequate to settle doctrinal or disciplinary differences in the Johannine churches. In Third John the presbyter-author sends a delegation to bear witness concerning the true tradition to Diotrephes, a presbyter whom he considers a false teacher (5–8, 12). That worthy who "likes to put himself first" refuses to receive the delegation (9, 10). It is a stalemate of appeals to the tradition guaranteed by the Counselor. Later history has shown that other structures are needed.

Consequently, while nothing in the church takes precedence over the *agape* of the supper discourse, in our sinful, fallen state love needs implementation. There is room in the church for clearly defined ministries—even hierarchically ordered ones—along with the pure democracy of love. There is a place in a community of charity for synods, open hearings, sanctions, committees, even budgets. Love, in other words, has consequences.

The willingness to die for one's friends may translate in our time into relinquishing posts that boost the ego, stepping down at retirement age, acknowledging the worth of other opinions on what the ancient faith both is and demands. A familiar painting which one sees reproduced shows a pair of friars in heated discussion before clerical onlookers, their faces contorted, the veins on their necks and foreheads straining. Its title: *Odium Theologicum,* the hate of God's defenders. An ancient adage says: "O liberty, what crimes have been committed in thy name!" The same is true of love. A "crime of passion" makes the hearer think of *eros.* In the long span of church life the basic crime tends to be hatred of the other, the death of *agape.* Often the quarrel is over true doctrine. Yet the church's one unequivocally true doctrine is love for one another. Ministers of the gospel must preach it often and live it always.

PREACHING ON JESUS' GREAT DISCOURSE IN JOHN

To preach on John 14—17 is easier said than done. Its sonorous phrases somehow bring out the banal in us and invite the hearer to boredom. In Greek the style is tolerable, every *hoti, hina, alla* and *de* having its place. Translation by even the most skilled persons fills the page with puzzles. What is the meaning of this transition which seems to be a *non sequitur* (e.g., 14:19, 31; 15:19*b;* 16:4*b*)? How does adversative phrase *A* follow immediately on phrase *B* in which the proposition not clearly affirmed above is vehemently denied (e.g., 16:26*b*)? The best solution seems to be John Calvin's—to teach every literate Christian Greek.

177

One modest way around the difficulty is never to preach on
any portion of this discourse extemporaneously or from an outline. The legend in Eusebius has it that John in his old age had
no other theme but love. That is endurable from one whose life
is a symphony of love. From the rest of us, the speech of the
Fourth Gospel can descend to the level of cliché fairly soon. The
Johannine flow, so like a Moebius band without beginning
or end, can tire the mind—even as it comes from the pen
of its creator. As paraphrased by a lesser expositor it can be
unbearable.

The inspired prose needs to be dissected or dismantled,
each part examined and related to every other, then all pol-
ished and reassembled like the parts of a watch if it is to function
for the hearer. A good technique is to say the words of John in
one's own words—painstakingly selected for aptitude—then
using John's words as the capstone of the segment. No word of
the discourse can be treated as an axiom. Unexamined, all the
great phrases that have become the world's heritage are like
pebbles worn smooth. Without exploration they have no sharp
edges, no bite; they challenge the hearer to nothing. Disen-
gaged one from the other, scrutinized under the magnifying
glass of faith, they invite the hearer to everything.

John 14:1–14

All of the lectionaries proclaim this passage on the Fifth Sunday of Easter
in Year A (1). The Catholic and Lutheran lectionaries terminate it at verse 12
(the believer in Jesus will do greater works than he does, "because I go to the
Father" [12b]; can stopping here provide an explanation?) while the other two
go on to verse 14. The Episcopal and Common Lectionaries seem to think that
asking things of the Father in the name of the now absent Jesus, precisely
because he is absent, is the reason given—which therefore must be read (vv.
13–14). Only the Episcopal does not resume at verse 15 on the next Sunday. It
picks up at 15:1–8.

"Let not your hearts be troubled" (v. 1), Jesus says. Who can
endure advice like that? Do not be nervous, anxious, shattered.
This kind of talk is meaningless, normally, to anyone to whom
it is addressed. Here, however, the speaker is Jesus and he
provides a means to the end. As you commit yourselves totally
to God in a relation of trust, he says, so must you do to me (v.1).
178 The pain of life, separation, the cross cannot last forever. Live
in hope. The present will yield to the future because I shall see

to it. A permanent place of abiding with God ("many rooms," *monai pollai,* v. 2) is in store for all who believe.

The destiny in store for Jesus is likewise laid up for his friends. He says that they know the way of his journey (v. 4). Their response is immediate consternation. The ignorance of his destination which they harbor, Thomas answers, makes talk of the way there pointless (v. 5). This is the kind of statement so dear to John which triggers his best responses. In this case it comes swiftly. Jesus himself is the route, the underlying reason for the journey. He is way and truth and life (v. 6). "All the way to heaven is heaven," an old Christian paraphrase of this passage has it, "for he said, 'I am the way.'" He alone is the way to the Father. All approach to God is through him (v. 6). Yet this approach is not only an eschatological future spoken of, like that of the Synoptics, but also a this-worldly abiding with God. To be on the way is to know truth and have life.

At this point the scope of Johannine theology, and by extension the Christian faith, comes under challenge. Images of bumper stickers arise in which a single index finger is held aloft. "One way," they proclaim, defiantly eliminating all who think otherwise about the gospel and all Jews and all Muslims; necessarily, too, eliminating the peoples of black Africa and India, and of China, Japan, and Korea, who have some good ideas about the "way" *(Tao, Do)* but distinctly non-Johannine ideas about God. Are all other approaches to God or to ultimacy in the universe eliminated by John's Gospel on the principle of "Jesus said: . . ."?

It was John who said it in the first place, and the church that made the saying its own. The Evangelist was throwing a challenge to all in his circle—pagans, Jews, and fellow believers in Jesus—announcing the necessity of the kind of faith in Jesus that he professed. What did he think about the faith of Parthians, Nubians, and the peoples of the western isles? Perhaps he did not think of it at all. John was exercised over what he knew. So must the Christian be. That means that Jesus must be proclaimed as the one way to God to whoever is willing to listen, while leaving the faith and the fate of those who have never heard the gospel to a God who is equal to the problem. The church will always be missionary because it is convinced it possesses in the gospel a peculiar treasure. In earlier times (but not the earliest time) it feared for the eternal salvation of those

179

who had not been baptized. Portions of it still do. But there is a much greater trust in the providence of God nowadays and of God's mysterious ways of self-disclosure to all the peoples of the globe.

Johannine thought is not a shouting match. Neither is it a denial of all that most people on the earth hold dear as their way to God, or simply their "way." John is calling Christians to go to the Father through Jesus and to bring a knowledge of Jesus to any who are disposed to hear of him.

Knowledge of Jesus, for those who know him in the Johannine way, is knowledge of the Father (v. 7a). Jesus is known by the way of the cross and the resurrection. "Henceforth you know him and have seen him" (v. 7b). There is a tone of reproach in Jesus' response which brings on Philip's question to follow immediately (v. 8; cf. 8:19). The relief Jesus holds out is that "henceforth," that is, from the completion of God's revelation in him, Jesus, as he departs in suffering/glory, it will be possible to know him and to know the Father through him. Indeed, the possibility of knowing the Father in Jesus already exists. Moses' desire to see the face of God (Exod. 33:19–20) surfaces in Philip's question. It seems to receive a different response in Exodus: "But my face you cannot see, for no one sees me and lives" (v. 20). In fact, though, verses 9–10 contain a reiteration of the Exodus passage in John 1:18, for here again it is God the only Son (the "only God" in the more difficult textual reading), ever at the Father's side, who as his messenger reveals the Father. The difference from the way of Moses and the prophets is that Jesus is in God, dwelling in the Father's godhead, and God dwells in him "doing his works" (v. 10) in a way the Bible never claims for any other human being.

Believers in Jesus have two ways to go. They may accept his word about the intimate Father-Son relation or be moved by the testimony of Jesus' works (v. 11). Clearly the latter can arouse faith (see 2:11). The former way of direct acceptance is better. A life of faith will unlock wonders to a community of believers, "greater works than these" (v. 12; cf. 1:50–51). Paradoxically, Jesus' return to the Father is the condition of performing these works (v. 12). Throughout the Gospel runs the theme that in Jesus' absence all that could not be achieved in his presence is possible. This firm stand against nostalgia is part of the writer's message to his contemporaries. The theological

180

reason is that while faith in Jesus in his lifetime was possible it was only an inchoate faith. Complete faith in him requires as its object the Father's deed of Jesus' death and glorification. Put another way, the gift of the Spirit which comes after belief in these is the *sine qua non* of right faith. In Jesus' absence he will give anything asked in his name, "that the Father may be glorified in the Son" (vv. 13–14).

This means that that homilist is on firm ground who finds the present graced existence or life of belief in the Son the high point of the Spirit's action in the world. The power of the person who trusts in the Son's intercession is immeasurable.

> Whatever you ask in my name, I will do it,
>   that the Father may be glorified in the Son;
>   if you ask anything in my name, I will do it (vv. 13–14).

John 14:15–31

All the lectionaries except the Episcopal propose verses 15–21 for the Sixth Sunday of Easter in Year A (1). Verses 23–29 containing Jesus' response are in good part the Gospel reading common to the four lectionaries on the Sixth Sunday of Easter, Year C (3).

In these seven verses, keeping Jesus' word or commandments is the condition of enjoying the Father's love and the abiding presence of Father, Son, and Counselor-Spirit. The "other Counselor" of this Gospel appears first in verse 16. Jesus' return to the Father makes possible an intercession with God through him that cannot go awry. "Whatever you ask . . . I will do" (vv. 12c, 13). The Father's glorification in the Son demands it. This advocacy of Jesus would seem to be enough—is, in fact, described as such (v. 14). Yet, another position is proposed as equally necessary. Its condition is love of Jesus and fidelity to his commands (v. 15).

> Not for any gains I see;
> But just the way that thou didst me
> I do love and I will love thee
> 　　　　　(G.M. Hopkins, "O Deus, Ego Amo Te").

is the believer's response to Jesus' demand of love and obedience. Why the need for the other Counselor? Jesus' absence, evidently. But there are other, more subtle advantages which will accompany this Gift at its bestowal. The Spirit of truth will dwell with those who obey Jesus and be within them as some-

181

one they know in a way that the world cannot (v. 17). There is the possibility for Christians of living in truth because Truth lives in them.

> Jesus that dost in Mary dwell,
> Be in thy servants hearts as well,
> In the spirit of thy holiness,
> In the fullness of thy force and stress . . .
> And every power in us that is
> Against thy power put under feet
> In the Holy Ghost the Paraclete
> To the glory of the Father. Amen.
>
> (Hopkins, "Oratio Patris Condren").

The next verse, 18, "I will not leave you desolate; I will come to you," has led some—like R. A. Culpepper in *The Johannine School*—to think that this Counselor is none other than Jesus upon his return. In fact, I John 2:1 calls Jesus Christ a "righteous advocate," using the same word, *parakletos*. Still, the word *"another"* [Counselor] appears in verse 16 and the whole context bespeaks an interim scheme until Jesus comes in glory. The temporary desolation (lit., "orphaning") is not fated to last (v. 18). This "other" is God's great gift for the meanwhile. The community lives, not in virtue of an absent Lord and Teacher, but a present and abiding Spirit of truth. Jesus is seen through this Spirit even when he, Jesus, is unseen. There is continuing life in Jesus for those who know the Spirit (v. 17).

The easiest understanding of the "little while" during which the world will not see Jesus (v. 19; cf. 7:33; 12:35; 13:33; 14:28; 16:16, 17, 18, 19) is the brief separation that his crucifixion and death will bring. This might have accounted for the cryptic use of the term as it appeared earlier. Here, however, the appended phrase about "living" or "having life," regardless of how the ambiguous *hoti* clause is interpreted (*"because* I live,"? *"that* I live"? v. 19), suggests strongly that Jesus is "seen" by his disciples and not by the world as a "living one," and they are seen as persons who shall live in him.

The Johannine knowledge or sight of Jesus is that of faith, not of the senses. Hence the office of the Spirit of truth will be to help disciples "see" Jesus throughout the still enduring time before the parousia. "That day" of verse 20 is a standard term from Jewish eschatology. John uses it to mean the day of Jesus' coming to his disciples (v. 18), but since they are to know on that day not only the coinherence of Father and Son but also their

182

own in him (v. 20*b*), it refers as much to the continuing presence of Christ to the believers for whom the Gospel is written as to the past disciple-witnesses of the resurrection. An awareness of the Christ life within is made the condition for knowing something of the relation of Jesus to the Father. It has been so in Christian life ever since John penned his Gospel.

Verse 21 is an expansion of the earlier verse 15, a technique we have encountered in John already and will see again frequently in the discourse. Obedience is the hallmark of Jesus' disciples, the proof that they love. God will love the lovers of the Son in a special way. The Son, in turn, will reciprocate the love of the individual disciple and manifest it in a way which is not further indicated (v. 21*c*). The parousia is the day of final disclosure. The resurrection of Jesus is its anticipation; but all through this discourse there runs the thread of a self-revealing of the glorified Jesus in his disciples well before the final day of revelation. This might be called the Johannine remythologization of Jewish eschatology. The future is made present in a way that everyone, whether steeped in the Jewish myth of the end-time or not, can understand.

The Judas who joins the rather large cast of foils for Jesus' remarks in John (v. 22) may well be the son of James of the Lukan Twelve-list (cf. Luke 6:16; Acts 1:13), but John does not use any such Synoptic tally of the disciples and the point is not important. Important is the way this query of Judas brings into focus the difference between a disciple and "the world." As to the disciple's form of address, the man born blind had called Jesus "lord" *(kyrie)* before he believed in him (9:36), an indication that the term there rendered the Aramaic *mar* or "sir." Here the intention may be the same from the aspect of written rhetoric, even though Judas ("not Judas Iscariot") is farther along the path of discipleship.

The difference between Jesus' disciples and the world is precisely the love that consists in faithfulness to his word (vv. 23–24). The Counselor, now called "the Holy Spirit" for the first time (v. 26), will act as teacher of the disciples, basically a recaller to mind of all that Jesus has taught (v. 26). Here the Spirit's function is akin to that of the comforting which is attributed to God through the prophets in the matter of the messianic age (cf. Isa. 40:1).

183

In the LXX and various New Testament writings, *paraklesis* is the consolation or encouragement that comes with prophecy (see Luke 2:25; I Cor. 14:3, 31). It seems to be the same here: God as guarantor of the first stage of the final days. Once again, the total unanimity of Jesus with God is underscored. Jesus wants his word kept (vv. 23–24; it becomes "words" in 24*a*, then back to the singular in 24*b*), but that word is always in origin the Father's. Jesus while still with his disciples makes a promise concerning the future (vv. 25, 29). It is that the Counselor/Holy Spirit will surely come (v. 26). The deed of Gift for the interim is centered on "peace," the total wellbeing that underlies this Hebrew word of greeting and farewell (v. 27). It has a meaning specific to Jesus in this Gospel, namely, the overcoming of fear and perturbation with which the chapter opens. Only he can give the gift of peace which is envisioned. Like love, it is a Johannine hallmark of being a disciple of Jesus.

If peace is the condition proper to the non-orphaned community, being with the Father who sent him is the condition proper to Jesus the Son. The total origination of everything in God, above all the plan to have humanity be with godhead, is underscored by Jesus' expressed reason for his return: "For the Father is greater *(meizon)* than I" (v. 28*c*). This declaration of implied *origin* is consonant with everything said about Jesus and God in John's Gospel, including the full divinity of the Word. It became a problem only with the Arian challenge. There, Jesus was seen as "less than the Father" by being a creature, although the firstborn of creation. Arius was neither the first nor the last to seize on this phrase for support in what he already believed. It happened that the church had already come to believe otherwise on the basis of the whole Gospel but it could not express its faith swiftly or easily. The debates of Nicaea and the aftermath of the next century and a half were needed to consolidate this as the faith of East and West.

The discourse is substantively over now. The nearness to hand of "the ruler of this world," the devil, is given as Jesus' exit cue (v. 30; cf. 12:31; 16:11). If he has no hold on Jesus, as the latter asserts (v.30), is there any Johannine sense in which this is the hour of the power of darkness? Luke (22:53*b*) seems to think so. Precisely *not*, thunders John. It is an hour of condemnation of the world's ruler, even if his "power" *(exousia)* as darkness is not destroyed in Luke until the resurrection. In Jesus, John says, he has nothing (v. 30*b*). The world will be forced to conclude from Jesus' death that obedient love led to

184

it, not any Satanic victory (v. 31*a*). This is the whole of Johannine soteriology in the size of a hazelnut.

The discourse seems to be over with Jesus' peremptory command to be up and out of the supper room (v. 31*b*). Was that ever the case, namely that it ended at the conclusion of chapter 14? Good arguments can be made for its once having capped the discourse. In such case, either the displacement of chapters or the addition of materials supervened. Perhaps the strongest of these arguments is Jesus' surprising statement, "I will no longer talk much *(polla)* with you" (v. 30), in light of all the words that follow. That phrase appears to be terminative in its intent. Alternatively, it may be the addition of a scribe who saw three more chapters of discourse material coming up and dealt with them in this minimizing fashion. Actually, the heart of Jesus' message is over by the end of chapter 14. What follows in chapters 15—16 will be a targum on chapter 14. The interconnections among Father and Son, Son and disciples, love and obedience and commandments, the absent Jesus and the present Counselor have all been set in place. In what follows they will only receive a reworking or be given a fresh look.

The Supper Discourse and the Church's Developed Faith

An important question remains before we conclude chapter 14 and take a fresh breath. It comes, not from the text itself, but from the use to which the Greek fathers of the church put it in their discussions of the mutual relations of Father, Son, and Spirit. Do we have the elements of the mystery of the triune God in this discourse as that doctrine was hammered out three centuries later? If so, do we have our Spirit doctrine in germ in its Eastern form ("proceeds from the Father") or Western form ("proceeds from the Father and the Son") or neither?

To answer the basic question briefly: John has a reciprocity of understanding, love, and activity between Father and Son that seems better accounted for by assuming the full participation of the Word in godhead (cf. 1:1–18) than by the sensitivity of a human son to a divine Father. The latter reality is there but it cannot be demonstrated that this and nothing more is present.

Secondly, the Spirit/Counselor who will come from God to do what Jesus does is a divine emissary in the same sense as the

185

Word/Son, or else the work the Spirit does is not a sharing with humanity of the very life of God. No creature could carry out that embassy. Hence there is to be found in chapter 14 the root concept of a God, self-manifested to the world, who offers it divine life *through* the Son and with undiminished vigor *in* the Holy Spirit. The expression of the mystery by the prepositional use indicated above (retained in the conclusion of the eucharistic canons or anaphoras and the collects) reflects the economy of salvation which came to prevail as the church's faith. The writers of the early centuries were convinced that this faith was to be found in the ways in which Jesus spoke of the Father and the Spirit in these chapters of John.

The Fourth Evangelist cannot be thought of as setting aside the primacy of Israel's God, the LORD, who has done all these things. When John uses the ordinary verbs of "sending" and "coming" (*pempein, ekporeuesthai,* 15:26) it is clear that he is describing God's activity in history through the Son and the Spirit. The Greek fathers took this language to describe an eternal dynamic within godhead which the saving drama in time reflected. Thus, they developed a *theologia* of "processions" or "goings forth" of Son and Spirit from the Father when in fact all John may have intended was an *oikonomia,* a description of God's deed for us in time. If the latter was the case, that does not render all inference invalid, but it does identify it as an inference. The Greek fathers, however, had no such doubts.

The Father will "give" another Counselor at the Son's request (v. 16); ten verses later (26) he will "send" him in Jesus' name; but Jesus also will "send" from the Father this "Spirit of truth, who proceeds from the Father" (15:26): the Jesus who is back in glory is the sender of the Counselor Spirit without qualification. From this it appears that neither the East nor the West has the better of it from the standpoint of the Evangelist's intent, that is, the primitive Eastern creedal phrase which says "who proceeds from the Father" or the later Western one "who proceeds from the Father and the Son." It was the church of Spain via Gaul that made the West totally vulnerable by adding the phrase *filioque,* "and from the Son," to the creed without consultation of the East. The East might indeed have agreed to the twofold procession but it took offense at Western arrogance in tampering unilaterally with the text of a traditional creed. When theological arguments were framed in the East after the eleventh-century split, those churches maintained that the Holy Spirit did indeed proceed from both Father and Son but not as from a single principle, as the West had begun to teach. Rather, said the East, Scripture is clear in teaching that the Spirit proceeds from the Father *through* the Son.

The question remains, was John entertaining any such ontic thoughts about godhead as the Greek fathers attributed to him in the days when *ekporeuesthai* meant simply to "go forth" or "set out on a journey"? Perhaps the term needs a good detheologizing in East and West so that both can agree to the very *least* that the Evangelist is saying as regards the Spirit's relation to God as Father. It is already quite a lot, namely the coming forth of the fullness of deity from the fullness of deity.

Homilists should not be discouraged from sharing a little of the history of doctrine with their congregations, who get precious little of it compared with their fellow believers of the East. They need to be taught to distinguish between the oak and acorn, namely, what John saw in his time and what the church, understanding itself to be a legitimate witness in his line, made of his teaching. This process, which is called the unfolding of tradition, is thought valid by all the major churches. Even the churches which deny it in principle transmit the teaching of the great christological councils and call it "the clear sense of Scripture." What no homilist can legitimately do is read out John's Gospel and find there the whole post-Nicaean development of trinitarian teaching as it is now held. The roots of such teaching are to be found in John, but not the teaching as later fashioned. If it were clearly available in Scripture, there would have been no need for the three hundred and fifty years of uncertainty and struggle up to Chalcedon (451).

What can and must be preached is the certainty that the Spirit is abroad in the world doing the work of advocacy, consolation, encouragement, and peace-making that only godhead can achieve. The whole of divinity is at work, as any rudimentary theology knows, not one-third of it. Consistent neglect by the West of its own pneumatology or Spirit-teaching has left it open to those protagonists of the Spirit who see the Spirit as some kind of God above God, not God of very God. This Spirit, being none other than the fullness of godhead, is to be glorified equally with Father and Son. In each of them there is likewise the sum of deity without remainder. This God active in our midst since Jesus' departure—the departure Jesus so longed for if the Counselor were to come—is the God of the church's present experience.

The Spirit "spoken of through the prophets" is the God poured out in fullness at the beginning of these last days. Without this Spirit there is no life for humanity of the sort the Son has from the Father. Jesus is empowered by the Father to give this Spirit by sending another, even as he has been sent. Whatever the hidden mystery of deity in itself, of this much we have an inkling: The totality of godhead is self-given as uncreated Gift to us from the Father ("God") through Jesus Christ. This Gift is bestowed on those who believe in Christ risen. We call the Gift *Creator Spiritus,* in the words of an ancient hymn. We can never have the Gift in sufficient measure—it is figurative language, of course, because quantitative—and so we pray: "Come, Creator Spirit!"

John 15:1–8

Verses 1–8 occur in all the lectionaries but the Episcopal (which reads 14:15–21) on the Fifth Sunday of Easter of Year B (2).

From this hymn sung to the consummate Gift in chapter 14, it may seem a step backward to return to the vine and branches allegory with which chapter 15 begins. This is not because the allegory is imperfect but because by all logic it precedes the conclusion which 14:31 once provided.

The figure is simple enough to one who has done any actual pruning, not just trimming. Without this experience the preacher should consult a person in the congregation who has— or else not go down the horticulturist's path! Being made "clean" *(katharos)* was evidently the right word for this pruning in the vine culture of the ancient world. A mastery of the biblical sources for this *paroimia,* which depicts Israel as the beloved vine, will not suffice (e.g., Isa. 5:1–7; 27:2–6; Jer. 2:21; 12:10–11; Ezek. 15). Is the vigilant vinedresser, who is clearly the Father, the chief actor? Or is it Jesus, the vine from whom the branches draw life? And how, if he is the vine, can he be the speaker of a cleansing word?

In 12:48 Jesus' spoken word had meant condemnation. Here it seems to bespeak healing. His utterances must abide in people if their requests are to be heard (v. 7; cf. 17:8). What is this word, anyway? Is it the whole oral teaching of Jesus or the

188

simple fact that he came from the Father who sent him? Message and medium—in this case a person—are the same in John. There is simply Jesus. His heavenly origins and his earthly task, which is to lay down his life for his friends (v. 13; cf. 3:16), are one with his person. Believing this and doing his commands is accepting his word or words. There is a note of productivity or yield in all this, as in the agricultural parables of the Synoptics. John calls it "bearing much fruit" (12:24; cf. vv. 2, 4, 5), meaning the glory given to God by discipleship of Jesus. The figure is natural when one considers that what is at stake is the transfer of God's own life.

John 15:9–17

Verses 9–17 appear for all the lectionaries as the pericope for the Sixth Sunday of Easter, Year B (2).

The verses are repetitive of what has gone before but they advance the idea of the vine and the branches. The reality behind the symbol is, as suspected, intimate friendship. Jesus invites to an abiding love of him, a love that is committed, that is sure. The sign of fidelity is the same as in all friendships: taking seriously what the friend takes seriously (here, expressed as "my commandments"). The measure of the mutual love of disciples is Jesus' love for them, even to death (vv. 12–13). Its outcome will be joy (v. 11). Since the disciples of the Gospel give little proof of deserving love in return for their love, the initiative lies with Jesus as lover and friend. That is the cue. In emulating him one loves not only those deserving of love but all in the company, lovable or not. Such was the Master's way with the disciples. It is God's way with the human family. This sounds like what Aristotle and Aquinas called *benevolentia,* the love that wills another's good. It comes from the stance of one situated above. In contrast is the love of desire, *concupiscentia,* in which one hopes to gain something from the person loved. Its primary motive is need of fulfillment. Better than both is *amicitia,* the love of friendship. That term sounds pallid to our modern ear, but the teachers who made the distinction ranked it as the highest of the three. It is the love God has for us and it puts us on a par with God. This is the *agape* of the New Testament.

189

Jesus said: "No longer do I call you servants . . . but . . . friends, for all that I have heard from my Father I have made known to you" (v. 15). As with perfect friendships from time immemorial all secrets are shared, both from above and below. Friendship at its fullest destroys the barriers of above and below.

Must it not be a fiction to say that the creature knows what God knows? It would be if what were meant were all those secrets of divine power with which the LORD taunted Job. Those majestic possibilities are not shared in this friendship. What is shared is the godliness of God which consists in the power to forgive, the initiative in acceptance of those who are inimical and the love that makes the unlovely lovable. "You did not choose me, but I chose you . . ." (v. 16a). That is the story of the first step. It could be intolerable if it were the story of the entire friendship. Reciprocity must set in, otherwise there is an awareness of the patron who cannot endure being a peer. Jesus puts matters directly quite early in the relationship, saying something like: "We shall be friends, you and I. No more of this I up here and you down there, you the object of my affection and I the subject of your veneration. We are both subjects undergoing the passion and pain of love." He speaks of the command to love one another (v. 17). But love is never mandated. Love is not available on demand. This command to love has to be Bible language for: "The Father wills that the children of God's love give themselves to one another freely." There is no other way to love. It is done freely or it is not love.

John 15:18–27

The world's hatred of genuine lovers, from which there seems to be no escape, appears at first in John to be the paranoia of the pious (vv. 18–19). It is, of course, an expression of the opposition in which Semitic thought delights. The Bible knew antithesis long before Hegel, and knew no synthesis by the fusion of opposites. That came with the Amoraim, the men of the Talmud. In the Scriptures there was only the conversion of one reality to the other or an unresolvable stand-off. This being so, the true nature of "the world" comes to the fore (v. 19). Here it does not mean the globe of earth, which is the human dwelling-place. No more is it the relatively ordered course of nature. It is all that is set against God and the Son; it is the opposite of the divine holiness. "The world" is the chaos of a conscious hell. The Christian therefore does ill to reduce "worldliness" to a description of foolish vanity or purposelessness. The worldly is a category of evil for John. "All this [viz., persecuting you, failing to observe your words] they will do to you on my account, because they do not know him who sent me" (v. 21). It is a culpable ignorance. As countryfolk say, "They had a right to know." The world did not see what it would not see. It is therefore without excuse. John speaks of hatred of Jesus as tantamount to hatred of God (v. 23). The bitterness of religious exchange in his day is, happily, almost impossible to recapture.

Jesus cites the Psalter (65:9) in what John identifies as "their law" against those who choose darkness over the Light which Jesus is (v. 25). There is no room for him in the law as some prefer to read it. The Counselor (v. 26) and Jesus' earliest disciples (v. 27) will give witness at the proper time.

Evil must be seen as evil and condemned, but nothing can ensure this except the Spirit of truth. Not everyone can exorcise or condemn, only the holy. Bearing witness in Jesus' name is a perilous business because it requires that full play be given to the Spirit of holiness who is the Spirit of truth. It is much easier to spout Johannine censures than let the Spirit of God suffuse one's whole being.

John 16:1–4

The persecution theme with which chapter 15 concludes continues through at least the middle of verse 4 before Jesus proceeds on another tack. It is not easy to know what to say about the Johannine theology of siege by the world. A persecution complex regarding the church or even one's congregation can develop all too readily. "They're agin' us," we say, the "they" often being outsiders who perceive shortcomings in our corporate conduct that we ourselves will not admit. There is undoubtedly a sociological basis for the Evangelist's entrenched position, but at this late date it is obscure. His explanation is theological. The "world" is pitted against the friends of Jesus because of Jesus' person (in Greek, his "name").

The modern counterpart to seeing opposition to the church everywhere is seeing the devil everywhere, taking the struggle of light and darkness so literally that evil powers are viewed as at work on every side. An obvious peg on which to hang contemporary discontents is the mention of expulsions from synagogues and attempts on disciples' lives (v. 2). Fortu-

191

nately, no Sunday lectionary features these early verses of chapter 16. They would almost certainly be heard in the modern period as Jewish violence directed at pious Christians. The contemporary belief referent is hatred for God and Christ by repressive regimes when Christians act clearly as the church.

The comments on 9:22 should be reviewed for the term *aposynagogoi* which recurs here in verse 2. In the rhetoric of verses 1–4, the threats on Jesus' life of chapters 5 and 7 and that of ostracizing his disciples of chapters 9 and 10 are repeated. All this is done in a context of the necessity of previous warning by Jesus (vv. 1, 4; cf. 14:25), lest when the events occur his followers be scandalized by what their prescient Master failed to tell them. "Their hour" of violent activity in verse 4 is the persecutors' hour. The testing of the disciples is thus compared to Jesus' hour (13:1).

A homilist is ill-advised to get into Jewish persecution of the early believers in Jesus' time or at any time. The Christian record of the centuries makes it ring hollow. That there was such persecution—understandable in light of Jewish zeal for the law which, it was thought, was being attacked—is something there is scattered evidence for elsewhere in the New Testament (see Acts 7:54–60; 8:3; Matt. 5:10–11; Mark 13:12–13; Luke 12:4; Gal. 1:13–23). All religious groups treasure their earliest trials and canonize their martyrs. Thus, Acts gives us Stephen, the "protomartyr" of Christian devotion. But the Jewish violence recalled in Christian sources was the normal religious response of the Middle East in those days. It had a biblical basis if blasphemy were suspected to be at work. The Evangelist no doubt has specific outbursts of violence in mind which were well known to his readers. They have not survived to us. Preachers today would do better to exhort to a holiness of life that would excite the hatred of "the world." Unfortunately, the one sure modern reality is the resentment caused by the Christians' use of New Testament rhetoric without deeds in the Spirit to match.

John 16:5–33

The Common Lectionary uses 15:26–27; 16:4*b*–15 on Pentecost in Year B (2). No other employs chapter 16 as generously as this. All use the shorter verses 12–15 on Trinity Sunday in churches which celebrate that feast as such.

We have already seen the theme of Jesus' return to the place from which he came (v. 5; cf. 7:33–34; 13:33). He speaks of it again to comfort his friends in their grief at losing him (v. 6), stressing the importance of his departure if the Counselor is to come (v. 7; cf. 14:16, 26). At the end of verse 7 Jesus is the sender of the Spirit of truth (v. 13), a phrase which, together with "he will have received from me" (vv. 14–15, *accipiet*, Vulgate), contributed heavily to the arguments employed by the West about a twofold procession of the Spirit (viz., from the Father and the Son). Jesus will send the Counselor "to you," that is, the believing community. It has already been established that the world cannot receive this Counselor (cf. 14:17). Hence, the Spirit's work of convincing (or condemning, v. 8), when he comes, will be exercised through the community. The laying of a burden on the world's conscience will be under three headings: sin, righteousness, and judgment. The meaning is cryptic, as early emendations of the text by scribes who were at pains to clarify it testify. John is probably saying that the Spirit will convict the world of the facts of *sin* in humanity and *righteousness* in Jesus with *judgment* residing in a correct discrimination between the two, an adverse judgment in the case of sin but favorable as regards him. The Counselor, verses 7–8 seem to say, will level sentence on the world through the community.

The world's sin takes the form of a refusal to believe in Jesus. His righteousness will be manifested in his return to the Father. Judgment will come on this world's ruler after Jesus' going back to heaven (vv. 9–11). All will come around right, in other words, *but only after Jesus' departure.* The Spirit of truth will make the separation endurable by speaking all that this Spirit hears (from God) and announcing the things to come (v. 13). The Spirit will be the proclaimer of the final age inaugurated in Jesus.

The Spirit will clearly receive a message from Jesus, both of truth and of things to come, and announce it to the disciples (vv. 13–14). The Spirit's passing it along will give glory to Jesus (v. 14), just as any transmission of a possession or a task among the three has the effect of generating the divine glory in the midst of believers (cf. 17:1). The phrase in verse 15*a* is unconditional ("All things whatsoever the Father has are mine" [author's trans.]). By force of words it means that Jesus possesses from the Father what he will proclaim to the disciples; hence he has full power to transmit what he has received to the Spirit. Yet it is no wonder that later Christians took "all things whatsoever" *(panta hosa)* to be the possession of the total divine

193

stance by the Son and his transmission of this fullness of deity, along with the Father's transmission of it, to the Spirit. In the West, Father and Son were understood to be a single principle or source of the Spirit. The tradition that flourished in the East, on the other hand (on the basis of the same Johannine data), was that the Father transmitted the fullness of deity through the Son to the Spirit.

Glory was traditionally a concomitant of the Messiah's coming. John does not hesitate, however, to speak of the Spirit's giving glory to Jesus well before the last day, because the Spirit has received from Jesus "what is mine," namely, what he will announce to the disciples (v. 14). Early speculation on these words saw here more than a message which would be proclaimed by the Spirit's power. It saw no less than the fullness of deity transmitted to the Spirit from the Son which came to him from the Father.

For a comment on the repeated "little while" (vv. 17–19), see the one on 14:19 above. Jesus' departure and return are here completely ambiguous. They may equally refer to the separation of his death terminated by resurrection or to the space between the resurrection appearances and the parousia—the "little while" of the church's life. Thus, the time of mourning may be the three days between the memorials of death and resurrection or the period that could be the countless millennia of Jesus' absence (vv. 20–24). In the former case the disciples' joy will come with seeing him as the risen one; in the latter, his return at the end will bring with it the full joy of the final days, but the presence of the Counselor to the community will create its own anticipated joy. Isaiah 26:16–17 and 66:7 are sources for the figure of the pains of labor that lead to delight and the forgetfulness of sorrow (vv. 20–21), here the birth pangs of the Messiah. The disciples' joy will be of an absolutely permanent kind (v. 23b). "On that day" of Spirit-guidance there will no longer be any need to ask Jesus questions like the ones they have put to him in chapters 13—16 (v. 23a).

A new thought begins at the "Amen, amen" of verse 23b. It has to do with the granting of requests and not the answering of questions. The sentiment is the familiar Synoptic one of asking and receiving (v. 24; cf. Matt. 7:7–8 = Luke 11:9–10) but John holds out the fullness of joy (cf. 15:11) as the response to expect, not just the things asked. He has in mind the Spirit-period of understanding all that was veiled in Jesus' earthly days (vv. 25,

29). Jesus places plain speech about the Father in that future-of-the-Paraclete, but the disciples take it as being already present. The day of the Johannine secret (*paroimia* = figurative speech) is over. There is a seeming shift back to "on that day" (v. 26a). It turns out to be needless for Jesus so to act because the Father is assured of the disciples' worth. They have loved the Son and believed that he came from God (v. 27). Already this guarantees the Father's love. No new intercessory deed is required. Verse 28 is in some confusion because of the textually doubtful status of 28a, "I came [forth] from the Father." Even if some over-explicit scribe thought it was needed, in naming Jesus' origin as Word it sums up the Johannine initiating love of God which sends the Son, then receives him back from a world despoiled of him.

In the exchange of verses 29–33 the disciples are actively entrapped by Jesus in John's ironic style. They are described as comprehending his whole message. No further problems! Jesus catches them up short: "Do you now believe?" (v. 31). If they believe truly theirs will be the time of grief (cf. vv. 20, 22), which is Jesus' immediate future. These verses are a prediction of what seems to have been his historical desertion by his friends. But, as usual, a theological corrective is added. The Father is always with him (v. 32; cf. 10:30).

The chapter ends as it began, with an explanation of why Jesus has given all this teaching (v. 33a; cf. v. 1). The lengthy disclosures were in the interest of the disciples' peace. Their suffering *(thlipsis)* in the world is unavoidable but they must take heart. Jesus has overcome the world (v. 33b). How, exactly, is not said, probably by rescuing the company of believers from the ruler of this world who dominates it. There are more who are to be saved (cf. 17:20). In general Jesus' prayer is successful in seeing that his disciples escape corruption. In sealed-off, sectarian Christian communities these passages are interpreted quite literally. Where, however, the close proximity of believing Christians to all the forces that constitute the world— success, money, a surplus of consumer goods—is accepted as normal, it is strength to know that God governs such forces and is not governed by them. No more need the creature be.

John 17:1–26

The lectionaries use chapter 17 in its entirety by dividing it into three parts and reading it in successive years on the Seventh Sunday of Easter, which precedes Pentecost; thus, Year A (1) uses 1–11, Year B (2) uses 11–19, Year C (3), has 20–26.

In a very influential modern book about this chapter we read: "The speaker is not a needy petitioner but the divine revealer and therefore the prayer moves over into being an address, admonition, consolation, and prophecy" (Ernst Käsemann, p. 5).

The supper-table discourse may be considered as ended here or not, as the "high-priestly prayer" of Jesus is taken to be a part of it or a fresh start because of its direct-address form. It is a proclamation and a thanksgiving (like the *berakah* of 11:41–42), not a petition. The proper place of chapter 17 in the Gospel has been argued (between 13:30 and 31 is Bultmann's suggesting for its primitive occurrence), but it recapitulates enough elements of the three previous chapters that it may well have started out in this place. A prayer to sum up a presentation, moreover, has a vigorous history in both biblical-Jewish and pagan worlds.

There is no mention of the Counselor in this chapter, only of the Father-Son relation. This may be owing to the confinement of that figure of consolation to the last days. The Father rather than the Spirit is asked to sanctify Jesus' friends in truth (v. 17). This may be highly oblique reference to the Spirit of truth, through whose offices above we should have expected it to be done. Jesus prays to his Father in this chapter as a real suppliant if not a needy one (see vv. 9, 11*b*, 15, 20). Yet his subordinate position is unique. What other utterer of a prayer has asked for an exchange of glory with God as if on equal terms with him (vv. 1, 5) or claimed authority over all humanity and the power to give the life of the final age (v. 2)? Who else has described himself as having "come from God" (v. 8*c*)?

The prayer is, in the last analysis, a plea for unity among believers. The paradigm proposed for this is the way in which the Father is in Jesus and Jesus is in the Father (v. 21). If disciples are at one in this fashion, this should provide a motive for the world's belief (v. 21). John's Gospel views "the world" so poorly that nothing less than the marvel of the unanimity of Jesus' followers could achieve its conversion. Jesus has revealed God's name to the ones God has given him out of this world (see vv. 6, 26). Jesus has also given them the glory he was given by the Father (v. 22)—evidently in sufficient measure to bring

196

them into unity, for greater glory lies in store later "with me where I am" (v. 24).

It is no more clear here than elsewhere whether the "glory" of the Fourth Gospel is godhead itself or a property of godhead or a gift transmissible from the divine to the human as a result of obedience. Is "glory" a proclamation of the greatness of the Creator by the creature or is it all of the above? Whatever the case, Johannine glory is based on a remarkable reciprocity between Father and Son except when it comes to mission. The Son never sends the Father and the Spirit-Paraclete does not send anyone. There also seems to be an interpenetration of the divine and the human: Creatures are "in" God as the Father and Son are "in" each other. Yet the hearer or reader is never tempted to equate the human possessor of everlasting life, defined as one who knows God and Jesus Christ (v. 3), with Jesus as the possessor and giver of that life. In a word, Jesus stays on the God side of the drama in a remarkable way, even while he prays as a man pleading for fellow humans. But the latter must mean that he never deserts the human side.

The prayer of chapter 17 calls on God to make a holy people of believers in God through Jesus. They are to be spared the world's corruptions, even while not withdrawing from the world in any gnostic way. Jesus expects the world to be a better place for his having been there, and his disciples' too. He has been on assignment below, as it were, and means to keep his influence strong after his necessary departure. The task is no less than the sanctification of the world through the sanctification of Jesus' disciples—a work which is chiefly his but is to be carried on equally by the Spirit's momentum. The latter concept, we repeat, does not occur in chapter 17, but nothing in the prayer of Jesus negates its presence in chapters 14—16.

The prayer of verses 1–11*b* supposes that the Son has been given authority over all humanity so that all whom the Father gave him may be given eternal life (v. 2). Who is being prayed for here? Is it the human race of all time or the believers of divine election? Early tradition opted to retain the ambiguity: not only those who would be saved but everyone in the world in need of the divine gift of the Father. Knowledge of the only true God (v. 3) and the words *(ta rhemata)* of Jesus which he faithfully passed on (v. 8) are identical in this prayer. The disciples referred to have kept Jesus' word *(ton logon sou,* v. 6)

197

because they recognized his origin from God (vv. 7, 8). These believers are the chief beneficiaries of Jesus' prayer—God's elect who are his (v. 9) and who are in the world as Jesus comes to the Father (v. 11*a*). The prayer is uttered, therefore, for the members of the believing community. But "all flesh" (*pases sarkos*, v. 2), even the "world" (v. 9) excluded from the prayer, are called to become members of this company.

As the prayer continues in verses 11*b*–19 Jesus tells the Father that he has protected the disciples with the Father's name which has been given him (v. 11*b*); he asks that divine guardianship from the evil one may continue (v. 15). The disciples, those believers who are no more "of the world" than Jesus is (v. 16), require continued sanctification in truth and Jesus asks for it (vv. 17–19). Up until now the prayer has been for those of Johannine faith. It is couched in the most familiar words of petition to any divinity, equivalently, "O *our* God, look especially upon *us*".

Verses 20–26 represent a branching out from the disciples of John's acquaintance to those who would come to believe through their evangelizing efforts. John cannot possibly have Jesus pray for all who believe in him, "each in his own way," as the modern phrase has it. Such latitude would be incomprehensible to John. He looks for unity of belief in Jesus' words as he sees it. A variety of Christologies he both knows and deplores. A variety of churches he could have no part or lot with. John's only prayer is for unity in God and Christ as he conceives it, namely, in terms of right faith.

The prayer is prayed with increasing confidence by Christians to include all who believe in Jesus on any terms, indeed, anyone anywhere in the world. There was a time when it was prayed *against* other believers in what may have been a more authentically Johannine spirit. But now that it is realized how unfaithful to Jesus all believers are, John 17 is being prayed in a newer, humbler tone.

Do preachers regularly invite their congregants to anything like the high standard of John 17, which actually is 13—16 summed up? Whether they do or not, they should. It may not be done in a sectarian spirit, as if the preacher has "seen" and "known" the Father through Jesus quite as the Evangelist has and hence has a unique possession of the truth. This possession of eternal life should be preached, but in a state of awe that the

Evangelist and his company did so know God, and in hope that preacher and hearer may do the same.

It was a remarkable time in the history of one infant church, the Johannine, when a vision of the world as it might be and the history of one actual community came together. The congruence of the world believed in and the world lived in may already have passed by the time the Gospel was written. Its author wants believers to live in hope until the parousia, but knows that the only way to make any sense out of that strange concept of the final coming is to live it *now:* in an "everlasting life" of entertaining the Spirit as a guest, not unlike the "ongoing now" *(nunc fluens)* of the philosophers. Go with the flow, says the Evangelist. All the way to heaven is heaven because Jesus said, "I am the way."

The lengthy discourse of 13:31—17:26 could be the purest gnostic speculation if it were not for John's gift of keeping one foot firmly planted in history. A church that forgets either Johannine realism or Johannine otherworldliness will find itself off the way, into the mire on the right or left of the path.

It is literally worth one's life to be a member of a church like the Johannine church.

John 18—19
Jesus Apprehended, Questioned, Condemned

These two chapters are proposed for reading in their entirety on Good Friday in all three years by the Catholic and Common Lectionaries; in the Episcopal likewise, but ending at 19:37. Since this may discourage preaching in an otherwise lengthy service, the wiser choice is made by the Lutheran and Common, which allow substitution of 19:17–30 for the entire two chapters. There is so much of importance in John's passion and so much likely to be misunderstood that less reading and more exposition is the better formula for proclamation. Christians may not forget how Jewish populations in Europe cowered in fear behind locked doors on Good Friday because the passion of Saint John's Gospel was read in its entirety that day. Nowadays not many hear it in full and those who do are often the least likely to be governed by passion and prejudice. Still, they above all are most open to a careful exposition of the symbolic rather than historical character of chapters 18—19.

An attractive option in dealing with the narratives in this Gospel of Jesus' apprehension by authority, his Jewish hearing and Roman trial, and his crucifixion (chaps. 18—19) is to desert

199

the search for the symbolism that has prevailed in the Gospel until now and deal with the material historically as if this were its chief orientation. The lengthy trial and execution pericopes invite the preacher and teacher to such a treatment. Comparison with the Synoptics, especially Luke, reveals that here as elsewhere John is drawing on sources. The temptation to see a window on history in these two chapters is understandable. It may not be forgotten, however, that in the Fourth Gospel consistency reigns. The author does not desert the established pattern in favor of an uncharacteristic historicity, to return to his familiar symbolism in the risen life accounts. He is concerned without interruption with the religious meaning of events, not with the events themselves.

And so he reports on the challenges of Annas and Pilate to Jesus, not as one who possesses a transcript or chronicle but as one who wishes to go behind the scenes he portrays to plumb the meaning of this testifier to the truth (see 18:37). The same is true of his presentation of the three Marys and the beloved disciple at the cross, the soldiers' abstention from breaking Jesus' legs, and his elaborate burial by two male disciples. All is told either to illustrate the world's disinterest in the truth (see 18:38) or to show the fulfillment of Scripture (see 19:24, 36–37). The outcome of true discipleship is painted starkly in the portrayal of Jesus' "hour" (see 19:27).

John 18:1–12

The company of disciples led by Jesus leaves the supper room for the orchard across the Kidron Valley for a purpose that is not announced. John omits a picture of Jesus in desolation, even though he seems to know of the tradition (see 18:11c; 12:27), probably because it does not suit his purpose. His Jesus is sovereignly in charge of his own movements and will freely lay down his life (cf. 15:13).

> "My hand held no sword when I met their armed horde,
> And the conqueror fell down, and the Conquered bruised his
> pride."
> What is this unheard before, that the Unarmed makes war;
> And the Slain hath the gain, and the Victor hath the rout?
> What wars, then, are these, and what the enemies,
> Strange Chief, with the scars of Thy conquest trenched about?
> ("The Veteran of Heaven," Francis Thompson).

John must get Jesus to the traditional place of his arrest, even though he does not name it Gethsemane or the Mount of Olives. He does this by identifying it as a place which Judas knew, as did all the rest, through having frequented it in Jesus' company (v. 2). Judas "took" the cohort there—surely not the literal six hundred men of a regiment at full strength of three thousand but a small fraction—along with "some officers from the chief priests and the Pharisees" (v. 3).

The historicity of the account cannot be judged readily since the temple guard ("officers") probably used the vocabulary of the Roman army. Hence "band" ("cohort") and "captain" ("tribune," v. 12), are not sure indications of Roman army presence at this early stage. That ambiguity is probably John's intent, however, since he like the other evangelists has the Roman and Jewish power classes working together against Jesus. He does not sort out which is the initiator. Commentators consistently take stands on what alignments of power were likely or unlikely in the circumstances, yet no one can be sure of the collaborative efforts employed during the pilgrimage feasts. John's interest in historical detail may be minimal. We are also back to the problem of the alleged common cause of temple priests and Pharisees (v. 3; recall 1:19, 24) which many characterize as historically impossible.

A Jesus aware of all that would happen to him, typically Johannine, steps forward to ask who is wanted (v. 4). The tradition of Judas as betrayer is retained. Jesus asks twice whom they want and is told who, by name and town, twice (vv. 5, 7). He declares himself to be the one sought. The phrase he uses, *"Ego eimi"* (cf. 13:19) is the ordinary, "It is I," of Greek speech. The fact that his challengers fall backward to the ground (v. 6) at this disclosure makes us wonder, as before in John, whether the Evangelist has in mind the name by which the LORD described himself to Moses at the bush (Exod. 3:14, LXX) or the recurrent phrase "I am he" from Isaiah 43. John may mean by the soldiers' reaction that the answer itself was fraught with power or else that the person of Jesus has this intimidating effect upon his apprehenders.

True to the spirit of Jesus' saying that his disciples are to abide in him and bear much fruit (15:2–5), he asks the crowd to release "these" if they seek only him (v. 8). This confirms the intimation of verse 1 that all of Jesus' disciples have stayed with him in the garden and not the favored, closer three only. But

201

this is not uppermost in John's mind. He wants to make it clear that the force of Jesus' word continues, which said that none that the Father gave him had been lost (v. 9; cf. 6:39; 17:12).

The story of the blow that severed the ear of the high priest's unnamed slave occurs in the Synoptic tradition, but only John describes Simon Peter as having done it (v. 10). The Evangelist deals with it not as the occasion for a miraculous healing (cf. Luke 22:51) but as a potential interference with Jesus' resolve to drink the cup the Father has decreed for him. Jesus will not be interrupted (v. 11). The soldiery arrests and binds Jesus without giving a reason; they only establish his identity (incidentally, without Judas' kiss of betrayal). A charge will be formulated at 19:7.

John 18:13–27

The sequence of questions seems to go from Annas (v. 13) to Caiaphas (v. 24), but the mention of "the high priest" as the one who does the questioning before Jesus is brought to Caiaphas (v. 19) is a problem. The older man had held the office A.D. 6–15 and was succeeded by three unknowns as to name (including one of his sons) for a year or so, then his son-in-law Caiaphas in the years 18–36. Conceivably the older man, Hanan, who had long ago been deposed by the perfect Gratus, was still known as "the high priest," retaining his honorific title. John's interest in an inquiry by Jewish authority is, in any case, minimal. He may think that judgment has already been passed on Jesus from that quarter (cf. Harvey's theory, see commentary on 10:22–42) and know that the judgment of Pilate was ultimately decisive. He may, in fact, reintroduce Caiaphas chiefly to have him reiterate as high priest an unwitting prophecy about Jesus' vicarious death (v. 14; cf. 11:49–52) and report on two separate interviews to take care of Peter's threefold denial (cf. 13:38). Peter denies Jesus once to a woman gatekeeper in conjunction with the Annas appearance (v. 17) and twice to others, including slaves, in relation to Caiaphas (vv. 25, 27).

The Fourth Evangelist's main interest throughout is in figure and fulfillment. He gives evidence of reshaping historical traditions in support of that interest. Thus, the disciple "known to the high priest" (vv. 15, 16) may simply be introduced to get the unknown disciple and Peter into a strategic place for Peter's denials. The relation of the high priest's slave to the man who

202

lost his ear (v. 26) likewise smacks of embroidered detail to establish a tie among Jesus' captors. John shows no concern for a preliminary Annas hearing, then a subsequent fullscale Sanhedrin inquest under Caiaphas' leadership, which some have thrust upon him. He possesses traditional materials and uses them in the way we have become accustomed to.

Thus, whereas the chief priests and the whole council in the Synoptics try to get Jesus to claim to be the Christ or Son of God, and thus deliver himself into their hands, John settles for an inquiry about his disciples and his teaching (v. 19). That is what "the world" wishes to challenge (see 17:6–10). Jesus' innocuous response of verse 20 is a declaration of openness and innocence similar to statements in the other Gospels (cf. Mark 14:49 = Matt. 26:55*b* = Luke 22:53*a*). The Judean crowds in the temple area could easily testify to his teaching. John wishes to maintain here, as throughout, that popular animosity to Jesus' claims was a matter of public record. His had been no hole-and-corner existence but a verifiable public career (vv. 20–23). This appears to be a remark on the illegality of the proceedings but is John's way of underscoring the public character of the message Jesus had delivered from his Father. It brought resistance through its very clarity and availability. The reference is to the later response of believers in Jesus on trial for their faith, making of Jesus' complaint at being struck despite his innocence (v. 23) a legal point which the Evangelist places in the record. Abusive conduct is a response to the preaching of the gospel with which he is well familiar.

John 18:28–40

Here begins the extensive and important exchange between Jesus and Pilate (18:28—19:16). John concurs with the Synoptics that the Roman trial was an early morning affair and that Pilate was inclined in Jesus' favor throughout. Aside from the later detail about the Pavement where a judge's bench was situated (*Lithostroton;* in Hebrew *Gabbatha*—"hill"?—19:13), there is nothing in the Johannine account that could not have been derived from Mark—even though some students of the Gospel require a separate historical source like the one employed by Luke. Still, in distinguishing carefully between the meanings of kingship and authority as held by the followers of Jesus and by political power, John does a service which no

203

other evangelist renders. His contribution is theological, not historical.

Pilate was of an uncompromising nature and a bully (cf. Josephus, *War* II, 169–177; *Antiquities* XVIII, 55–62; 85–89). The softer picture of him which John shares with the Synoptics may result from early Christian attempts to gain concessions from the empire. The proclaimers of Jesus as Lord could not avoid mentioning his crucifixion, a punishment normally inflicted only by the Romans, which would identify him as condemned under capital sentence. What they could do, and appear to have done, is attenuate the imperial participation in the execution (which was total) and heighten the complicity of the priestly and the learned leadership. The latter, especially the priestly, could have been considerable, but John's deemphasis of the Roman activity goes far to render his account of the Jewish role suspect. The Gospel picture of a high priesthood getting a Roman prefect to do its will is certainly doubtful. Yet there is nothing to require that a Jewish power class should have had no interest in Jesus' elimination. Indeed, for political rather than religious reasons, the opposite would seem to have been true.

Nothing is said about Caiaphas' dealings with Jesus (but see 11:49–52). The latter is simply brought by "them" to the military headquarters *(praetorium),* the governor's temporary residence. Pilate lived permanently in another praetorium in the seacoast town of Caesarea and came to this one during the turbulence of pilgrimage feasts. A handsome stone flagging, complete with the tracks of iron wheels, has been found underneath the modern Convent of Our Lady of Zion on the Via Dolorosa and identified by some archaeologists as the *Gabbatha* of John. This has been disputed by others as the judgment site in favor of the still-standing Phasael tower of the palace of Herod ("David's Tower") near the Jaffa Gate.

When the Evangelist observes that Jesus' opponents were scrupulous about avoiding impurity while pressing for his death, he is almost certainly being ironical (v. 28). It is not clear from the Mishnaic tractate which speaks of ritual impurity (*Pesaḥim* 8, 9) just how it operated with regard to the Passover; but then the entire operation of laws on ritual cleanliness in Jesus' day is in doubt. Seemingly an impurity of seven days is in question here which would have made scrupulous observants put off eating the Passover for a month, not just a day-

204

long impurity that could have been terminated by a bath at sundown.

Pilate comes on the scene without introduction as if he were already a known personage. He was an imperial functionary of the equestrian order who served as prefect of Judea 27–36, under the senatorial legate to Syria. The exchange with Jesus has to be entirely the work of John, a reconstruction on the basis of the faith of the author and his knowledge of the judicial outcome. Pilate's first question is improbable and the people's response even more so (vv. 29–30). From the start, John clearly wants Jesus to be guilty of the death sentence according to Jewish law. As to whether the Jewish community of the time had the authority to kill by stoning (see v. 31)—one of its four traditional modes of execution—the experts are divided. Jean Juster, a Jewish scholar of France, concluded that they could (1914), Edwin Sherwin-White, an Englishman, that they could not (1963). There may have been a different practice between Jerusalem and the city where the Evangelist wrote. In any event, John explains that the ambiguous status of Jewish power meant for him that since Jesus "had to die" by being "lifted up from the earth" (3:14; cf. 12:32–33), crucifixion was required for the fulfillment of prophecy (v. 32). Numbers 21:8–9 tells the story of the healing serpent mounted on a pole. This prophetic image and not that of the Passover sacrifice—which included seven yearling lambs—is probably intended (see Num. 28:19).

No charge has yet been brought against Jesus, only the vague one that he is a "malefactor (evil doer, RSV)" (v. 30). In the dialogue that follows, the charge on which he in fact was condemned (see 19:19) surfaces: "Are you the king of Judea (v. 33; lit., the Judeans)?" Only the term "king of Israel" (1:49) has occurred thus far, when the whole people as a religious unity was meant. Here Pilate, whom Luke has correctly designated "governor [*praefectus*] of Judea" (cf. 3:1), is rightly exercised over a threat to his power. Galilee and Perea already had a Jewish king, the puppet Herod Antipas. Diaspora Jews accepted the name *"hoi Ioudaioi"* in place of "Israel" well before the New Testament period, but in Palestine "Israel" is virtually the only self-name of the people throughout the Mishnah (200 C. E.). In First Maccabees the leader *"ton Ioudaion"* means "of Judea" (13:42; 14:47; 15:1) whereas by Second Maccabees the usage has changed. Diodorus Siculus likewise calls the Hasmonean ruler Aristobolus king *"ton Ioudaion"* (*Lib. Hist.* XL, 2). "King of Israel" would have been a meaningless title on Jesus' cross, at least to the Romans. To them he was thought to pretend to the political title of King of Judea; hence Pilate's question.

Jesus parries with one of his own about the origin of the charge (v. 34) and Pilate is quick to dissociate himself from the people of the country to which he is assigned (v. 35). The Jesus matter is a Judean one from start to finish, an internal affair of "your own nation and the chief priests" as Pilate supposes. Jesus' Galilean status never comes up at the John trial. When Pilate presses to learn the political charge that Jesus' fellow Jews think him guilty of, he receives a theological response. Jesus' kingship is not of this world, it is of another place not "from here" (*enteuthen,* v. 36). That is why neither Pilate nor John's contemporaries should have been surprised that no political or military force was raised in support of Jesus and his claims. The words "king" (v. 37) and "kingship" (v. 36) touch on a different sphere than this world. The latter term *(basileia)* has been allowed as valid in 3:3, 5. Here it is given new meaning. It is the sphere of belief in him who came into the world to testify to the truth (v. 37). This belief is both a hearing and a heeding of Jesus' voice. Proclaiming the truth, being the truth (cf. 14:6) is what makes him a king. His dwelling is not in some far off land of Platonic exemplars. He comes from, and brings a knowledge of, a world that is real with the reality of God.

Pilate's famed question, "What is truth?" (v. 38) has been freighted with many meanings, including that of Francis Bacon's "jesting Pilate" who did not wait for an answer. A jest is the last thing John intended. He wishes it to bear a single meaning. Indeed, it answers itself. "Truth" is all that Pilate and the "world" which he inhabits is not. The Evangelist conducts no polemic against the power of the Empire such as is found in Revelation. He does not provide the raw material for anything like a church-state confrontation. What he presents is a pagan protagonist of unbelief to balance off his Judean ones who, because of their background, should have believed. Sympathetic Pilate may be in John, but a crypto-believer he is not. Although his personal portrait looms large, he is just another foil for the Evangelist's presentation of the true or genuine world of belief in God.

The questioning of Jesus is described as having taken place inside the praetorium (v. 33) after an initial appearance of Pilate (v. 29). Pilate goes out to the Judeans "again" (v. 38) and says he finds no case against Jesus. At this point John employs the Barabbas tradition and makes short work of it (vv. 39–40). It is found in Mark and is probably legendary; a "son of the Father" (*bar abbas,* not a known Hebrew name) who *is* guilty of sedition is set free in place of the true Son of the Father who is not. The Judeans "shout" to Pilate (v. 40; cf. 19:6) but they are never represented as a crowd, as in the Synoptics. John conceives of them as a small band of dedicated antagonists against all that Jesus stands for.

John 19:1–16

The chapter break is not a natural one. It was dictated in the thirteenth century by considerations of length more than sense. Sentence has not been passed, yet Jesus is scourged at Pilate's order (v. 1), then mocked as a king (vv. 2–3). John fits the details of Jesus' mockery in here although they come well after his sentence in the other accounts. The heart of the ridicule is Jesus' patently false claim to political rule (v. 3). Pilate comes out "again" (a third time; cf. 18:29, 38) and tells "them" that he is going to bring Jesus out "that you may know that I find no crime in him" (v. 4). Merely putting him on display, it is thought, will establish his innocence. Pilate then proclaims as "the man" that one in whom the believing readers of the Gospel have placed their trust. It is a remarkable declaration of faith by the Evangelist in the Word become man, this miserable human, this weak flesh. There is a passage in Zechariah 6 so suggestive of the present scene that one wonders if John could fail to have had it in mind:

> . . . go the same day to the house of [the exiles who have arrived from Babylon]. Take from them silver and gold, and make a crown, and set it upon the head of Joshua, the son of Jehozadak, the high priest; and say to him, "Thus says the LORD of hosts, Behold, the man *(LXX, idou aner)* whose name is the Branch: for he shall grow up in his place, and he shall build the temple of the LORD (vv. 10–12).

The passage had been written with a king in mind, Zerubbabel, but revised with reference to a priest whose name is given as

"Iesou" in the LXX. John designates Jesus a human being *(anthropos)*, not a male as in the Greek version of Zechariah.

The chief priests and the officers (the Pharisees of 18:3 have long since dropped out) then cry out for Jesus' crucifixion and, as in Matthew (27:24c), Pilate suggests that they crucify him (v. 6). Crucifixion by Jews was thoroughly repugnant but it seems to have happened in the Hasmonean period, notably the crucifixion of eight hundred Pharisees by Alexander Janneus (cf. Josephus, *War* I, 97f.; *Ant.* XIII, 380–83). Herod the Great evidently broke from this tradition, since not a single crucifixion is reported by Josephus from Herod's time. As John reports the suggestion of Pilate, it is probably a taunt meaning, "Take the responsibility for his death yourselves." It is then that the totally new idea of Jesus' death for making himself the Son of God rather than for sedition is introduced (v. 7). The law of "We have a law" is probably the prohibition of blaspheming the Name in Leviticus 24:16 which M. *Sanhedrin* (7, 5) spells out, saying that the blasphemer must pronounce the Name itself and be attested by witnesses to have done so. There is oblique mention of the sentence of death, and the judges are described as rending their garments which they may not later mend.

Interestingly, no religious charge was raised against Jesus before the high priest in John where it might have been expected. "Blasphemy" figures heavily in the night trial of Mark and its derivatives in Matthew and Luke. The last-named, however, omits mention of the term blasphemy (22:71) as if he knows that technically no such offense has occurred. John has reported extreme tensions between Jesus and fellow-Jews over speech-patterns of his that seem to the hearers to claim equality with God (see 5:18; 10:33, with blasphemy raised as a question by Jesus when he said that he was Son of God in 10:36). If the nature of the blasphemy is obscure in Mark and Matthew, it is slightly less so in John, but on terms not previously conceived. Here it describes the claim by a human to be so closely related to God that uttering the divine Name in that connection can be taken as blasphemous. Leviticus 24:11 makes clear that the capital offense is "blaspheming the Name, and cursing" (the verbs *killel* and *kavav* are roughly synonymous). It describes a formal attack on the LORD and has nothing to do with uttering the Name loosely, least of all merely vocalizing the word YHWH, against which practice the rabbis never invoked Leviti-

208

cus 24 on blasphemy. What we seem to have in John is the record of a late first-century Jewish classification of the Christian claims made for Jesus as "blasphemy," even though the offense does not coincide with the biblical one. The usage that survives in the Gospels (since no matching usage does in Jewish sources) is a piece of human behavior totally outside biblical categories.

Pilate enters the praetorium "again" (v. 9), presumably with Jesus. This is his third return to the shelter of the garrison where his conversations with Jesus have taken place (cf. 18:33). He will make a public appearance for the fourth and last time before he allows Jesus to be taken off (v. 13). Once inside he asks Jesus, with a studied Johannine ambiguity, where he comes from. This *pothen* (v. 9) is the ordinary adverb for "whence," similar to the *enteuthen* (hence) of 18:36, and is so used by John in a number of places, for example, to describe where the wine (2:9) or the wind (3:8) or the flowing water (4:11) has come from, or will. Here the reference is to Jesus' ultimate origins as in 8:14 (cf. 9:29–30). In a parallel place the Lukan narrative (at 23:6) has Pilate ask Jesus whether he is from Galilee. Once more John displays his skill at using traditional material to raise non-traditional questions. Jesus is silent (it does not happen often in John), but the question both answers itself for the reader and leads to an important exchange about authority (*exousia*, vv. 10–11). Pilate's power is said by Jesus to come "from above" (v. 11), hence the imperial edict to crucify him will somehow fall under the divine decree. More than that, Pilate's guilt is that of a tool of the real culprit, the one who did the handing over *(ho paradous)*. This is normally a word for Judas but here it could mean Satan or the opposition to Jesus whom Judas had served as an instrument. It is, in any case, part of the Johannine exculpation of Pilate.

The prefect grows even more desirous of freeing Jesus but the Judean antagonists remind him of the peril of his political status if he yields to such a temptation (v. 12). "Friend of Caesar" seems to have been a technical term in one word in Greek, although it is not used in this Gospel. Stung by the reminder that he has a case of an attack upon imperial dignity on his hands, Pilate brings Jesus outside for final disposition (v. 13). John reminds his readers that it is midday on the day of "preparation for the feast" (v. 14). Calling Jesus "your king" is heavy

209

sarcasm at the literal level, as if the charge were too absurd for anyone to take seriously, but is also a Johannine distancing between worldly power and those who acknowledge Jesus' rule. Pilate tries to enlist the sympathy of the chief priests. In a peculiarly Johannine twist they will have none of Jesus but declare their fealty to the Caesar (v. 15). Pilate weakly hands Jesus over "to them" for crucifixion (v. 16).

John 19:17–22

If John knows the story of Simon of Cyrene (Mark 15:21), he does not use it. Jesus carries the cross "by himself." John's description of the death of Jesus in one verse (18), like Luke's 23:33–34, is a masterpiece of restraint. Pilate has a "title" written (v. 19) and placed on the cross. It is the most complete title of the four in that it identifies Jesus by his town and has survived in Christian iconography probably for that reason. The "I.N. R.I." of Western art abbreviates the Vulgate translation of John's *títlos* in three languages. *"Iesus Nazarenus* [the Greek has *Nazoraios*] *Rex Iudaeorum.* Only John has the story of the attempt of the chief priests and the Judeans to get Pilate to change what he has written, perhaps because only John has them claim the Caesar as their king. The opponents of Jesus, having gone on record so strongly as loyal to the imperial cause, would look particularly foolish in having any association with this tatterdemalion King of Judea.

The ironical contrivance of the chief priests' asking Pilate to change the wording is the Evangelist's, of course, since the fact is lost to history—as it was probably lost to him—of what exact part the temple priesthood had in the Roman *processus.* The best we can say is that there lingered in the Christian memory the fact of collaboration. Pilate's response, in any case, like his query about truth, has passed into the literature of the West in its Vulgate form, *"Quod scripsi, scripsi,"* "What I have written I have written." It is a Christian version of the pagan proverbial saying, *"Scripta manent,"* "What is written remains."

By virtue of the disparate fourfold wording (hence no Gospel copied another), the inscription on the cross is thought by many to be an authentic historical reminiscence. In any case, what Pilate wrote in mockery remains.

210

John 19:23–30

Only John has the detail of the coat without seam (v. 23), although an indebtedness to the tale of the rending of the temple curtain (Matt. 27:51) may be conjectured. Only John cites the psalm verse (22:18) which the Synoptics hint at. Josephus describes the high priest's linen tunic similarly, but without the Gospel adjective "unstitched" (*Ant.* III, 161). It is doubtful that John wishes to make a priest of Jesus here except by a stroke of allusion. His interest in verse 24 is in the psalm which the other evangelists used so freely to describe the suffering Jesus, "They divide my garments among them and for my clothing they cast lots" (cf. v. 28 below, dependent on Ps. 22:16 but also 69:21).

The Synoptic tradition on the Galilean women of Jesus' band was that they were in Jerusalem for his death but stood "afar." John has three women—or four or two depending on how one punctuates—"standing by the cross." Of these, Jesus' mother is the one John uses for a typological purpose. Along with the "disciple whom he loved" the women stand near. The "woman" (cf. 2:4) is given over to her anonymous adoptive son and this son to his new mother. He takes her "to his own" (v. 27), a pregnant phrase because identical with that used by Jesus to describe the scattering of his disciples who would leave him quite alone (16:32), each going "to his own." Jesus as Word had, at the very outset, come *eis ta idia* and *hoi idioi* had not received him (1:11). Now a spiritual son reverses that tragic history and receives a mother from "the Son," to begin a community of believers in that only Son who speaks with power from the cross.

The final word but one spoken by Jesus, "I thirst" (v. 28), is reported as part of a traditional story. John alone has the spongeful of vinegar placed on hyssop rather than a reed, probably a bit of Passover symbolism out of Exodus 12:22. In instance after instance the historically probable yields to the symbolic in this Gospel. Jesus' last spoken utterance on tasting the vinegar or sour wine will be, "It is finished" (v. 30; cf. v. 28), not finished in the sense of over and done with but brought to consummation. His food had been to complete his Father's work (4:34). He had given God glory on earth by completing the

211

work God had given him to do (17:4). Now the completion of his task must be observed. He has shown his love for his friends "to the end" (13:1). Does he then "transmit the Spirit" to them in the phrase John has chosen to describe his dying (v. 30)? Probably not. That is deferred until the "Receive the Holy Spirit" of 20:22. What we have here is a peculiarly Johannine way of describing Jesus' death, a yielding up of his last breath. But, knowing him for the incurable player on words that he is—especially the word *pneuma* (cf. 3:8)—we would be unwise to say that he surely did not have the double meaning in mind.

John 19:31–42

John's final conveyance of truth by symbol in the crucifixion narrative is his account of the known custom of "leg-breaking" as the Romans called it, *crurifragium*. It was sometimes done as a cruelty but mostly as a mercy. It is thought to have hastened the death of those who had been suspended many hours or days, a cleat between their buttocks, by removing them from the cleat and thereby rendering the legs limp, bringing on the collapse of the organs in chest and abdomen.

We cannot know whether the fact that the morrow was the sabbath and a "high day" (v. 31; according to John, the Passover began with it) would have heightened the biblical prescription that a body hanging on a tree be taken down before nightfall (see Deut. 21:22–23). John is interested in the typology of the legs that were not broken and does not scruple at details. Often the families of criminals lost all rights to the disposition of the victims' bodies, so it is not as if the precepts of Deuteronomy were regularly observed. A subject people salvages such concessions as it can from its oppressors, whose soldiery frequently loathes the tasks it must do. In any case, Jesus was found upon inspection to be dead, says John. His relatively brief time on the cross is reported by all the evangelists as part of his voluntary expiration. John, above all, has insisted that no one takes his life from him, that he lays it down freely (10:18). The allegory of the unbroken legs would be impossible if Jesus were already dead, hence in no need of the hastening that the *crurifragium* brought. But it is to fulfill the precept about preparing the Passover lamb without breaking any of its bones (Num. 9:12)—coupled with the LORD's care for the just (Ps. 34:20)—that requires the omission of this custom in Jesus' case (v. 36).

A second text is quoted from Zechariah 12:10, which speaks of an unnamed sufferer thrust through by the very people who mourn him. In the original this is an indication of a blunder or an impetuous act immediately regretted. John is not interested in the biblical context, only the text. He gives it a new setting by applying it to Jesus. Whether grief was being expressed in the book of the prophet at the death of King Josiah is unimportant. The Evangelist only knew (like all the N. T. writers) that Jesus was being spoken of on every page of Scripture.

One important question remains. What does John mean to convey by the lance-thrust into Jesus' side that immediately drew blood and water? As a historical occurrence it is improbable, whether intended as an added fillip of cruelty or a *coup de grâce*. The incident is narrated, according to verse 35, in the interests of belief, not belief that it happened but in order to beget faith in another unseen reality. This much, at least, is meant: that the mixed stream which came forth from Jesus in death achieved life for believing humanity.

The life-giving properties of water are clear in this Gospel (see 3:5; cf. 4:14; 7:38; 13:5–10). Blood too, specifically Jesus' blood, is believed to give life (6:53–56). Could the one "who saw it" (v. 35) and who testifies to the unusual stream be someone who, privy to a marvel, has attributed religious significance to the event from earliest times? That is conceivable, but by now we know that John's "witnesses" are conveyors of the authentic religious tradition. Their testimony is that of faith, not of the senses.

We have been told by John that Jesus was put to death on Preparation Day, and from the references to Exodus 12 in verses 29 and 36 that he sees in Jesus a fulfillment of the type of the Passover lamb. The Mishnaic tractate *Pesaḥim* 5 tells of the slaughter of the Passover offering on the eve of the feast. The priests are to catch the beast's blood in basins of silver and gold, tossing it against the base of the altar. In *Pesaḥim* 5.8 the blood is spoken of as "mingled." In 5.5 fear is expressed lest the blood set down to rest might congeal. Is there any connection here with the sprinkling of sin-offering water (6.2)?

Oholoth ("Tents") 3.5 defines "mingled blood" as that which issued from a body while it was still alive and that which issued after the person was dead. Different positions are taken on the relative amount of each required to constitute it "mingled blood." Rabbi Eleazar bin Rabbi Judah says [of the before-

213

and-after components]: "These both alike are but as water. What counts as 'mingled blood'? If beneath a man that was crucified, whose blood gushes out, there was found a quarter-*log* of blood, it is unclean; but if beneath a corpse, whose blood drips out . . . this is clean." Rabbi Judah thinks that the opposite is true. John is in agreement with Rabbi Judah. He believes Jesus to be eminently clean or *kosher*. As a Johannine disciple will later write: ". . . the blood of Jesus his Son cleanses us from all sin" (I John 1:7).

Later patristic writers distinguished between water and blood as symbolic of baptism and the Eucharist. It scarcely seems that the Evangelist has any such symbolism in mind— only the "mingled blood" of the paschal lamb. Eastern iconography delights in showing priests catching blood in bowls from Jesus' side, while the West is familiar with a gushing, sevenfold stream to represent the sacraments.

The soldier of verse 34, meanwhile, has become St. Longinus ("The Spearman") for the life-giving stream which he initiated.

John's final vignette in his passion account, like so much else, could have come from Mark and been coupled with John's fruitful imagination. He makes Joseph of Arimathea a secret believer in Jesus from the ruling class in 12:42 and joins him to Nicodemus, whom he has already so identified (vv. 38–39; cf. 3:2, where the reason for his coming at night is not made explicit). Most bodies were left to rot on their crosses or plucked at as carrion by dogs and vultures. Not so this one, which is treated with spices in an exorbitant amount (to convey the wealth of the two men? the preciousness of Jesus body?). The two bury it in a new tomb in an orchard or cultivated place, seemingly in proximity to the place of execution, and in haste because of the oncoming sabbath sundown (vv. 41–42).

PREACHING ON THE JOHANNINE PASSION

Now that this lengthy segment of two chapters has been commented on, what is to be said of it as a whole? First, that when John conducts himself as a narrator of events without extensive development of their significance, he is as skilled literarily as any of the evangelists. He does not have Luke's stylistic smoothness, but he never misses the point as a Semitic story-teller, something Luke at times seems to do. If anything, John heightens the power of his brief narratives by his spare use

214

of words. In this part of his Gospel too he resembles Matthew with his formula-quotations: "This happened that the Scriptures might be fulfilled which says" (see 18:32; 19:24). The symbolism which heretofore has been covert becomes overt. Signs of one sort contributing to belief yield to signs of another sort, namely, explicitly biblical signs that this is indeed God's Son who must die in this way and in no other.

The preacher is well advised not to see in John a chronicler of the events of Jesus' last days. He is not that. He pits antagonists to Jesus from among the Jewish ruling classes against a Pilate who seems to be Jesus' protagonist. But this is not the point of the tale, and it would betray the narrative badly to read it in such simplistic fashion. Here, as throughout the Gospel, light and darkness, belief and unbelief, this world and those whom Jesus has called out of this world are in combat. There is no simple ethnic alignment reported, nor indeed a religious one in the ordinary sense. Those who were Jesus' "own" in his lifetime were all of them Jews. Some who "refuse to hear his voice" are likewise Jews. The gentile world scarcely appears here. When it does, in the person of Pilate and the soldiers, they do not represent paganism but only another power class. It is not in virtue of Pilate's and the Roman soldiers' connection with the Empire that is persecuting God's people, the Jews, that they are "of this world," but that in condemning and executing Jesus they are set against God. All of John's alignments are fresh ones: those who believe and those who fail to believe are measured by a new standard—Jesus. Yet John insists that it is identical with the old standard—namely all that Moses in the Torah foretold of him.

If John 18—19 are understood in depth, popular preachers will be robbed of many of their favorite conceits. Pilate's question about truth is unrelated to cynicism or skepticism. It has to do with one truth only, the *aletheia* that is God's deed in Jesus Christ. Similarly, ringing declamations of the evils of the power of the state over the church have no place here. What may fit in is the paradox (a construct of John) of an empire that is briefly sympathetic to Jesus' plight while religious leadership is unsympathetic to it. Such an application is a twentieth-century possibility, to be sure: a Jesus persecuted in his own church while civil authority at times arrives at more moral settlements. But identifying the Gospel elements of such a theme for modern use is risky, beginning with the false assumption that we possess in

215

the Fourth Gospel an account of the actual alignment of powers and of Pilate's conduct in Jesus' last days. Since we know that we do not have either, it is unwise to assume for preaching purposes that we do. It is important always to tell congregations or students that we are preaching and teaching from the parabolic narratives which the evangelists so artfully created.

What we have in John's Pilate story is a parable of the way "the world" is set against the Jesus in whom faith must be reposed. That this "world" of John's contrivance is partly Roman and partly Jewish is irrelevant to the preaching of the Gospel. The matter of consequence here is openness to the possibility of faith in Jesus. As John describes it, this faith is God's doing but it is not without a component of human responsibility. The refusal to believe is by all means presented as a conscious choice of darkness over the Light.

In modern preaching it must be made clear that historicity is not to the fore in the Fourth Gospel's passion account—beyond the indisputable fact that Jesus as a man of Jewish history was executed by the Romans. The spirit of faith and the spirit of this world remain the important considerations. "This world" of John can be realized in the culture, in political regimes, in the church. Any congregation of believers which faces the fact of this opposition can hope to be saved. But it needs to be guided carefully by a homilist who is consistently preaching on what the spirit of truth and the spirit of this world consist in. Good Friday, after the entire Pilate pericope has been read, may not be the best day to make this development. The paradoxical reason is that the graphic character of the story can lead both homilist and congregation astray. That is why it is better to choose a segment of it for public reading that does not give the appearance of historicity and let the antithesis between Jesus and "this world" come fully into the light.

There are thus good reasons for improving on the Common Lectionary option and preaching on a brief reading like 19:17–18, 23–30, whether at a eucharistic or other Good Friday service. This passage conveys the basic redemptive fact, with its stress on Jesus' deliberate choice of death as the consummation of his work. It includes the fidelity of the women disciples to the end, which may be the primitive recollection. And it transmits the spirit of faithful, uninterrupted discipleship (see 19:25) as represented by Jesus' mother and the disciple who "took her to his own home." The totality of chapters 18—19 should only be read in congregations where there is the leisure to develop much that is going on in this symbolic narrative. Otherwise, worshipers can easily come away with the impression of a Roman-Jewish antithesis which would leave their last state worse than the first. In an exposition of the narrative, the tragic possibility of *their* being Annas and Caiaphas and Pilate and Peter as "the world" can be brought home. The holy women and the disciple whom Jesus loved and the receivers of the testimony of "him who saw it" can equally be presented as their role models. Only a preacher who has studied the text carefully, meditated on it long, and worked hard at conveying a portion of its riches can do this. Those who are unwilling to submit themselves to this discipline can only present a soteriology of "enemies," thereby falling under Nietzsche's censure that Christianity is basically a religion of resentment.

PART FIVE

Easter and After

JOHN 20—21

John 20
Jesus Risen

The Catholic Lectionary proposes verses 1–9 on Easter in all three years. The Common offers a choice between verses 1–18 and a Matthew, Mark, or Luke pericope in successive years.

All Four Gospels in their canonical form contain appearance stories of the risen Christ. All tell of the discovery of the empty tomb. Close examination of these two types of narratives shows each to be independent of the other in origin. It cannot be established, in other words, that the appearance stories originated as a result of the tradition that the tomb was found empty or vice versa. Both kinds of accounts, in turn, are without clues as to their having come from the resurrection-kerygma of I Corinthians 15:3–7. Only Luke, of the Four Gospels, has a kerygmatic statement that relates to First Corinthians in any way: "The Lord has been truly raised and has appeared to Simon" (24:34, author's trans.). John E. Alsup in his study *The Post-Resurrection Appearance Stories of the Gospel Tradition* thinks that the risen-life narratives are not demonstrably antihistorical and that form and redaction-critical examination of them dispels the notion that they are late and legendary (in the sense of totally unhistorical). They do not seem to stem from the sermon summaries in Acts, hence they may be dated as early in their tradition-origins as the time in which the Hellenist-Palestinian communities that composed them were able to absorb them. Since the choice of expression in the narratives makes it impossible to understand them correctly outside the context of that choice—namely, as told in the manner of the anthropomorphic theophany stories of Genesis 18; Exodus 3—4; Judges 6 and 13; I Samuel 3; Tobit 5, 12; Testament of Abraham—"It would seem that the farthest point in the origins of the tradition to which we may reach back is the *Gattung* [literary type] itself which declared that the risen Lord encountered and re-established fellowship with his own and sent them out in his service" (p. 274). Exactly how early that was we cannot say. The above theory, it should be noted, goes contrary to the widely-held view of Dibelius that the appearance stories arose as illustrations of the Pauline-Jerusalem kergyma for preaching purposes.

John 20:1–18

John's first resurrection narrative combines an appearance to Mary Magdalene—who does not occur in any Synoptic story—with an empty-tomb account proper to him in which the beloved disciple is featured (vv. 1–18). Verses 14–18 are the bridge which provides a transition between tomb and appearance, somewhat as Matthew 28:9–10 unite them. The Evangelist uses the familiar terminology of "seeing" and "believing," in this case to commend the disciple whom Jesus loved for believing, presumably in Christ risen upon seeing the empty tomb (v. 8). This puts that disciple ahead of Peter and the others, certainly above Thomas, who asks for evidence of the senses before he will believe (vv. 24–29). Mary Magdalene sees Jesus but she does not "see" him, that is, with the eyes of faith, until he discloses himself to her (vv. 14–16). Also to be found in the narrative are the Johannine themes of the ascent of Jesus to the Father (v. 17) and the disciples' incomprehension of the biblical message, in this case that Jesus had to "rise from the dead" (v. 9; cf. 2:22; 7:39; 10:6).

Why John chooses to mute the glory of the resurrected Jesus is a puzzle. For example, a special self-disclosure is necessary before the Magdalene, having first heard his voice, recognizes him (v. 16). She saw two heavenly messengers in dazzling robes (v. 12) but presumably not the Lord himself in any such guise of glory. The same holds for Jesus' mysterious reticence in forbidding her to continue to cling to him (v. 17). It may be that, since for John Jesus' true glory consists in his being lifted up from the earth in crucifixion, the glory of the risen appearances is anticlimactic. More convincing is the theory that this

220

portion of Jesus' earthly time is a transition from his historical existence to his heavenly glorification, hence in the nature of the case an ambiguous interval: a kind of glory but not his ultimate glory. Jesus has promised in his supper discourse to come to his disciples, but he has not yet come in the sense promised.

Early in the morning of "the first day of the week" (v. 1) would be our Sunday before dawn. It would not be very early in the Jewish day, however, which had begun at sundown the evening before. Mary the Magdalene is identified again (cf. 19:25) by her village on the west shore of the Sea of Tiberias. Magdala was called Taricheae by Josephus, meaning "salted [fish]." In the Talmud it has the fuller name Migdal Nunaiya, "fish tower." It is still there to be visited—a beach area full of recreational vehicles and bathers at the foot of gently rising Mount Arbel. There is no satisfactory explanation for the absence of Mary the mother of Jesus from the narratives about women going to the tomb. Christian piety of the patristic age (first in a poem of Sedulius, *Carmen Paschale, ca.* 392) settled for an unrecorded first appearance of Jesus to his mother, on the supposition that it could not have been otherwise. As to the visit of Mary Magdalene alone, we can only say that John possessed or modified a tradition to this effect. The Marcan story of the three Marys or the Matthean version of the two may be that tradition.

The stone before the sepulchre here makes its first appearance in this Gospel. Its removal is hinted at as mysterious (v. 1). "Simon Peter" (v. 2) is a frequent form of the name in this Gospel (1:40; 6:8, 68; 13:6, 9, 24; 18:10) but see 1:42 for *Kephas.* Mary rushed toward him and the other disciple, the one Jesus loved (v. 2), to share her discovery. Peter when last heard from had been denying that he was one of Jesus' disciples (18:27), but the one whom Jesus loved was described as standing near the cross (19:26). Mary tells them of her suspicion that the grave has been robbed, a common crime of the time. She describes Jesus by the honorific title "Lord." This designation has occurred before to describe Jesus in the third person (6:23; 13:13) and often as a form of address (6:34; 11:3; and trans. "sir" at 4:11; 12:21), but here it seems to connote his new status as the risen one.

Mary has not actually seen the empty tomb, only made a deduction from the removal of the stone (v. 1). Hence the be-

221

loved disciple is the first one actually to arrive at it (v. 4) and the first to peer in (v. 5). Everything about this tale of the two hastening disciples indicates a primacy of the unnamed one, who nonetheless defers to Peter (v. 6). It is hard to know how the Evangelist conceives Jesus' getting free of the grave clothes, that is, whether he wishes to portray him as miraculously leaving them behind, as in his appearance through closed doors, or merely to suggest that the body was not stolen fully swathed. In any event, Peter who gets the first and best view of the interior of the tomb (vv. 6–7) does not believe in the resurrection of Jesus by that fact. The beloved disciple does (v. 8). The vignette is abruptly over. It is, however, linked to an appearance of Jesus to the Magdalene as the disciples retrace their steps (v. 10).

The fact that there is no contact whatever between the men and the women at the tomb suggests that two narratives have been joined. Although stricken with grief, Mary too peers inside and sees two luminous angels, presumably in the antechamber where Jesus' body had lain before final entombment preparations after the sabbath. They address her as Jesus has twice addressed his mother, "Woman" (2:4; 19:26). She gives as the reason for her grief the disappearance of the body of her friend Jesus and is immediately caught up in the Johannine technique of coming to understand through an initial failure to do so.

She first supposes that the person she "turns round" to speak to (v. 14) is the custodian of the property (v. 15), addressing him as "Sir" *(kyrie)*. Her remark is not terribly lucid, beginning with the inquiry as to whether he is the thief and ending in the offer to carry off the heavy corpse herself. But she is not supposed to make sense, any more than any poser of a Johannine question is. She is meant to recognize the sound of the master's voice when he calls her by name (cf. 10:3). Mary addresses him in a slightly different form than the "Rabbi" of 1:39 but John translates both in the same way, "Teacher." The Semitic words mean something closer to "My great one," but he is the teacher of the way to God for her, as he is for so many.

We assume that she grasps him in embrace, for his negative imperative translates into something like, "Let go of me" (RSV, "Do not hold me"), not the prohibition, "Do not touch me." The latter is enshrined in the Vulgate phrase, *"Noli me tangere,"* which connotes that there has been as yet no bodily contact.

222

John's meaning is that the close bond between disciple and teacher cannot be resumed on the old terms. Jesus must proceed to his glorification by ascending to his Father (who is her God and Father too, made such by the bond of belief in Christ risen). Precisely this is what she must report to the company of believers-to-be, "my brethren" (v. 17). Jesus' stay is but an interim from an earthly standpoint, even though his final glory at the Father's side has been achieved.

Her report to the disciples, "I have seen the Lord," had as one result the interesting fact that the Roman Mass rite of pre-Vatican II days recited the creed on her feast day (July 22) by analogy with apostles and evangelists. This liturgical custom acknowledges the priority of a woman as first herald of the Gospel, something of which I Corinthians 15:5–7 does not know. The Lukan tradition retains it with "Mary Magdalene and Joanna and Mary the mother of James and the other women with them" who told all this to the apostles [to the eleven and to all the rest, v. 9] (Luke 24:9–10).

John 20:19–31

The four lectionaries employ verses 19–31 on the Second Sunday of Easter in all three years.

The Gospel according to John clearly ended at 20:31 in the form in which it had been before the final revision we possess. The last two incidents in this chapter happen one week apart, the first on the evening of the day Jesus rose from the dead (v. 19), the second a week later (v. 26). The appearance to the disciples, whom Paul's traditional kerygma speaks of as "to Cephas, then to the twelve" (I Cor. 15:5), is described in John as if it might once have been the final sign in a book of signs (cf. v. 30). Its closest parallel in the Synoptics is the narrative of Jesus' appearance in the midst of his friends in Luke 24:36–49, which is likewise told as if it happened on the evening of the day he was raised from the dead. In Luke the assembled group is "the eleven gathered together and those who were with them" (24:33). There is no indication of the size of the group in John.

The doors of the place where the disciples were assembled were "closed," not locked, but since this is described as a precaution taken in fear of Judean antagonism the difference is insignificant. The Evangelist seems to wish to point up the paradox of a risen Christ who can appear at will without regard to physical hindrance, while establishing at the same time the reality of his bodily risenness. On any reckoning, this Gospel is anti-docetist. Luke has Jesus deny in so many words that he is a ghost (24:37–39). In John the net effect is the same.

P. Seidensticker in a 1967 study, "The Resurrection of Jesus in the Kerygma of the Gospels," holds that there was a single Easter experience of the risen Christ by "more than 500 brethren, once and for all" which took form, variously, as the group appearance stories of Matthew 28, Luke 24, and John 20. He may be right. The question as it reaches us here is, Does John present a scene with a large ("the disciples," v. 19) or a small group ("Thomas, one of the twelve," v. 24, "the twelve" being a phrase found previously only at 6:67, 70, 71)? It is impossible to say from the data John provides. The smaller number would serve as representatives in a commission to the whole community (vv. 21–23), but we cannot know whether this is intended. Jesus appears in the midst of the company that can assemble in one dwelling. There he wishes them "Peace" (v. 19; again at 21, 26). It is no longer a conventional greeting by the time the Gospel is written but one laden with community significance (cf. 14:27; 16:33). The disciples rejoice at seeing him (v. 20), as he had predicted would be the case after brief separation (cf. 16:20, 22).

Jesus' display of his wounded side is something we might have expected (v. 20; cf, 19:34), but there has as yet been no mention of wounded hands. "Nailprints" will occur in verse 25, the only time nails are spoken of in any of the Gospels. Because lashing with ropes or leather thongs was the usual means of affixing a victim to the stake, this detail is thought to be late and perhaps influenced by the account of the spear-thrust. The significant point, of course, is that the very person who was crucified is risen.

There are two verbs for "sending" which seem to be used indiscriminately in John. In verse 21 both appear without apparent distinction. The Father is described as sending the Son and Jesus is described as sending the Counselor or the disciples numerous times in this Gospel. Verse 21 seems to resemble most closely 13:20 and 17:18. The word *apostolos* occurs once in John (13:16) but it does not have a technical sense, being generally a messenger who is sent by a sender. Here in verse 21 we have a solemn commissioning, not just the mission of disciples as spoken of before. The disciples must conduct themselves in perfect obedience "just as" the Son has done in being sent by the Father. This is the commission and constitution of the community of believers. The breath image of verse 22 is obviously patterned on the first creation of humanity (cf. Gen. 2:7; Wis. of Sol. 15:11). This is the beginning of the new life of believers in the risen Lord. The resurrection of Jesus, his appearances as glorified, and the giving of the gift of Spirit may all have been experienced as unitary in the community's earliest days. The separate stories will then have come later.

Jesus gives the gift of the Holy Spirit to make his followers a community in which forgiveness is firmly lodged (v. 23). As in the Matthean rabbinic binding-loosing texts (16:19 and 18:18 derived ultimately from the shutting and opening mandate given to Eliakim, master of the palace, in Isa. 22:22; cf. Rev. 3:7), there is the power to forgive and to withhold forgiveness. When Jesus declared, "Your sin remains" (9:41, author's trans.), he was making a statement of fact about the blind who would not see. The Spirit of truth would likewise pass correct judgments in the realm of sin and righteousness—in effect, judgments of condemnation—because those who resisted left the Spirit no choice (see 16:8–11). Jesus may be doing here what he does in Matthew 28:19 in holding out to his church the gift described there as baptism. By the Spirit's power Jesus is making his disciples corporately remitters of sin. Failure to receive such remission will come only when this is the sinners' choice.

The Thomas vignette is divided into two incidents which take place one week apart. This is not the only Gospel instance of the disciples' doubt about Jesus' resurrection (cf. Matt. 28:17; Luke 24:11, 25, 37, 41; Mark 16:14 is stitched from the above). Thomas, rather than being thought of as the sole or even an egregious doubter, should be considered the subject of John's dramatizing technique. He stands for a spirit that was abroad in the early community. The Evangelist makes Thomas a caricature in the specificity of his demands about touching the wounds (v. 25). Jesus accedes to the latter one week later (v. 27). John's intent is doubtless apologetic and tells us something of the doubts and denials voiced in his day. This situation of the assembly of the disciples on the first day of the week makes us

225

wonder whether the first day has emerged with any liturgical significance by the time the Gospel is written.

We are not told if Thomas accepted Jesus' invitation, only that he engaged in an outburst expressing faith (v. 28) and was challenged over believing through having seen (v. 29a). Those who do not see and yet believe are in a superior condition (v. 29b). Their lot is a happy one (see note on 13:17).

The exclamation of Thomas at looking on Christ risen is in the nominative case and each noun, "Lord" and "God," is prefixed by an article. The form of the vocative case could be the same. Whatever the case intended, Thomas is uttering a faith statement. Whether speaking to Jesus as his Lord and God or invoking divinity upon experiencing the epiphany of God in Jesus, he means to express the Johannine community's faith. The phrase could be an early creed, meant to balance off 1:1 at the end of chapter 20, in the form the Gospel had before chapter 21 was added. "Lord" and "God" were often coupled as the "YHWH Elohim" of the Hebrew Scriptures, not to speak of the "Dominus Deusque" of Roman inscriptions attributing deity to emperors. Here the conjunction of the two nouns is probably the result of reflection in the Johannine community on Jesus' cultic status as human Lord of the faith community and fully divine figure who is believed in as "God the only Son" (1:18). The one who has been raised up from the dead is the fully human being to whom divine honors are being paid—perhaps on the first day of the week in the assembly of believers "who have not seen."

The Gospel closes, in its earlier form, with a statement of the author's purpose. The signs were recorded to nourish faith, a faith that gives life (v. 31). The titles of Jesus considered to be significant at the end of the Gospel are worth noting. He is "the Son of God." One might also have expected the designation "Son of man" that is so important for John in its uniquely non-eschatological sense, but perhaps this is subsumed under "the Christ." In any case, faith is not thought to be a possibility apart from the witness of the earliest community which John was obliged to transmit. He does not report signs in any grudging sense, as if there should have been faith without them on the basis of Jesus' words alone. There is just a touch of regret that the stories recounted for the confirmation of faith might have become a refuge, even a substitute for faith. That would have pained the Evangelist deeply.

226

PREACHING ON MARY MAGDALENE AND THOMAS

As to the preacher's pulpit performance regarding the resurrection narratives of chapter 20, there should be neither a bullying of Thomas nor a setting of the Magdalene on a pedestal of faith. Both are used by the Evangelist to convey pictorially states of mind with regard to the risen Lord. The wide range of faith positions regarding Jesus are of great interest and importance to the believer. Dealing with the New Testament texts literally is a little too easy and it misses John's point besides. There may be a strong temptation to go the route of apologetics exclusively: proving to congregations that the risen One is the crucified Jesus, demonstrating that Jesus cannot be clung to humanly in his now glorified state, establishing that he must be believed in as divine because he has risen from the dead. Nothing works quite that way, of course, in matters of faith. That is not to say that there cannot be intelligent argument in religion or an apologia which shows that it is not unintelligent to believe. But belief itself comes from another source than evidence. It is a gift of God.

John knows this well. He is betrayed if his clear perception of the fact that it is a gift is missed. Regarding faith, John is a "hard-liner" by a modern standard. He thinks that those who do not believe, once faced with the reality of the risen Christ, must be in bad faith because they have had the grace of God held out to them. The evangelist John is not a modern man. He is, at the same time, a very modern one when it comes to reporting psychological states, rationalizations, nuances. He may praise Jesus for knowing uniquely "what was in man," but he has a few excellent insights himself. These must be extracted with care, pondered deeply, and shared with believers.

Chapter 20 does not, cannot disclose the mysterious revelation embodied in Jesus' resurrection from the dead. It hints at it in the most marvelously allusive way. In doing so it is a strong aid to belief in this central mystery of faith.

John 21
An Editor's Appendix

227

Chapter 21 is rightly considered to be an appendix to chapters 1—20 written by another hand. Not only are there major differences in vocabulary and style but this is obviously an added account of the relation between Peter and the disciple whom Jesus loved, written when both are dead. It could not well have been worked into the narrative any earlier.

John 21:1–14

In Year C (3) on the Third Sunday of Easter verses 1–14 are read in the Lutheran, Catholic, and Episcopal Lectionaries.

The initial story of the miraculous catch of fish (vv. 1–11) is a problem. No doubt it testifies to a tradition known from the Synoptics of appearances of the risen Christ in Galilee (cf. Matt. 28:16–20; Mark 14:28; 16:7). It is also so close to the story of a similar catch in Luke that the question of mutual dependence or dependence on a common source arises. Verses 1–14 contain an account of a miraculous catch joined awkwardly to one of Jesus feeding the disciples with fish and bread which he has already prepared (vv. 9–10, 12–13). This resembles what Luke does in two separate places, 5:1–11 and 24:41–43. In the first Lukan account, however, Simon the catcher of human beings is the only important figure besides Jesus (vv. 4–10). Two other disciples are named and others are alluded to (v. 10), but they are of no consequence. Jesus is accompanied in chapter 21 by Simon Peter and six others whose names follow his (v. 2, the last two, "two others of his disciples"). This is the closest the Fourth Gospel comes to the Synoptic tradition of naming Peter first in a list of the Twelve. Jesus calls them *"lads,"* (*paidia;* v. 5), not the usage of chapters 1—20 but found in First John twice.

Simon Peter takes the initiative in the fishing operation in this Johannine addendum (vv. 3, 11). The exact significance of the catch of a hundred and fifty-three fish is not spelled out. We are left to deduce that it stands for all in the believing community. (It may derive from Ezek. 47:10, where a river filled with fish, like those of the Mediterranean, flows from the temple; and the place name [En-]eglaim yields a total of 153 if the customary numbers are assigned to Hebrew letters.)

This narrative appears to be thoroughly Peter-centered, but the detail should not be missed that the disciple whom Jesus loved recognized Jesus first, using a possible creedal formula, "It is the Lord" (v. 7). He then told Peter, the man of action. The conflict of Jesus' having fish already on the fire and his asking for more from the immense catch (v. 10), which he seemingly foreknew (v. 6), is not resolved. Hence there is the suspicion of a seam at verse 9 introducing the distinct story of 9–14, into which verses 10–11 have been inserted from the tale of the miraculous catch. The echo of the multiplication of bread and fish narrated earlier in this Gospel (6:11) is unmistakable.

Much more mysterious, of course, is the placing of this chapter here at all. The disciples are back at their old trade without any indication of how the Judean events have changed their lives and why they are back in Galilee. They do not at first recognize Jesus (v. 4), and they act as if he had not given them a solemn charge (cf. 20:21–23)—even though all this supposedly happened "after these occurrences" (v. 1). The mystery is somewhat dispelled when we learn that the setting at the lakeshore is not essential to the main point of the chapter. The final redactor who wrote chapter 21 possesses a traditional narrative and decides to use it. But he does so in subordination to his account of how Peter and the beloved disciple (whom he has inserted into the narrative at v. 7 and perhaps v. 2) end their respective careers. Their relationship has evidently been a matter of concern for the community and its first evangelist, the author of the unedited chapters 1—20. The redactor thinks he has some new information on the problem—so important that a supplement is required.

It is not clear to all who study the Fourth Gospel minutely whether this editor is thoroughly sympathetic to the Evangelist's positions or sets himself to correct them. Both could be the case if he thinks he possesses new insights. The obvious difficulty throughout consists in identifying the redacted material. There are twenty-eight words used in chapter 21, for example, that have not previously occurred in the Gospel and a number of uncharacteristic constructions. These do not supply the necessary verbal clues, being by definition not found in chapters 1—20. This leaves the problem of identifying redacted pericopes as one of content. When a passage is clearly retouched it is easy to identify (e.g., 4:2; 6:71). Failing to discover stylistic or vocabulary indications, scholars fall back to what they think the original evangelist could not have written consistent with himself. This often proves to be what they would not have written. Bultmann's aversion to anything redolent of sacraments as distinct from—he might say as contrasted to—faith is an example

229

of the redactive procedure practiced by moderns. We shall indicate below how chapter 21 may depart from the spirit of 1—20.

Knowing of the two appearances of Jesus to his disciples one week apart in chapter 20, the author of chapter 21 identifies the meal at the Sea of Tiberias as the third time Jesus was made manifest as risen from the dead (v. 14). It bears the earmarks, however, of a first appearance.

John 21:15-23

In Year C (3) on the Third Sunday of Easter a choice between verses 1–19 or 15–19 is offered in the Common Lectionary.

Jesus' exchange with Simon Peter (vv. 15–23) is given here for a twofold purpose: to confirm his importance in the community as a great lover of the Lord who has responsibilities to match and to describe his death as no surprise but something foreknown by Jesus. Two verbs are used in this colloquy for "love" and "feed" and two nouns for "sheep." No nuance appears to be indicated, merely diversity in word use. The threefold question and answer could easily correspond to Peter's threefold denial of Jesus during the hearing (18:17, 25–27). It is impossible to prove this but equally pointless to deny it.

"More than these" (v. 15) has a strange history in internal Christian polemic. People concerned not to rank Peter too high in the early church have been at pains to show that the question could mean "more than you love these others," a fairly meaningless question in the context, or "more than you love these possessions," that is, the equipment of your fishing trade. The latter makes a wild kind of sense, but Jesus is probably asking the more obvious question: "Do you love me more than these others do?" Upon Peter's thrice-repeated and intense response (he was "grieved" by the question, v. 17), Jesus tells him to shepherd his sheep (cf. 10:1–16, 26; Acts 20:28; I Peter 5:2–4). We must conclude that some elements in the Johannine community have questioned Peter's primacy and the writer wishes to affirm it. Some think that he may be doing it more vigorously than the author of chapters 1—20 would like. Yet in verses 20–23 a proper balance is struck. Meantime, verse 18 is a solemn prediction by Jesus that Peter in his maturity will lose the freedom of youth and be lashed or bound in the manner of those crucified (see commentary on 20:25). "Stretch out your

230

hands" is a technical term in the crucifixion process. The phrase "by what death" (v. 19*a*) is the one used in Jesus' case (12:33); both are the editorial comments of the Johannine authors. To die obediently is to give glory to God.

The center of gravity in this chapter is verse 19*b*. If verse 18 is an early piece of evidence for Peter's death by crucifixion, hence a special reason for the community to honor him, the half-verse of instruction Jesus gives him sets him solidly in the framework of discipleship. From the first days, to be Jesus' disciple was to "follow" him (cf. 1:37). This assured a person of being with Jesus and being honored by the Father (12:26). Following Jesus later was to become a possibility which it was not "now" (13:36). In the view of the author of verse 19*b* that "now" has come. Peter was to follow Jesus in discipleship in a way he never dreamed. It would end in the witness of the martyrdom of blood, but that is not identified as being the essence of following Jesus.

Peter then looked at the disciple whom Jesus loved—identified here as the man at the supper of 13:35—and found him "following" (v. 20). Once again Simon the son of John is upstaged by his nemesis, the man beloved, who always gets there first. The disclosure that this one is the follower *par excellence* is the main message of the chapter. Curiosity had evidently grown widespread over the fate of the person so well known as the one loved by Jesus. Chapter 21 puts in the mouth of Peter the question which the whole community had come to ask: "Lord, what about him?" (v. 21*b*). How will he end? What is God's plan for him? Jesus resolves the speculation by answering cryptically (vv. 22*ab*). What comes through is that the beloved disciple's ultimate outcome is God's business and not a human affair. Being a follower is every disciple's affair, not just Peter's (cf. v. 22*c*).

Verse 23 then discloses what the whole hypothetical conversation between Peter and Jesus was about. There had been talk regarding which of the two disciples was greater, what God had in store for Peter, and how the disciple whom Jesus loved would probably be spared death. Loose talk, all of it, says the author in a chapter written to set the record straight, probably after the death of the two. There was a saying of Jesus abroad which hinted that the beloved would be kept alive until the *parousia*. A fruitful imagination must have coined this guess. The author of chapter 21 has Jesus say, in effect: "What if I did

231

say it? That is my business. You have more important things to do than speculate. Follow me."

John 21:24-25

Having made a valid point, the author (authors? "we know," v. 24) then engages in overkill. He (or they) identifies the beloved disciple as both a witness to these things and the one who wrote them down. Witness he surely was, but not likely the composing author of chapters 1—20. The verb "wrote" probably means "stood behind what is written," "vouched for it." In any case, Peter's question "What about him?" is richly answered. He is the one who testifies in his own person to all that has gone before. The beloved disciple stands behind the Gospel in its entirety, much as the Righteous Teacher was the validating figure for the Qumran community and John the son of Zechariah was for all the baptizing sects that survived him. Verse 24 is an echo of 19:35 and is meant to be, just as verse 25 is a poor copy of 20:30–31. The testimony is true. It is provided so that you may believe.

The signs that Jesus worked were so many that a selection had to be made—lest the world be crowded to unlivability with the ledger of his deeds (v. 25).

PREACHING ON CHAPTER 21

There is a rich harvest for the pulpit in this final chapter, whoever may have written it. Chapter 21 poses squarely the problem of who are important before God in the work they do for the gospel. Congregations are much taken up with this problem. The clergy above all have it as a threat to their peace. The answer is a marvel of balance. Peter comes first in the quality of his love, the beloved disciple in his discipleship. But being a follower of Jesus—the call itself—is so important that the question of who happens to exercise it fades to insignificance. Some will die young, some will last for decades. Always the question will arise: "How did she qualify for that post? What lies behind his move to that congregation?" We forever want to know who gets what and why. Jesus' answer is that the lovers get the highest rewards—little tokens of his esteem like crucifixion or a long, hard life of service.

The great matter is to give the witness required: truthful, faithful witness. Not the lying witness of an inauthentic life but

232

the Jesus-like testimony of a career—long or short—that is *ale-thinos:* genuine, real. True with the truth of God.

The Fourth Gospel is so unrelievedly christological, not just Christ-centered, in its concerns and so censorious in its judgments that it has long served as an arsenal of dogmas and the encouragement of pathological Christian states. Not without reason did various gnosticisms look to it as their charter. They considered it intellectual, "spiritual," a thinking-man's Gospel (the gender specificity is conscious), and contemptuous of the carnal as they were. John has had a lot to overcome with the passing of the centuries.

Is there in it the concern for the poor which marks the Synoptic Gospels; the attention to the way the church or various churches are to be governed; the ethics of life's difficult choices? Absent, all of it, with heavy doses in its place of "truth" and "love" and "judgment" (meaning condemnation). John is a disciple of clear-cut black and white in a life where much is gray, even for the most devoted follower of Jesus. Of what earthly use can this Gospel be except to the most mindless Bible-thumping sectarian or the dedicated apostle of affectivity for whom "love" is a three-syllable word?

We answer with Paul: "Much and in every respect." The use of John's Gospel is above all *earthly* use. But its secrets are not yielded up lightly. It requires both belief and infinite painstaking *study.* John is a treasure of the church as a document of faith. It is betrayed if it is interpreted as a charter of complacent exclusiveness or an instrument of divine wrath. The Evangelist's profoundest hope is that he has written a book calculated to bring about belief in Jesus Christ in fuller measure. It must always be preached and taught in the church in that Johannine spirit.

Bibliography

1. For further study

BAMMEL, ERNST. "Jesus und der Paraklet in Johannes 16," *Christ and Spirit in the New Testament: Studies in Honor of C.F.D. Moule.* B. Lindars and S. S. Smalley, eds. (Cambridge: At the University Press, 1973), pp. 199–218.

BARRETT, CHARLES KINGSLEY. See section 2, Bibliography.

BOWMAN, JOHN. *The Fourth Gospel and the Jews: A Study in R. Akiba, Esther and the Gospel of John* (Pittsburgh: Pickwick Press, 1975).

BRAUN, F. M. See section 2, Bibliography.

BROWN, RAYMOND EDWARD, S.S. See section 2, Bibliography.

BULTMANN, RUDOLF. See section 2, Bibliography.

COLLINS, RAYMOND F. "Mary in the Fourth Gospel. A Decade of Johannine Studies," *Louvain Studies* 3:99–142 (1970).

CULLMANN, OSCAR. See section 2, Bibliography.

DODD, CHARLES HAROLD. See section 2, Bibliography.

DUKE, PAUL D. *Irony in the Fourth Gospel* (Atlanta: John Knox Press, 1985).

FORTNA, ROBERT T. "Theological Use of Locale in the Fourth Gospel," *Gospel Studies in Honor of Sherman E. Johnson.* Massey H. Shepherd, Jr. and E. C. Hobbs, eds. ANGLICAN THEOLOGICAL REVIEW SUPPLEMENTARY SERIES 3:58–95 (1974).

HAENCHEN, ERNST. *John,* translated by Robert W. Funk; Funk and Ulric Busse, eds. HERMENEIA (Philadelphia: Fortress Press, 1984).

KYSAR, ROBERT. *The Fourth Evangelist and His Gospel: An Examination of Contemporary Scholarship* (Minneapolis: Augsburg Press, 1975).

LINDARS, BARNABAS, S.S.F. See section 2, Bibliography.

MALATESTA, EDWARD. "Blood and Water from the Pierced Side of Christ (Jn. 19.34)," *Segni e Sacramenti nel Vangelo di Giovanni,* Pius Ramón Tragan, ed. STUDIA ANSELMIANA (Roma: Editrice Anselmiana, 1977).

MEEKS, WAYNE A. *The Prophet-King: Moses Traditions and the Johannine Christology.* SUPPLEMENTS TO NOVUM TESTAMENTUM 14 (Leiden: E. J. Brill, 1967).

———. " 'Am I a Jew'?—Johannine Christianity and Judaism," *Christianity, Judaism, and Other Greco-Roman Cults: Studies for Morton Smith.* Part One: New Testament, Jacob Neusner, ed. (Leiden: E. J. Brill, 1975), pp. 163–86.

———. "The Man from Heaven in Johannine Sectarianism," *Journal of Biblical Literature* 91:44–72 (1972).

MORRIS, LEON. *The Gospel according to John: The English Text with Introduction, Exposition and Notes.* THE NEW INTERNATIONAL COMMENTARY ON THE NEW TESTAMENT (Grand Rapids: Wm. B. Eerdmans Publishing Co., 1971).

ROBINSON, JOHN A. T. "The Use of the Fourth Gospel for Christology Today," *Christ and Spirit in the New Testament.* B. Lindars and S. S. Smalley, eds. (Cambridge: At the University Press, 1973), pp. 61–78.

SCHEIN, BRUCE E. *Following the Way: The Setting of John's Gospel* (Minneapolis: Augsburg Publishing House, 1980).

SCHNACKENBURG, RUDOLF. See section 2, Bibliography.

SLOYAN, GERARD S. "Recent Literature on the Trial Narratives of the Four Gospels," *Critical History and Biblical Faith: New Testament Perspectives.* HORIZONS, Thomas J. Ryan, ed. (Villanova, PA: The College Theology Society, 1979), pp. 136–76.

———. " 'Come, Lord Jesus': The View of the Post Resurrection Community," *Who Do People Say I Am?* F. A. Eigo, ed. (Villanova, PA: Villanova University Press, 1980), pp. 91–122.

SMITH, D. MOODY. *Johannine Christianity: Essays on Its Setting, Sources, and Theology* (Columbia: University of South Carolina Press, 1984).

———. *John.* PROCLAMATION COMMENTARIES, second edition (Philadelphia: Fortress Press, 1986).

2. Literature cited

ALSUP, JOHN. *The Post-Resurrection Appearance Stories of the Gospel Tradition* (Stuttgart: Calwer, 1975).

AMBROSE, SAINT. *On the Sacraments, Studies in Eucharistic Faith and Practice.* Henry Chadwick, ed. (London: A. R. Mowbray, 1960).

———. *On the Mysteries,* translated by T. Thompson-Srawley (London: S.P.C.K., 1950).

AUGUSTINE, SAINT. *Miscellanea Agostiniana.* TESTI E STUDI, 2 vols., (Rome: Tipografia Poliglotta Vaticana, 1930–31).

———. Sermon 9 (Guelf. VII) in Philip T. Weller, ed., *Selected Easter Sermons of Saint Augustine* (St. Louis: B. Herder, 1959).

BARRETT, CHARLES KINGSLEY. *The Gospel according to St. John: An Introduction with Commentary and Notes on the Greek Text,* second edition (Philadelphia: Westminster Press, 1978). First published 1955.

———. *The Gospel of John and Judaism,* translated from the German by D. M. Smith (Philadelphia: Fortress Press, 1975). First Published 1970.

BETTENSON, HENRY, ed. *Documents of the Christian Church,* second edition (London: Oxford University Press, 1963).

BORNKAMM, GUENTHER. "Die eucharistische Rede im Johannesevangelium," *Zeitschrift für die Neutestamentliche Wissenschaft,* 47:161–69 (1956).

BRAUN, F. M. *Jean le Théologian,* 3 vols. (Paris: J. Gabalda, 1959, 1964, 1966). See especially III, *Sa théologie: Le mystère de Jésus-Christ* (1966).

BROWN, RAYMOND EDWARD, S.S. *The Gospel according to John.* ANCHOR BIBLE 29 and 29A (Garden City, N.Y.: Doubleday, 1966, 1970).

————. *The Community of the Beloved Disciple* (New York: Paulist Press, 1979).

BULTMANN, RUDOLF. *The Gospel of John. A Commentary,* translated by Beasley-Murray, Hoare and Riches from the 1964 edition with the Supplement of 1966 (Philadelphia: Westminster Press, 1971).

CHESTERTON, GILBERT KEITH. *The Collected Poems* (New York: Dodd, Mead, 1932).

COMMON LECTIONARY: *The Lectionary Proposed by the Consultation on Common Texts* (New York: The Church Hymnal Corporation [800 Second Avenue], 1983). Foreword by Horace T. Allen, Jr.

CULLMANN, OSCAR. *The Johannine Circle,* translated by John Bowden (Philadelphia: Westminster Press, 1976). First published 1975.

CULPEPPER, R. ALAN. *Anatomy of the Fourth Gospel: A Study in Literary Design.* FOUNDATIONS AND FACETS (Philadelphia: Fortress Press, 1983).

CYRIL OF ALEXANDRIA, SAINT. *In Johannem Libri,* II, V (Migne Patrologia Graeca) 73, 337.

CYRIL OF JERUSALEM, SAINT. *Lectures on the Christian Sacraments: The Protocatechesis and the Five Mystical Catecheses.* F. L. Cross, ed. (London: S.P.C.K., 1951).

DEAD SEA SCROLLS IN ENGLISH, THE. Translated by Geza Vermes (with revisions; Baltimore: Penguin Books, 1968).

DIODORUS SICULUS. *Diodorus of Sicily,* translated by C. H. Oldfather, et al., 12 vols. LOEB CLASSICAL LIBRARY (Cambridge: Harvard University Press, 1961–83).

DODD, CHARLES HAROLD. *The Interpretation of the Fourth Gospel* (Cambridge: At the University Press, 1958).

————. *Historical Tradition in the Fourth Gospel* (Cambridge: At the University Press, 1958).

EUSEBIUS OF CAESAREA. *Ecclesiastical History,* Vol. I translated by Kirsopp Lake; Vol. II translated by J.E.L. Oulton (Cambridge: Harvard University Press, 1926, 1932).

FARRER, AUSTIN M. *A Rebirth of Images* (Westminster: Dacre, 1949).

FINEGAN, JACK. *The Archaeology of the New Testament. The Life of Jesus and the Beginning of the Early Church* (Princeton: Princeton University Press, 1969).

FOWLER, ROBERT M. *Loaves and Fishes. The Function of the Feeding Stories in the Gospel of Mark* (Chico, CA: Scholars Press, 1981).

GUILDING, AILEEN. *The Fourth Gospel and Jewish Worship* (Oxford: At the University Press, 1960).

HARVEY, A. E. *Jesus on Trial. A Study in the Fourth Gospel* (Atlanta: John Knox Press, 1976).

HOPKINS, GERARD MANLEY. *The Poems of Gerard Manley Hopkins.* W. H. Gardner and N. H. MacKenzie, eds., with additional footnotes and foreword, fourth edition (Oxford: Oxford University Press, 1967).

237

IGNATIUS OF ANTIOCH. "The Epistles of Ignatius" in *The Apostolic Fathers*, 2 vols., translated by Kirsopp Lake. LOEB CLASSICAL LIBRARY (Cambridge: Harvard University Press, 1912).

JEREMIAS, JOACHIM. *The Rediscovery of Bethesda*. NEW TESTAMENT ARCHAEOLOGY MONOGRAPHS, Jerry Vardaman, ed. (Louisville: Southern Baptist Theological Seminary, 1966).

JOSEPH AND ASENETH. *The Old Testament Pseudepigrapha*, translated by C. Burchard, in James Charlesworth, ed., Vol. II (Garden City, N.Y.: Doubleday, 1985).

JOSEPHUS. *The Jewish War*, translated by H. St. J. Thackeray. LOEB CLASSICAL LIBRARY. 2 Vols. Books I–III and IV–VII (Cambridge: Harvard University Press, 1927, 1928).

———. *Jewish Antiquities*. Books XV–XVII, translated by Ralph Marcus and Allen Wikgren; XVIII–XX, translated by L.H. Feldman (Cambridge: Harvard University Press, 1963, 1965).

JULIAN OF NORWICH. *Showings*, translated by Edmund Colledge, OSA and James Walsh, SJ. THE CLASSICS OF WESTERN SPIRITUALITY (New York: Paulist Press, 1978).

JUSTER, JEAN. *Les Juifs dan l'Empire Romain: Leur condition juridique, économique et sociale, 2 vols.* (Paris: Geuthner, 1914).

JUSTIN MARTYR, SAINT. "The First Apology," edited and translated by Edward Rochie Hardie in Cyril C. Richardson, *Early Christian Fathers*. THE LIBRARY OF CHRISTIAN CLASSICS, Vol. I (New York: Macmillan, 1970).

———. *The Dialogue with Trypho*, translated by A. Lukyn Williams (London: S.P.C.K., 1930).

KAESEMANN, ERNST. *The Testament of Jesus according to John 17*, translated by Gerhard Krodel (Philadelphia: Fortress Press, 1968).

KOESTER, HELMUT. "Geschichte und Kultus in Johannesevangelium und bei Ignatius von Antiochien," *Zeitschrift für Theologie und Kirche*, 54:56–59 (1957).

LINDARS, BARNABAS, S.S.F. *The Gospel of John*. NEW CENTURY BIBLE (Greenwood, S.C.: Attic Press, 1972).

MARTYN, JAMES LOUIS. *History and Theology in the Fourth Gospel*, second revised edition (Nashville: Abingdon Press, 1979). First published 1968.

———. "We Have Found Elijah," *The Gospel of John in Christian History: Essays for Interpreters* (New York: Paulist Press, 1978).

MISHNAH, THE. Translated from the Hebrew with Introduction and Brief Explanatory Notes, by Herbert Danby (Oxford: Oxford University Press, 1933).

NAG HAMMADI LIBRARY IN ENGLISH, THE. Translated by Members of the Coptic Gnostic Library Project of the Institute for Antiquity and Christianity, James M. Robinson, ed. and director (San Francisco: Harper & Row, 1977).

NESTLE-ALAND. *Novum Testamentum Graece*, twenty-sixth edition prepared by Kurt Aland and Barbara Aland (Stuttgart: Deutsche Bibelstiftung, 1979). First published 1898.

NEUSNER, JACOB. *Midrash in Context: Exegesis in Formative Judaism*. PART ONE: *Method; Messiah in Context: Israel's History and*

Destiny in Formative Judaism. PART TWO: *Teleology; Torah: From Scroll to Symbol in Formative Judaism.* PART THREE: *Doctrine.* THE FOUNDATIONS OF JUDAISM (Philadelphia: Fortress Press, 1983, 1984, 1985).

NORRIS, RICHARD A., JR. *The Christological Controversy. Sources of Early Christian Thought.* Patristic texts translated and edited (Philadelphia: Fortress Press, 1980).

NUTTALL, GEOFFREY. *The Moment of Recognition: Luke as Story-Teller* (London: Athlone Press, 1978).

ORIGEN. *Commentaire sur saint Jean . . .*Texte grec, avant propos, traduction et notes par Cécile Blanc, r. a. SOURCES CHRÉTIENNES, 120 (Paris: Cerf, 1966).

PETERSEN, NORMAN R. *Literary Criticism for New Testament Critics* (Philadelphia: Fortress Press, 1978).

PHILO OF ALEXANDRIA. *Philo,* with an English translation by F. H. Colson and G. H. Whitaker. LOEB CLASSICAL LIBRARY, Vol. 5 (Cambridge: Harvard University Press, 1934).

RHOADS, DAVID and MICHIE, DONALD. *Mark as Story: An Introduction to the Narrative of a Gospel* (Philadelphia: Fortress Press, 1982).

RICHTER, GEORG. *Studien zum Johannesevangelium* (Regensburg: Pustet, 1977).

ROBBINS, VERNON K. *Jesus the Teacher* (Philadelphia: Fortress Press, 1984).

SCHILLEBEECKX, EDWARD. *Ministry: Leadership in the Community of Jesus Christ,* translated by John Bowden (New York: Crossroad, 1981). First published 1980.

SCHNACKENBURG, RUDOLF. *The Gospel according to John,* 3 vols., translated by Smyth, Hastings, McDonagh, Smith, Foley, and Kon (New York: Herder and Herder, 1968, I; Crossroad, 1982, II, III).

SEIDENSTICKER, PHILIPP. *Die Auferstehung Jesu in der Botschaft der Evangelien.* STUTTGARTER BIBLISCHE BEITRAEGE, 26 (Stuttgart: Verlag Katholisches Bibelwerk, 1967).

SHERWIN-WHITE, A. N. *Roman Society and Roman Law in the New Testament* (Oxford: Clarendon Press, 1963).

SLOYAN, GERARD S. "The Samaritans in the New Testament," *Horizons* 10, 1:7–21 (1983).

TALBERT, CHARLES. *Reading Luke: A Literary and Theological Commentary on the Third Gospel* (New York: Crossroad, 1982).

THEODORE OF MOPSUESTIA. *Commentary . . . on the Lord's Prayer and on the Sacraments of Baptism and the Eucharist,* translated by Alphonse Mingana. WOODBROOKE STUDIES VI (Cambridge: Cambridge University Press, 1933).

THOMPSON, FRANCIS. *Poetical Works* (New York: Oxford University Press, 1965).

WILDER, AMOS N. *Early Christian Rhetoric: The Language of the Gospel* (Cambridge: Harvard University Press, 1971).